The German Element of the Shenandoah Valley of Virginia

John W. Wayland

HERITAGE BOOKS
2019

HERITAGE BOOKS
AN IMPRINT OF HERITAGE BOOKS, INC.

Books, CDs, and more—Worldwide

For our listing of thousands of titles see our website
at
www.HeritageBooks.com

A Facsimile Reprint
Published 2019 by
HERITAGE BOOKS, INC.
Publishing Division
5810 Ruatan Street
Berwyn Heights, Md. 20740

— Publisher's Notice —
In reprints such as this, it is often not possible to remove blemishes from the original. We feel the contents of this book warrant its reissue despite these blemishes and hope you will agree and read it with pleasure.

International Standard Book Number
Paperbound: 978-0-7884-1645-3

Preface.

One who was born in the Shenandoah Valley, who has dwelt there during the greater portion of his life to the present, and who is by blood three-fourths German or German-Swiss, may doubtless be excused for writing about the German Element in the Shenandoah Valley of Virginia. He may also be excused, perhaps, for regarding such a subject as naturally attractive, and for believing that it is well worthy of careful investigation. As a matter of fact, the field has proved most fruitful: so much so that the writer has been surprised at the abundance and wealth of material that may be secured for historical, economical, sociological, political, religious, linguistic, and even literary studies. He hastens to say, however, for the reassurance of the reader, that he has not attempted to follow out all these lines of investigation in the present treatise: what he has attempted is merely a plain, unvarnished picture of the people in their homes, in their churches, in their schools, in their fields and workshops, and in the larger relations of church and state as affected by peace and war. As preliminary to this picture, a brief account of the exploration and settlement of the country has been deemed necessary and appropriate.

In addition to a natural inclination toward the subject in hand, the writer has felt in some measure what he is pleased to call a sense of duty. It is a patent fact that the German element in Virginia—and that chiefly means the Germans in northwestern Virginia—is a subject that has received but slight attention, either in the thought and literature of our larger Virginia, or in the thought and concern of the German element itself. And the fact is not singular. The prevailing element of our State is English; our language is English:

and not even a German would have it anything else: hence our books and our thought are English and of England. So the fact is not singular that the German element of the Valley of Virginia and adjacent sections should be overlooked in the more familiar life and interests of the larger part. It is only analogous to the larger fact in our country as a whole. The German fifth or fourth of our American nation is often forgotten—we love old England so well. And yet the student at least should not be so forgetful—he loves the German schools too well. Hugo Münsterberg is reported as saying that the German and American nations are more alike, in mind and temperament, than any other two nations of earth, and must eventually adopt the same form of civilization and government.[1] We hesitate to accept this statement in its entirety, because Münsterberg is a German, and Germans are apt to be enthusiastic; but we do put a good deal of confidence in what Andrew D. White says; for he is one of us. Mr. White says: "Although Great Britain is generally honored as the mother of the United States, Germany has, from an intellectual standpoint, become more and more the second mother of the United States. More than any other country, Germany has made the universities and colleges of America what they are to-day—a powerful force in the development of American civilization."[2] In view of these facts, therefore, the writer feels like saying a word for his own kind and to them. He is gratified, moreover, to observe a gradual awakening of conscience, so to speak, among them. A few have always kept the faith, and have tried to keep the language, though against overwhelming odds; but lately—and this is the gratifying fact—many of the young men and women of the Valley of Virginia, in whose families the language and literature of the Fatherland have been practically dead for two or three generations, are now turning back to them in their courses of higher

[1]The Inglenook, Elgin, Ill., of recent date.

[2]Report of U. S. Commissioner of Education, 1901, vol. I, p. 543.

education, and are taking up for their own accomplishment and culture what their great-grandfathers and great-grandmothers tried to get rid of as soon as possible, in order to be like other people.

In enumerating the sources from which the facts presented in this treatise have been gathered, the writer ventures to mention first his own life and experience among the people of whom he writes, together with a first-hand acquaintance—often familiarity—with nearly every locality named. For definite facts of time and place, relating to the early settlements, the archives of the several counties of the Valley and adjacent sections have been consulted: namely, in the order of their organized establishment, Spottsylvania (1721), Orange (1734), Frederick (1743), Augusta (1745), Shenandoah (1772), Rockingham (1778). In Rockingham County many of the earliest records were destroyed, or partly destroyed, by fire during the Civil War; but the burnt records have many of them been restored to a serviceable form. In Spottsylvania County, also, the records suffered considerably, if not from hostile soldiery, at least from the "underground" methods necessary for their hiding. Although the valley of the Shenandoah was first settled while the district was still a part of Spottsylvania County, I have not been able to find any references in the records of this county to persons or places in the Valley. There are, however, frequent entries referring to the Germans of Germanna; to some that must have lived in the territory now constituting Madison County; as well as to a few that seem to have been locating about Fredericksburg. In the counties of Orange, Frederick, Augusta, and Shenandoah the records, at least of deeds and wills, are complete, almost without exception. Many of the original documents in these counties were written and presented in German script; and I am told that in Frederick County some of them, like so many German family names, have suffered not a little in the translation and transcription by English clerks; and I have no doubt that the same is true to a greater or less degree in the other counties also.

As sources for the earliest history of the Valley, I have found most valuable a series of documents edited and annotated by Mr. Charles E. Kemper of Washington City, and published during the past year or two in the *Virginia Magazine of History and Biography*: "The Early Westward Movement of Virginia, 1722-1734, As Shown by the Proceedings of the Colonial Council." These documents, together with the series of Moravian Diaries covering some ten years in the middle of the eighteenth century, translated from the German and annotated by Mr. Kemper and Prof. William J. Hinke of Philadelphia, and published recently in the same magazine, furnish a substantial basis for the historical study of beginnings in the Valley section. Hening's Statutes at Large have been found a rich storehouse of facts and figures for the first three-quarters of a century of Valley history. These, together with Palmer's Calendar of Virginia State Papers, Stanard's Virginia Colonial Register, and Kennedy's Journals of the House of Burgesses, have been freely consulted. Among the many other publications that have been found helpful, two must be mentioned here: John Lederer's Journal, translated by Sir Willam Talbot and printed first in London in 1672; and Prof. I. D. Rupp's Collection of Thirty Thousand Names of German, Swiss, Dutch, and other Immigrants to Philadelphia, from 1727 to 1776.

All of the publications above mentioned will be found enumerated and briefly described in the appended Bibliography. To this bibliography special attention is invited. In it two things have been attempted: first, an atonement for the necessary brevity of this treatise; second, some real help in practical form to those who may wish to follow out the present subject in any particular lines. It is hoped that the latter object at least may be regarded as in some measure accomplished.

Among the individuals in different parts of the country

who have given valuable assistance in the preparation of this monograph, I gratefully mention the following:

Rev. Dr. D. M. Gilbert, deceased, Harrisburg, Pa.; Mr. J. G. Rosengarten, Philadelphia; Bishop L. J. Heatwole, Dale Enterprise, Va.; Mrs. Charles G. Johnson, Radford, Va.; Mr. Charles E. Kemper, Washington City; Mr. Elon O. Henkel and Mr. Ambrose L. Henkel, New Market, Va.; Mr. A. H. Snyder, Harrisonburg, Va.; Dr. H. J. Eckenrode, Richmond, Va.; Dr. B. W. Green, University of Virginia; Mr. D. S. Lewis, Harrisonburg, Va.; Hon. J. A. Waddell, Staunton, Va.; Pres. George H. Denny, Washington and Lee University; Dr. W. H. Ruffner, Lexington, Va.; Gen. Gilbert S. Meem, Seattle, Wash.; Eld. J. H. Moore, Elgin, Ill.; Col. S. R. Millar, Front Royal, Va.; Maj. R. W. Hunter, Richmond, Va.; Hon. A. C. Gordon, Staunton, Va.; Miss Sarah M. Spengler, Front Royal, Va.; Mr. E. Ruebush, Dayton, Va.; Dr. J. L. Miller, Thomas, W. Va.; The A. S. Abell Company, Baltimore; Mr. W. G. Stanard, Richmond, Va.; Mr. W. H. Sipe, Bridgewater, Va.; Mr. T. K. Cartmell, Winchester, Va.; Hon. J. G. Neff, Mt. Jackson, Va.; Mr. Samuel Forrer, Mossy Creek, Va.; Prof. J. Carson Miller, Moore's Store, Va.; Gen. John E. Roller, Harrisonburg, Va.; Capt. J. H. Grabill, Woodstock, Va.; Rev. S. L. Bowman, Daphna, Va.; Dr. Thomas Walker Page, University of Virginia; Mr. John Van Horne, Charlottesville, Va.

As opportunity is afforded in the succeeding pages, I shall gladly makes specific acknowledgment to as many as possible of the more than one hundred other persons who have contributed facts, either personally or in writing.

It is with special gratitude that I acknowledge in this place my indebtedness to my honored friend and teacher, Professor Richard Heath Dabney, of the University of Virginia; who, at no time during the past seven years, has failed to respond readily and liberally to my every call upon his scholarship and my every claim upon his friendship; whose mature and even judgment has repeatedly been an aid and a guide in the difficult field of historical research, and whose broad and thorough learning has been a constant inspiration.

If an appendix may be allowed in a preface, it may be worth while to state here that in the course of the preparation of this monograph a great many particular facts of interest have been collected concerning a number of the German families of the Valley of Virginia. It was a first intention to include these notes in this publication; but that procedure, owing to the considerable bulk of the material in question, has been deemed impracticable. If conditions appear to warrant the undertaking, these collections may be enlarged and published independently at a subsequent period.

J. W. WAYLAND.

University of Virginia,
February 27, 1907.

Contents.

CHAPTER I.

The Shenandoah Valley of Virginia: A Geographical Outline.

The great Valley of Virginia lies near the present northwestern border of the State, between the Blue Ridge and the first ranges of the Alleghanies. Its total length, measured from the Potomac River at Harpers Ferry southwest to the line of Tennessee, is upwards of 300 miles; its average width is twenty-five or thirty miles. About midway, that is, near the line between the counties of Rockbridge and Botetourt, the Valley is cut across by the James River, flowing eastward; sixty miles further southwest, by the New River, flowing westward. Some forty miles northeast from the transection of the James, the headwaters of the Shenandoah rise and flow northeastward 140 miles into the Potomac, parallel with and between the Alleghanies and the Blue Ridge, draining the counties of Augusta, Rockingham, Shenandoah, Page and Warren, Frederick and Clarke, of Virginia; with Berkeley and Jefferson of West Virginia. These nine counties named, beginning with Augusta, form the Shenandoah Valley of Virginia.

The Shenandoah River joins the Potomac at Harpers Ferry. If one should ascend its channel from the mouth, he would find that for forty miles or so, to Riverton in Warren County, it washes the western base of the Blue Ridge. Then its course shifts slightly to the west, and its waters are divided by an isolated wedge of mountain, fifty miles long, known as the Massanutten Range, which, at a distance of six or eight miles, parallels the Blue Ridge along the greater length of Warren County, the whole length of Page, and half way into Rockingham. If one could look down upon the Valley from an eyry in a cloud, the oblong expanse below, bordered by its tiers of mountains, might suggest an immense hippodrome, or circus; only the Titanic *spina*—the Massanutten Mountain—would not be found quite midway between the sides, but a little nearer the eastern border. Turning the figure into fact, we find it true and real: the Shenandoah Valley has been the race course of giants, and the Massanutten Mountain was more than once the wall of separation about which the contests were waged.

The two great branches of the Shenandoah River go sluggishly to their meeting point at Riverton, in many a sinuous fold on either side of the Massanutten Mountain. The north branch washes the northwestern base of the Massanutten throughout the entire length of Shenandoah County, after having struggled out with some haste through Brocks Gap from its sources in the mountains of western Rockingham. The main river—the south branch of the Shenandoah, or simply the "South River"—washes the Massanutten on the southeastern side, from the point in Rockingham at which the mountain rises up out of the plain with a suddenness that is equalled only by the abruptness with which it drops off into the plain at Strasburg and Riverton. The South River heads mainly in Augusta County, combining the three forks known respectively as South River, North River, and Middle River. North River and Middle River join on the line between Augusta and Rockingham, near the village of Mt. Meridian; together they flow on three miles and then join the South River at Port Republic, in Rockingham County; and thence the mingled waters continue in their course to the line between Rockingham and Page, where they come under the afternoon shadows of the Massanutten Mountain; to Riverton, where they receive the washings from the western side of the Massanutten in the waters of the North Branch; thence, under the morning shadows of the Blue Ridge, to the Potomac at Harpers Ferry.[1]

1. In connection with this account of the Shenandoah Valley and River, it may be worth while to tabulate some of the different forms

The Potomac River (Cohongoruton) flows across the Shenandoah Valley and bounds it on the northeast; and at the northeast corner of the Valley the Shenandoah River meets the Potomac at right angles. Out in the valley ten miles, parallel to the Shenandoah, is Opequon Creek; on another parallel line, ten miles further toward the Alleghany ranges, is Back Creek. These two creeks also meet the general course of the Potomac at right angles, and drain the lower end of the Valley. The Massanutten Mountain is cleft throughout the lower half of its length—the part toward Strasburg and Riverton; and out of the narrow valley or gorge between its long parallel walls, known as Powell's Fort, flows Passage Creek, joining the north branch of the Shenandoah River about four miles above Riverton. Almost opposite the mouth of Passage Creek, Cedar Creek joins the north branch of the river from the other side, after having marked the dividing line for the greater distance between the counties of Frederick and Shenandoah, and for a little

in which the name "Shenandoah" has been found, namely: Chanador, Chanetor, Chanithor, Gerando, Gerundo, Scandar, Schanathor, Shanando, Shanidore, Shannando, Shannandoah, Sharrandoa, Shenandoare, Sherandoah, Sherrendo, Sherundo, Sherundore, Thanadore, Tschanator, Zynodoa. One might almost conclude that we have here a series of attempts to demonstrate the law of permutations, could he only escape the suspicion that it is chiefly a case of bad spelling. Doubtless, to make the matter worse, imperfect pronunciation and defective hearing often contributed. For example, a German soldier in the British service during the Revolution—or as much of it as he was allowed to participate in—wrote in his diary of wading through the river "Scandar or Jonathan" on the way across the Valley to Winchester. The same writer puts the Rappahannock down as the "Krappa Hannah," and the Potomac as the "Bett Thommak." (Popp's Journal, pp. 24, 25.) On the north branch of the Shenandoah, in what is now Shenandoah County, a tribe of Indians, called the Senedos, are said to have lived in early times. It seems probable that they took their name from the river and adjacent country, or that the latter were named from this Indian tribe; though other derivations for the term "Shenandoah" are suggested.

way between Shenandoah and Warren. Four more considerable streams enter the north branch, or "Little Shenandoah," much further up its course: Stony Creek near Edinburg and Mill Creek near Mt. Jackson, both from the west; Smiths Creek near Mt. Jackson and Linville Creek at Broadway, both from the east. One of the principal tributaries to the South River is the Hawksbill Creek, flowing in from the eastern side, near Luray. The Norfolk & Western Railway follows the general course of the main river throughout the Valley; the Baltimore & Ohio Railway and the celebrated Valley Turnpike follow the line of the Little Shenandoah, and extend beyond it north and south.

In early times "South Mountain" was the name applied to the Blue Ridge in the upper Valley, southeast of the Massanutten range; and the latter, in consequence, is referred to in some of the old deeds as the "North Mountain." Latterly, however, "North Mountain" is the name applied to one of the great ranges on the northwestern border of the Valley. From an early period to the present, the abrupt southwest end of the Massanutten range, near Harrisonburg in Rockingham County, has been called "Peaked Mountain": variously corrupted into "Pickett," "Pinquet," etc. The term Massanutten, or "Massanutting," etc., has been applied from very early times to a small district at the eastern foot of the mountain of the same name, and to a small stream that drains the section and flows into South River several miles above the mouth of the Hawksbill. "Massanutting" seems also to have been the name applied occasionally to the whole of the larger district between the Massanutten Mountain and the Blue Ridge, roughly identical with what is now Page County.

In geological formation, the greater part of the Shenandoah Valley is what is known as Lower Silurian. Most of the soil is of the limestone variety, with occasional stretches of sand or gravel, and now and then a ledge of slate. One of the most notable of the last is found in the lower Valley, on a line of continuation from the end of the Massanutten range to the Potomac River. This tract of slate, drained chiefly by the Opequon Creek, is six or eight miles wide and over forty miles long. It has been suggested by scientists that this region of slate was once covered by a mountain, which in ages past was razed by some convulsion of nature or abraded by less violent but more persistent processes. It is well known, of course, that in the opinion of many the whole lower Valley was once a great lake, until the pent up waters burst through the mountain walls at Harper's Ferry and escaped, leaving only the rivers to follow and mark the course they took.

It appears to be a well established fact that in early times much of the Valley was a prairie. Kercheval says, "This region, * * * when the country was first known to the white people, was one entire and beautiful prairie, with the exception of narrow fringes of timber immediately bordering on the water courses."[2] According to Bishop Meade, parts of the Valley were prairie in early days,[3] and other sections were covered only by a growth of small saplings. Foote records that much of the Valley "was covered with prairies abounding in tall grass, and these, with the scattered forests, were filled with pea vines"; and that "much of the beautiful timber in the valley has grown since the immigrants chose their habitations."[4] Confirmation of these statements will be found in a less familiar but no less credible quarter further on.

The Valley abounds in beautiful landscapes and wonders of nature. The water gap at Harper's Ferry and the gorge of Powell's Fort are justly celebrated. The Natural Chimneys of Augusta County and the Narrow Passage of Shenan-

2. History of the Valley, 3d edition, p. 312.

3. Old Churches, Etc., Vol. II, p. 279.

4. Foote's Sketches, p. 15.

doah are no less remarkable, if less imposing. There are caverns of rare beauty and grandeur in the vicinity of both Harrisonburg and New Market; and at Luray and Shendun are the Luray Caverns and Weyer's Cave, two natural wonders of almost world-wide renown. The Luray Caverns, in a hill between the Hawksbill Creek and the South River, were discovered first about the year 1793, by a son of Joseph Ruffner, the owner of the land; Weyer's Cave, in a bluff on the Mohler farm, on the west bank of the same river, thirty-odd miles farther up its course, was found in the year 1804 by Bernard Weyer. The Ruffners, the Mohlers, and Bernard Weyer, it may not be impertinent to remark here, were all Germans.

CHAPTER II.

THE FIRST WHITE MEN IN THE VALLEY.

On a summer's day in the year 1716, Governor Alexander Spotswood, with a party of twenty or thirty horsemen, set out from Williamsburg, the capital of the Virginia colony, to ascertain for himself what sort of country lay west and north of the great "Blue Mountains." There was good reason to believe that several Indian tribes of uncertain friendship might be found there; and who else or what else nobody seemed quite certain, save the ignorant and superstitious, who declared that there were monsters and mysteries numerous and dreadful enough. The Governor may have had predominantly in mind objects much more commonplace and practical than the simple clearing up of superstitions and mysteries. Doubtless the elements of romance and danger afforded a considerable stimulus toward a jaunt; but he must have been seriously in earnest about something, to undertake an expedition of nearly two hundred miles up country, past the very frontiers and into the wilderness.[1] At any rate he came, and a gallant company with him. They crossed the Blue Ridge, probably by Swift Run Gap, into what is now the county of Rockingham; and one day early in September watered their horses in the Shenandoah River—the "Euphrates," they called it. They may have gone across the Valley to the first ranges of the Alleghanies; but this point

1. In a letter to the London Board of Trade, August 14, 1718, Governor Spotswood said: "The chief aim of my expedition over the great mountains, in 1716, was to satisfye myself whether it was practicable to come at the lakes."—Waddell's Annals of Augusta, pp. 19, 20.—It was a delusion of the time that the lakes of Canada were just a little way beyond the Blue Ridge, and many attempts were made to find a "northwest passage" through the mountains to them.

does not seem quite definitely settled. Somewhere, on a couple of prominent peaks of either the Alleghanies or the Blue Ridge, they went through a formal ceremony of drinking King George's health in nobody knows how many kinds of wine;[2] and, upon their return, endeavored to provide for the perpetual commemoration of their achievements in the order of the "Knights of the Golden Horseshoe."

Governor Spotswood is usually regarded as the first white man to look upon the great Valley of Virginia; and yet Governor Spotswood himself tells of other Europeans who saw it six years earlier. Writing on December 15, 1710, to the London Council of Trade, he says that a company of adventurers reached the mountains "not above a hundred miles from our upper inhabitants, and went up to the top of the highest mountain with their horses, tho' they had hitherto been thought to be unpassable, and they assured me that ye descent on the other side seemed to be as easy as that they had passed on this, and that they could have passed over the whole ledge (which is not large), if the season of the year had not been too far advanced before they set out on that expedition."[3]

These men are supposed to have ascended the Blue Ridge somewhere near the James River Gap, and to have looked upon the Valley from the vicinity of Balcony Falls; though no description is given of the country seen by them.[4]

2. Fontaine, the historian of the party, says: "We had a good dinner, and after it we got the men together and loaded all their arms, and we drank the King's health in champagne and fired a volley, the Princess's health in Burgundy and fired a volley, and all the rest of the royal family in claret and a volley. We drank the Governor's health and fired another volley. We had several sorts of liquors, viz: Virginia red wine and white wine, Irish usquebaugh, brandy, shrub, two sorts of rum, champagne, canary, cherry punch, cider, &c."

3. Spotswood Letters, Vol. I, p. 40.

4. Waddell's Annals of Augusta, p. 17.

Half a century earlier still, further to the southwest, other white men had penetrated and probably crossed the Valley. In 1654, Colonel Abraham Wood, who lived near or at the site of the present city of Petersburg, first discovered and named New River, going through the Blue Ridge probably by the way of "Wood's Gap," near the line between Virginia and North Carolina.[5] Between 1666 and 1670, Captain Henry Batte, with fourteen white men and fourteen Indians, started from Appomattox and, crossing the Blue Ridge, followed the New River some distance; likely going by the same route as Colonel Wood.[6]

But it may fairly be said that these men, particularly Wood and Batte, do not properly belong to the explorers of the Shenandoah Valley. Even the party that gazed down from the heights above Balcony Falls in 1710 did not look upon the Valley of the Shenandoah: they too were far to the southwest of it. Even yet, therefore, we might reserve the place of pre-eminence for the gallant Governor, were it not for a few stubborn facts and a "Dutchman" or two.

In the year 1722, Michael Wohlfarth, a German sectarian, visited Conrad Beissel, the famous Pennsylvania mystic, at the Mühlbach, while on a journey to North Carolina by way of the Valley of Virginia.[7] In 1705, the General Assembly of Virginia passed an act encouraging trade with the Indians; and, among other things, it was provided that any person who should make discovery of "any town or nation of Indians, situated or inhabiting to the westward of or between the Appalatian Mountains," should enjoy for the space of fourteen years the exclusive right to trade with them.[8] On

5. Hale's Trans-Alleghany Pioneers, pp. 20, 21.

6. Idem, pp. 21, 22; John Esten Cook's History of Virginia, p. 234.—In 1671 Batte and others seem to have reached the falls of the Great Kanawha.—Lewis' Handbook of West Virginia, pp. 29, 30.

7. Sachse's German Sectarians, Vol. II, p. 332.

8. Hening's Statutes, Vol. III, pp. 468, 469.

October 10, 1704, Dr. John Kelpius, a religious leader residing near Philadelphia, wrote a letter of twenty-two pages in German to Maria Elizabeth Gerber, in Virginia.[9] These facts make it not improbable that there were white settlers, or at least explorers, traders, or missionaries, in the Shenandoah Valley much earlier than is generally supposed. The Act of Assembly in 1705 ought certainly to have urged some hardy adventurer across the Blue Ridge long before Spotswood came. And besides, the question arises, where was Maria Elizabeth Gerber, the disciple of Kelpius, in 1704? Can we locate her in eastern Virginia? Dr. Julius F. Sachse thinks that the great valleys west of the Blue Ridge were known to the Germans of Pennsylvania and Maryland long before they were known to the English.[10] And it is hard to believe that Wohlfarth would have chosen the Shenandoah Valley for his line of travel to North Carolina in 1722, if there had been no white settlers from one end of the 300-mile stretch to the other. And yet we are left uncertain in the midst of many possibilities. Maria Elizabeth Gerber may have been, and probably was, either permanently or transiently in eastern Virginia;[11] the Act of 1705 may have been too weak to drive even the knights of trade into the hardships

9. Sachse's German Pietists, p. 226.

10. Sachse's German Sectarians, Vol. II, p. 333.

11. Under date of February 10, 1907, Dr. Sachse writes me as follows:—"In reply to your letter of 28 ult., will say there is nothing to indicate where Elizabeth Gerber was located—as you will see from my foot note, p. 37, in Falckner's Curieuse Nachricht von Pennsylvania, 1700. There were German settlements in Virginia prior to the beginning of the XVIII century, as per MSS. Petrus Schaffer, 1699. I have in my collection two old maps, one French, date 1687, which gives the location of the German settlement at the head waters of the Rappahannock; also an English map of the same period (n. d.), which marks the same location 'Teutsche Staat.' On this map another location on the head waters of the James is marked 'Meister Krugs plantasie.' I have no doubt that this map offers a solution, partial at least, to the location of some Germans in Old Virginia."

and dangers and uncertain terrors beyond the great mountains; and Wohlfarth may have traversed the Valley in 1722 alone; with a friend or two; or making his friends as he found them among the savage tribes.

But there is another person of whom we may speak with the greater assurance of more complete knowledge: one who likely was, so far as we now know, the first white man to cross the Blue Ridge; and the first also, doubtless, to look upon the fair valley of the Shenandoah. In the year 1669, the same in which La Salle came down to the falls of the Ohio, and ten years before he set out from Canada to complete the work of Joliet and Marquette, and find the mouth of the Mississippi; twelve years before Penn's "Holy Experiment" in the forests west of the Delaware; and forty-seven years before Spotswood and the Knights of the Golden Horseshoe crossed the Blue Ridge, he came to the Valley, crossed it, mapped it, and described it, together with other sections east, south, and southwest. This man's name was John Lederer; and he was a German.

But little is known of John Lederer, except that he is said to have been once a Franciscan monk;[12] and he was evidently a man of some learning. He was commissioned by Governor Sir William Berkeley, to make explorations; and under this commission he made, from March, 1669, to September, 1670, three distinct tours or "marches," on two of which he crossed the Valley; on the other he went far into the southwest, possibly into the present boundaries of North Carolina and Tennessee. Soon after his return from the third expedition, he was forced to leave Virginia: because, he says, of the jealousy and misrepresentation of those he had outdone in the work of exploration; because, it may be, of debt.[13] Probably race prejudice was a factor in the case,

12. J. G. Rosengarten, in Lippincott's Magazine, April, 1902.

13. Virginia Magazine of History and Biography, Vol. VIII, p. 324; Vol. X, p. 112.

whatever may have been the conditions in other matters. Upon leaving Virginia Lederer went to Maryland, where, under the friendship and patronage of Sir William Talbot, the governor of the colony, he prepared a map of the districts he had explored, and wrote out in Latin an accompanying account of his adventures and observations. Talbot translated this journal into English and had it published, with the map, in London, in 1672. For years the work has been rare and but little known; and the small edition recently reprinted for a bookseller of Rochester, New York, will not likely go very far toward making it familiar to the general reader.

Sir William Talbot's preface may serve to introduce Lederer and his work to us more fully.

TO THE READER.

That a stranger should presume (though with Sir William Berkly's Commission) to go into those parts of the American Continent where Englishmen never had been, and whither some refused to accompany him, was, in Virginia look'd on as so great an insolence, that our traveller at his return, instead of welcom and applause, met nothing but affronts and reproaches; for indeed it was their part, that forsook him in the expedition, to procure him discredit that was a witness to theirs; therefore no industry was wanting to prepare men with a prejudice against him, and this their malice improved to such a general animosity, that he was not safe in Virginia from the outrage of the people, drawn into a perswasion, that the publick levy of that year, went all to the expense of his vagaries. Forced by this storm into Maryland, he became known to me, though then ill-affected to the man, by the stories that went about of him: Nevertheless finding him, contrary to my expectation, a modest ingenious person, and a pretty scholar, I thought it common justice to give him an occasion of vindicating himself from what I had heard of him; which truly he did with so convincing reason and circumstance, as quite abolished those former impressions in me, and made me desire this account of his travels, which here you have faithfully rendred out of Latine from his own writings and discourse, with an entire map of the territory he traversed, copied from his own hand. All these I have compared with Indian relations of those parts (though I never met with any Indian that had followed a southwest-course so far as this German) and finding them agree, I thought the printing of these papers was no injury to the author, and might prove a service to the publick.

WILLIAM TALBOT.

According to Lederer's account, he, with three Indians whose names he gives, set out upon the ninth of March, 1669, "from an Indian village called Shickehamany," at the "falls of Pemaeoncock, alias York-River in Virginia." After crossing the Pamunkey to the south side, at the confluence of the two main branches,—the North Anna and the South Anna,—he followed the south branch to its source. "The thirteenth," he says, "I reached the first spring of Pemaeoncock, having crossed the river four times that day, by reason of its many windings; but the water was so shallow, that it hardly wet my horses patterns. * * * The fourteenth of March, from the top of an eminent hill, I first descried that Apalataean mountains, bearing due west to the place I stood upon: their distance from me was so great, that I could hardly discern whether they were mountains or clouds, until my Indian fellow travellers prostrating themselves in adoration, howled out after a barbarous manner, *Okée paeze* i. e. God is nigh."

Lederer was now evidently within the present limits of Albemarle County. He must have found the head waters of the South Anna (the south branch of the "Pemaeoncock") somewhere near the northeast corner of that county; and the "eminent hill" was doubtless one of the spurs or peaks of the Southwest Mountain, east or northeast of Charlottesville. From that point he could easily have seen the Blue Ridge at a distance of twenty or twenty-five miles. The reason he did not see it before was evidently due to the fact that he was coming up under the eastern side of the Southwest Mountain.

"The fifteenth of March," he continues, "not far from this hill, passing over the South-branch of Rappahannock-river, I was almost swallowed in a quicksand. * * * Thus I travelled all the sixteenth; and on the seventeenth of March I reached the Apalataei. The air here is very thick and chill; and the waters issuing from the mountain-sides, of a blue color, and allumish taste."

Here is a slight difficulty or discrepancy in geography that had better be noticed before we follow our traveler further. He either turned rather sharply out of his course to the northeast after leaving the "eminent hill," or else he mistook the Rivanna or Mechum's River for the south branch of the Rappahannock. He did the latter thing, more probably; for he is evidently pressing forward all the time toward the high mountains, which he speaks of as due west from the "eminent hill." Again, at the outset of his narrative he describes this expedition as made 'from the head of Pemaeoncock * * * *due west* to the top of the Apalataean Mountains.' This course would not have taken him across any branches of the Rappahannock, but would have taken him along the general course, and toward the sources, of Mechum's River. Moreover, he could much more readily have been mistaken in the identity of a small stream than in the points of the compass.

Having spoken of reaching the mountains on the seventeenth, he continues:

The eighteenth of March, after I had in vain essayed to ride up, I alighted, and left my horse with one of the Indians, whilst with the other two I climbed up the rocks, which were so incumbered with bushes and brambles, that the ascent proved very difficult: besides the first precipice was so steep, that if I lookt down, I was immediately taken with a swimming in my head; though afterwards the way was more easie. The height of this mountain was very extraordinary: for notwithstanding I set out with the first appearance of light, it was late in the evening before I gained the top, from whence the next morning I had a beautiful prospect of the Atlantick-Ocean washing the Virginia-shore; but to the north and west, my sight was suddenly bounded by mountains higher than that I stood upon. Here did I wander in snow, for the most part, till the four and twentieth day of March, hoping to find some passage through the mountains; but the coldness of the air and earth together, seizing my hands and feet with numbness, put me to a ne plus ultra; and therefore having found my Indian at the foot of the mountain with my horse, I returned back by the same way that I went.

Here are more difficulties. It appears uncertain from the

narrative whether Lederer crossed the Valley or not. And yet, traveling at the rate he seems to have maintained most of the time,—some fifteen or twenty miles a day,—he could easily have gone from the eastern part of Albemarle to the western border of the present Augusta County from the fourteenth of March to the seventeenth. What he can mean by his reference to the Atlantic Ocean, is a mystery; for it would be equally impossible to see it from either the Alleghanies or the Blue Ridge. His description of the prospect to the north and west, of the mountains near at hand higher than the one he stood upon, fits exactly the conditions west of the Valley, but does not fit the conditions on the eastern side. Moreover, persons who are familiar with both localities can readily understand how he could have wandered in snow from the eighteenth of March to the twenty-fourth on the first ranges of the Alleghanies without finding a passage through; but must be considerably at a loss to know why he could not, in six days, have gone down into the Valley from the top of the Blue Ridge. But the strongest evidence that Lederer did cross the Valley upon this first expedition is found in his map. There he indicates his route as extending westwardly across the Valley, and into the western mountains at the gap made in the first ranges by the north branch of the James River, now known as Goshen Pass, in Rockbridge County; and as terminating on one of the great peaks in or near the western border of the present county of Bath. It is probable that Lederer's Indian guides were somewhat familiar with the trails through the outlying range of the Appalachians,—i. e., the Blue Ridge; that it in consequence was passed without difficulty, and hence without special notice or remark.

On his second expedition, extending over the sixty days from May 20 to July 18, in the year 1670, Lederer went far into the southwest, and apparently did not get into the Valley proper. It was upon this tour that he was accompanied at the start by a Major Harris, "twenty Christian horse, and five Indians"; but this company turned back on the fifth of June, and Lederer had thenceforth only a single companion, a Susquehannah Indian. The circumstances at this point may be given with most brevity and appropriateness in Lederer's own words:

> The third of June we came to the south-branch of James-river, which Major Harris observing to run northward, vainly imagined to be an arm of the lake of Canada; and was so transported with this fancy, that he would have raised a pillar to the discovery, if the fear of the Mahock Indian, and want of food had permitted him to stay. Here I moved to cross the river and march on; but the rest of the company were so weary of the enterprize, that crying out, one and all, they had offered violence to me, had I not been provided with a private commission from the Governor of Virginia to proceed, though the rest of the company should abandon me; the sight of which laid their fury. * * * The fifth of June, my company and I parted good friends, they back again, and I with one Sasquesahanough-Indian, named Jackzetavon, only, in pursuit of my first enterprize, changing my course from west to southwest and by south, to avoid the mountains. Major Harris at parting gave me a gun, believing me a lost man, and given up as a prey to Indians or savage beasts; which made him the bolder in Virginia to report strange things in his own praise and my disparagement, presuming I would never appear to disprove him. This, I suppose, and no other, was the cause that he did with so much industry procure me discredit and odium; but I have lost nothing by it, but what I never studied to gain, which is popular applause.

Whatever Lederer's reception may have been upon his return from the second tour, he evidently still enjoyed to no slight degree the confidence of some men of influence, the Governor likely being still among the number; for on the twentieth of August he set out upon a third expedition, with a Colonel Catlet of Virginia, nine English horse, and five Indians on foot. This time he went "from the Falls of Rappahannock-River * * * (due West) to the top of the Apalataean Mountains."

The party set out from the house of Robert Talifer, and spent the first night at the falls of the Rappahannock—the site of Fredericksburg. The next day, having crossed to the neighborhood of Falmouth, the company proceeded up the north bank of the river to the fork; there they crossed the north fork to its south side, but continued to follow it toward its sources in the Blue Ridge. It will be seen, therefore, that this part of the route followed a direction northwest, and not "due west." On August 23, three days after the start, the stream was found so shallow that it wet only the horses' hoofs. By this time the party was near the summit of the divide, in the vicinity of Markham, or perhaps of Linden, on what is now the northwest border of Fauquier County. "The four and twentieth," says Lederer, "we travelled thorow the Savanae amongst vast herds of red and fallow deer which stood gazing at us; and a little after, we came to the Promontories or spurs of the Apalataean-Mountains."

Here beyond a doubt we find our explorer in the great valley, though again he has said nothing in particular of crossing the Blue Ridge.

It is worth while to notice that both on his map and in his narrative Lederer calls the Valley the "Savanae"—a tract of level or comparatively level land covered with the vegetable growths usually found in a damp soil with a warm or temperate climate; as grass or reeds; but destitute of trees. Here is found, then, a confirmation of the statements quoted in the preceding chapter, to the effect that in early times the greater part of the Shenandoah Valley was a prairie. Lederer's further description is interesting:

> These Savanae are low grounds at the foot of the Apalataeans, which all the winter, spring, and part of the summer, lie under snow or water, when the snow is dissolved, which falls down from the mountains commonly about the beginning of June; and then their verdure is wonderful pleasant to the eye, especially of such as having travelled through the shade of the vast forest, come out of a melancholy darkness of a sudden, into a clear and open skie. To heighten the beauty of these parts, the first springs of most of those great rivers which run into the Atlantick ocean, or Cheseapeack bay, do here break out, and in various branches interlace the flowery meads,

—2

whose luxurious herbage invites numerous herds of red deer to feed.[14]

The route by which Lederer and his party crossed the Valley upon this expedition was some seventy or eighty miles lower down than his crossing place of the preceding year; and must have taken them by or near the sites of the present towns of Front Royal and Strasburg.[15] He says:

> The six and twentieth of August we came to the mountains, where finding no horseway up, we alighted, and left our horses with two or three Indians below, whilst we went up afoot. The ascent was so steep, the cold so intense, and we so tired, that having with much ado gained the top of one of the highest, we drank the kings health in brandy, gave the mountain his name ['Mons Car Reg' it is marked on the map], and agreed to return back again, having no encouragement from that prospect to proceed to a further discovery; * * * we unanimously agreed to return back, seeing no possibility of passing through the mountains: and finding our Indians with our horses in the place where we left them, we rode homewards without any further discovery.[16]

"King Charles' Mountain," marking the western limit of this expedition, is probably within the present boundaries of Hampshire or Hardy County, West Virginia.

Thus we take leave of John Lederer, his friends and his foes; only remarking upon the coincidence that a German

14. The main cause for the Valley being so largely prairie is doubtless given by Hon. J. A. Waddell, in his Annals of Augusta, page 18:—"The face of the country between the Blue Ridge and the North Mountain was, of course, diversified by hill and dale [at the beginning of the 18th century], as it is now; but forest trees were less numerous than at the present time, the growth of timber being prevented by the frequent fires kindled by hunting parties of Indians."

15. Prof. Virgil A. Lewis is evidently mistaken in saying that Lederer and his party crossed the Blue Ridge in the vicinity of Harpers Ferry.—See Lewis' History and Government of West Virginia, p. 35; and Lewis' Hand Book of West Virginia, p. 29.

16. The Discoveries of John Lederer, p. 25.—None of the preceding quotations have been located by number of page, for the reason that the book containing the several accounts is altogether a small one, and the various statements from it may readily be found.

should have been the first white man to explore that portion of the Valley of Virginia that was to be so largely settled by Germans a little more than a half century later. It is not impossible that his sojourn in Maryland may have had some influence upon subsequent emigration from that quarter and the adjacent sections of Pennsylvania; but upon this point we find no record.

CHAPTER III.

THE GERMANS OF THE SHENANDOAH VALLEY: WHENCE THEY CAME; WHY; AND WHEN.

The great majority of the Germans in the Valley of Virginia came across the Potomac above Harper's Ferry, from Maryland and Pennsylvania. Pennsylvania was the chief distributing center; and the counties of Lancaster, Lebanon, Berks, and York, with those surrounding Philadelphia, sent south the greatest numbers. The narrow neck of western Maryland was soon traversed; and the Shenandoah Valley lay next beyond. In addition to the great body from Pennsylvania, there were a few who came from New Jersey and New York; a few from the East Virginia counties of Spottsylvania, Orange, and Madison—chiefly of the Germanna families; and also a few, doubtless, from the German settlements in North Carolina. In and following the period of the Revolutionary War, the German element in the Valley was considerably increased by Hessian soldiers who came over in the English service, and remained in America; and by others of their friends and countrymen who followed them after the establishment of peace. Some of these Hessians appear to have been skilled workmen; and a few, trained students. Most of them were a valuable addition to the growing country, despite the fact that they were looked upon for many years with much contempt and no little bitterness. In consequence, they and their descendants often tried to hide as soon as possible their origin and identity, under the new language, new forms of family names, and half-learned English manners. At this day, when time has long since erased those early prejudices, it is easy for us to see that much of the obloquy and scorn heaped upon the Hessians rested upon no good reason. It may seriously be doubted whether the tales of "selling soldiers," etc., are in many cases well founded. At any rate, there was abundant reason, aside from mercenary inducements, why the Hessians of the last quarter of the eighteenth century should fight with and for the English. The English had for many years been fighting with the Hessians in Germany. "For a century and a half Hessian soldiers fought shoulder to shoulder with the English troops, mainly against France."[1] What was more natural, therefore, than that when Frenchmen fought with Americans against Englishmen, Hessians should fight with Englishmen against Americans?[2]

During the latter part of the Revolution and immediately following that struggle, a considerable number of Germans belonging to the religious body known as Dunkers came into the Valley, and established homes. But they, too, were from Pennsylvania, almost without exception; and did not differ materially in racial or social qualities from the earlier immigrants. Barring individuals and small companies from time to time, the Dunkers appear to have been among the latest comers.

It will be observed, therefore, that the German element of the Valley of Virginia is chiefly made up of the descendants of early immigrants: families who, for the most part, came into the country prior to the year 1800; who bought lands and established homes, and handed their growing possessions down from father to son. The great influx of Germans to the United States during the last century scarcely touched the Shenandoah Valley: most of them went into the far North and West: so that comparatively few new families have come into the Valley during the last two or three generations. Among these few, however, there are some notable instances.

1. Pennsylvania Magazine, Vol. XXIII, p. 157.

2. On the Hessians, see the article above referred to; also, Popp's Journal; Rosengarten's German Allies and The German Soldier; Palmer's Calendar of State Papers, Vol. I, pp. 483, 486, 500, 508, 553, 554, 556, 560, 564; etc.

There are at present in the Shenandoah Valley, living for the most part in the larger towns, from 300 to 400 Jews, chiefly enterprising and successful tradespeople, generally good citizens, rapidly growing in public spirit. Most of them are natives of southern Germany, and nearly all of them have come in since 1850. The oldest among them came direct to the Valley, upon their arrival in America; the later comers usually stopped awhile in the seaport towns. They have come chiefly, it appears, because of the agreeable surroundings and excellent business opportunities afforded here; but many left the Fatherland because of the war in 1870-71 between Germany and France.[3]

Among the late coming German families have been a number of individuals that have already won distinction; but for want of space only two of these, F. A. Graichen and Charles B. Rouss, may be mentioned. Mr. Graichen, mayor of Winchester from 1886 to 1888, and founder of the well known glove factory of that city, was born in Altenburg, Germany, in 1827. He came to Baltimore in 1848, and located at Winchester in 1853. Mr. Rouss comes of an Austrian family, and was born in Frederick County, Maryland; but, coming with his parents early in life to the Valley of Virginia, he got his schooling in both books and business at Winchester. There, too, he made his first fortune as a tradesman; and there his body rests in a magnificent mausoleum.

The causes that brought the German people from Pennsylvania to Virginia were no doubt chiefly economic, though race prejudice growing out of the close association of heterogeneous nationalities, and real or fancied neglect on the part of the Pennsylvania government may have contributed to the same effect.[4] But the Pennsylvania Germans, having

3. For most of the facts herewith presented in reference to the immigration of the Jews, their number at the present time, etc., I am indebted to the kindness of Mr. B. Ney, of Harrisonburg, Va.

4. Schuricht's German Element in Virginia, Vol. I, p. 85; Waddell's Scotch-Irish of the Valley of Virginia, p. 90.

passed the stressful period of their history, wanted land for their children: good land, cheap land, much land. William Beverley, writing April 30, 1732, to a friend in Williamsburg concerning lands on the Shenandoah, says: "Ye northern men are fond of buying land there, because they can buy it, for six or seven pounds pr: hundred acres, cheaper than they can take up land in pensilvania and they don't care to go as far as Wmsburg."[5] Therefore, after the best farms in Pennsylvania had been taken, and the narrow breadth of Maryland had been occupied, the next and most natural thing was to go across the Potomac into the Shenandoah Valley. There they found a free, open, and fertile new land; and there they chose to invest their savings and fix their dwellings.

When we raise our eyes to the broader horizon, and ask the larger question, Why came the Germans to America?—which is a fair question, and one that can scarcely be disregarded here—we are confronted with a problem more intricate and complex, yet not difficult of solution. The great German immigration began practically with the beginning of the eighteenth century: some came to the Carolinas; some to Virginia; some to New York; but most of them came to Pennsylvania;[6] and the chief causes for their leaving Europe were religious persecution, devastating wars, political oppression, and social unrest.[7]

The German is by nature and training a lover of home and of the home land; he is conservative in temperament, and is not easily given to new opinions or new paths. It is evident, therefore, that a combination of strong influences must have been necessary to get the tide of emigration started—to overcome his racial inertia, and to drive him into the un-

5. Palmer's Calendar, Vol. I, p. 218.

6. Sachse's German Sectarians, Vol. II, p. 332.

7. Kuhns' German and Swiss Settlements, pp. 1-30; 62-82; Schuricht's German Element in Virginia, Vol. I, pp. 60-65; 76; Rupp's Thirty Thousand Names, pp. 1-18; 420; Stapleton's Memorials of the Huguenots, pp. 34, 72, 101, 112, 118; Virginia Magazine, Vol. XIII, No. 3, p. 287.

certainties, hardships, and dangers that two centuries ago beset a journey across the seas and lurked in the wilderness of the New World. But sufficient incentives were not wanting: the Old World drove him out, while the New, with all its untried possibilities, yet said "Come" in a language that was unmistakable.

It is doubtless true that the great German exodus of the eighteenth century had its preparation from 1618 to 1648, in the Thirty Years' War: that devastating scourge of fire, blood, and sin, kindled in the name of religion and fed to its bitter end with every human ambition and every human passion. The embers of this burning were still red when another series of wars began, which harried out the century and put their destroying blight heavily upon the next: the war respecting the Spanish Netherlands, 1667-1668; the war with the Protestant Netherlands, 1672-1678; the war of the Palatinate, 1688-1697; and the war of the Spanish Succession, 1701-1714.

One of the districts that suffered most severely in these wars was the Lower Palatinate, a country lying near France, on both sides of the Rhine, to the northeast of Alsace and Lorraine. Conditions there during the War of the Palatinate are described by a well known historian in the following words:

> Seeking a pretext for beginning hostilities, he [Louis XIV of France] laid claim, on the part of his sister-in-law, to properties in the Palatinate, and hurried a large army into the country, which was quickly overrun. But being unable to hold the conquests he had made, Louis ordered that the country be laid waste. Among the places reduced to ruins were the historic towns of Heidelberg, Spires, and Worms. Even fruit trees, vines, and crops were destroyed. Upwards of a hundred thousand peasants were rendered homeless.[8]

This war lasted till 1697. We are not surprised, therefore, that a great tide of emigration began almost immediately, continuing, as well as it could, throughout the next fierce

8. Myers' Modern Age, p. 211.

conflict, and for many years thereafter; nor are we surprised that a larger number of emigrants probably went out from the Palatinate during the next century than from any other part of Germany.

But even the Treaty of Utrecht, following the War of the Spanish Succession, was not to leave the stricken lands of the Rhine and Elbe long in peace. In 1740 began the eight-year struggle of the Austrian Succession; and, in 1756, the Seven Years' War. Thus we have in outline some of the great disturbing causes that were making many of the people of Europe long for new homes—or, indeed, homes of any sort. Added to these larger movements were the various disturbing forces, political, social, economic, or religious, peculiar to each locality. For example, at Heidelberg the Elector Palatine, Frederick II, became a Lutheran; Frederick III, a Calvinist; Ludovic V restored the Lutheran Church; his son and successor re-established Calvinism; and next came a Catholic prince, to insist upon the spiritual allegiance of his subjects to his creed.[9] No wonder that the Old World and its people became "well tired of each other." Scotch Refugees, Quakers and Dissenters, Huguenots and Hollanders, and with them the Germans in thousand after thousand, sought homes beyond the western seas.[10]

After the tide of Teutonic emigration had once become well started, the influence was often contagious; the *Wanderlust* siezed many, as when their ancestors of old pressed down from the north and overran the Roman Empire. Many who came to America found things well pleasing to them; and the reports they sent back to their friends lost nothing in the perspective of distance, novelty, and strong desire. Daniel Falckner, an educated German who had spent some time in Pennsylvania, went over to Halle about 1700. His friend, the influential August Hermann Francke, propounded to him

9. Pennsylvania Magazine, Vol. X, p. 382.

10. For an excellent presentation of this whole question, see the Pennsylvania Magazine, Vol. X, pp. 241-250; 375-391.

in writing one hundred and three questions, relating to the people and things in Pennsylvania, to which Falckner responded at length. The manuscript of the questions and answers covers 197 folio pages. This manuscript was published in 1702 at Frankfurt and Leipzig, and doubtless had a strong influence in stimulating emigration.[11] William Penn visited Germany, and large numbers of the people accepted his invitation, and settled in his new colony. The Dutch ship-owners hired influential Germans, living in America, to return to the Fatherland as emigration agents, and by artful methods, fair and unfair, to stimulate enthusiasm in the movement.

The hardships of the journey, over land and sea, have already been referred to; many died upon the long voyages; many arrived sick; and some who lived and escaped disease never saw the New World. Great numbers of Germans flocked to London, with an innocent confidence, which recalls the Children's Crusade, that a way would speedily be provided them for transportation to the English colonies in America. In the predicament, the Lord-Lieutenant of Ireland petitioned Queen Anne that some might be sent to the Emerald Isle. His request was complied with, at least in part; and by February, 1710, we find that no less than 3800 Germans had been carried to Munster, where they settled, and where their descendants have maintained their characteristics of probity, honor, and thrift.[12]

We have now before us not only the causes of the German immigration to America, but also, in Falckner's book and Penn's visit to Germany, at least two of the influences that drew them to the colony of Pennsylvania, rather than to any other colony. In the early days a considerable number came to New York; but most of them soon became dissatisfied.

11. Publications of the Pennsylvania-German Society, Vol. XIV, pp. 39-256.

12. Pennsylvania Magazine, Vol. X, p. 381; Rupp's Thirty Thousand Names, p. 4; Kuhns' German and Swiss Settlements, pp. 62-82.

Many of them seem to have got into trouble, through their financial embarrassments or ignorance of the law, in respect to their land titles and other interests; and because of this they reached the conclusion, often with good reason, that the authorities in the colony were unjust to them. The majority of them removed to Pennsylvania and, sending word back to the Fatherland, warned their friends against New York, advising them to come to Pennsylvania.[13] But, most of all, perhaps, Pennsylvania was generally looked upon as a place of religious liberty, a place of refuge; and so those distressed in heart and conscience, as well as those seeking a good investment for their money and labor, came to Pennsylvania.

From 1682 to 1702 comparatively few Germans arrived at Philadelphia: the movement was just beginning; but the period from 1702 to 1727 was epoch-making: between 40,000 and 50,000 came to the Quaker colony.[14] In the year 1719, alone, 6000 landed.[15]

In Professor Rupp's valuable collection, "Thirty Thousand Names of German, Swiss, Dutch, and French Immigrants," we have reproduced the names of many of the Germans that landed at Philadelphia from 1727 to 1776, together with other facts in many cases concerning the country from which they came, the vessels in which they sailed, etc. The original lists of signatures were taken by requirement of law; and, although in most cases they contain only the names of the men over sixteen years of age, in numerous instances the number of each sex, or the total number of both sexes in each vessel, is recorded. From the given figures as a basis, a fair estimate may be made of the totals in the other cases. Proceeding upon this basis, with a care to be conservative in all my estimates, I have gone over Rupp's work, and present

13. Pennsylvania Magazine, Vol. X, pp. 387, 388; Rupp's Thirty Thousand Names, p. 452.

14. Rupp's Thirty Thousand Names, pp. 1, 2.

15. Pennsylvania Magazine, Vol. X, p. 391.

herewith some of the results obtained,—not only those in regard to the number of arrivals each year, but also some in regard to the various countries from which the immigrants came.

German Immigrants, Male and Female, Landing at Philadelphia.

Year.	No. of Arrivals.	Year.	No. of Arrivals.
1727	c. 1250	1750	c. 4000
1728	c. 400	1751	c. 4000
1729	c. 310	1752	c. 4600
1730	c. 450	1753	c. 4000
1731	631	1754	c. 4500
1732	c. 2000	1755	c. 300
1733	c. 1500	1756	109
1734	c. 400	1761	c. 50[17]
1735	c. 230	1762	———
1736	c. 850	1763	c. 600
1737	c. 1800	1764	2129
1738	3116	1765	c. 800
1739	1673	1766	c. 600
1740	1131	1767	840
1741	c. 1000	1768	c. 800
1742	c. 850	1769	c. 325
1743	c. 1300	1770	c. 500
1744	c. 900	1771	c. 900
1745	———	1772	c. 800
1746	c. 350	1773	c. 1500
1747	c. 800	1774	c. 550
1748	c. 1500	1775	c. 200
1749	c. 7000[16]		

16. Lecky, following Kalm, says that nearly 12,000 came to Pennsylvania in 1749.—American Revolution, Woodburn's Ed., p. 21.

17. Rupp makes this note:—"Owing to the hostilities between France and England, German immigration was completely suspended from 1756 to 1761."—Page 351.

A glance over the above table, giving the approximate numbers of arrivals in the several years from 1727 to 1776, will reveal some rather striking facts in confirmation of the statement that the European wars were one of the great causes of German emigration. Take, for example, the War of the Austrian Succession, 1740 to 1748. During the actual progress of the conflict only a few could get away; but immediately following its close great numbers crowded the ships. On the other hand, war in America repelled immigrants. During the Seven Years' War, there was also war in America, and in consequence there was practically no immigration from 1756 to 1763. The American Revolution also put a decided check upon German immigration, which continued to be sluggish until after the fall of Napoleon.[18]

The following figures, prepared from statistics given in Professor Seidensticker's *Die Erste Deutsche Einwanderung in Amerika,* will afford additional illustration in this connection. From 1820 to 1831, the average yearly number of German immigrants to the United States was slightly over 845; from 1832 to 1836, the five years following the European disturbances of 1830, the average yearly number was 12,777 1-5. From 1845 to 1849, the yearly average was 56,979 2-5; from 1850 to 1854, the five years following the revolution of 1848, the yearly average was 130,850 1-5.[19] From 1861 to 1865, slightly more than 46,610 Germans came to the States yearly; but from 1866 to 1870 the annual number was 117,791.

The following facts, collated with reference to the places of nativity of those immigrants who came over from 1727 to 1776, are of particular interest in the face of our question, Whence? For the names of practically all the German fam-

18. Seidensticker's First Century of German Printing, p. viii.

19. On the influence of the revolutions of 1830 and 1848 upon German emigration, see Carl Schurz's article in McClure's Magazine, December, 1906.

ilies of the Shenandoah Valley are to be found in Rupp's collection. From 1727 to 1739 each ship-load of arrivals are designated "Palatines," almost without exception. During the years 1740 and 1741 they are also called "Palatines," except that one ship-load, registered on September 23, 1740, are labeled "Palatines and Switzers." From 1742 to 1748, "Foreigners" is the designation employed. In 1749 we find a pleasing variety: there are "Foreigners," "Wirtembergers," "Wirtembergers from Erbach," "Palatines," "Foreigners from Wirtemberg, Alsace, and Zweibrucken"; and more "Foreigners" from various places: Zweibrucken, Nassau, Hanau, Darmstadt, Eisenberg, Swabia, Mannheim, Durlach, Rittenheim, etc. From 1750 to 1753 the immigrants are not identified as to place of former residence; but they are sometimes identified with respect to religion, as "Calvinists," "Mennonites," "Catholics," etc. In 1754 their places of former residence are usually given: Alsace, Lorraine, Franconia, the Palatinate, Wirtemberg, Darmstadt, Zweibrucken, Hesse, Westphalia, Hanau, Switzerland, Hamburg, Hanover, Saxony. From 1755 to 1775 they are not identified as to place of birth or former residence; a few ship-loads, only, are identified with respect to religion; but, as in nearly every case from 1727, the name of the ship, of the ship-master, and the names of the foreign ports from which the ship last sailed, are given. From the foregoing particulars, it will be observed that the great majority of immigrants of the 18th century were from South Germany.

In closing this chapter, the fact is emphasized that the Germans of the Valley of Virginia are descended almost entirely from the immigrants of the early eighteenth century: people who left the Fatherland, not for economic reasons alone, but largely because of religious persecution, political oppression, or military outrages. Such forces always move the best classes,—people who at such times are seeking most of all liberty of conscience, health of the state, and safety for the morals of home and family.[20] The German pioneers of the Valley, like their neighbors the Scotch-Irish,[21] were such a people. They came when facilities for travel and transportation were at a minimum, and when the perils of the undertaking were at a maximum. Let us hope that their descendants will never lose the love of liberty and the love of virtue that burned in the bosoms of the fathers, and that drove them far forth in the face of danger.

20. See Report of U. S. Commissioner of Education, 1901, Vol. I, p. 562.

21. Peyton's History of Augusta, p. 79.

CHAPTER IV.

Early Settlements.

Attention has been called to the fact, in Chapter II preceding, that it is possible, and even probable, that other white men besides John Lederer and his companions were in the Shenandoah Valley ahead of Governor Spotswood, who came in 1716. However, if this be true, it is not likely that any permanent settlements can be placed nearly so early as his visit. Those white men who might have been found west of the Blue Ridge prior to 1726 or 1727, were all doubtless explorers, missionaries, hunters, or Indian traders. About the year 1725 John Van Meter, a Dutchman from New York, was in the valley of the South Branch of the Potomac, twenty-five or thirty miles west of the valley of the Shenandoah. He was a trader, and spent much of his time among the Delaware Indians, in Pennsylvania; but also journeyed far to the south to traffic with the Cherokees and Catawbas. Later, upon his advice, his two sons, John and Isaac Van Meter, came to Virginia and secured large tracts of land, not exclusively in the valley of the South Branch, but first in the lower valley of the Shenandoah.[1]

It is evident that about the same time that Van Meter the elder was traversing the valley of the South Branch, other adventurers, from eastern Virginia, were pushing out toward the head fountains of the same stream, where the waters turn southwestward, toward the James; for the Cowpasture River was known and named as early as 1727. In that year Robert Lewis, William Lynn, Robert Brooke, Jr., James Mills, William Lewis, and Beverly Robinson petitioned the Governor in Council for 50,000 acres of land "in one or more tracts on

1. Lewis' History and Government of West Virginia, pp. 40-42; Kercheval's History of the Valley, pp. 46, 51.

the head branches of James River to the West and Northwestward of the Cow Pasture," with a view to procuring settlers for the same.[2] Whether the petition was granted or not does not appear; but it seems to be an established fact that white people located in the designated region at the time of, or soon after, the settlement of the Scotch-Irish about the site of Staunton, in 1732.[3] Why Lewis, Lynn, Brooke, and their friends, in their search for lands, should have passed by the fertile tracts in the Valley is a mystery.

It was in 1730 that the younger Van Meters, John and Isaac, obtained their first grants of land. John got 10,000 acres in the forks of the Shenandoah, including the places called Cedar Lick and Stony Lick, together with 20,000 acres lower down; Isaac got 10,000 acres in the lower valley.[4] These grants, as most others of the time, were made upon the condition that within two years a family should be settled on each thousand acres. In 1731 the Van Meters sold portions of their tracts to Jost Hite, who, in 1732, settled in the Valley with his three sons-in-law, George Bowman, Jacob Chrisman, Paul Froman, and others. On June 12, 1734, patents were ordered to be issued to the "Several Masters of Families" residing on these lands, as well as on part of another tract granted conditionally to Hite, Robert Mackay, and others.[5] These patents were issued upon proof that the required number of families had been brought in; so that we here find evidence that, by the early part of this year (1734), some forty families were settled on and near the Opequon, east, south, and southwest of the site of Winchester.

2. Palmer's Calendar of State Papers, Vol. I, p. 214.

3. Waddell's Annals of Augusta, p. 21.

4. Virginia Magazine, Vol. XIII, No. 2, pp. 115-119.

5. Idem, No. 4, p. 354.—George Bowman's house, erected on Cedar Creek in 1734, is said to be still standing.—English's Life of G. R. Clark, Vol. I, p. 116.

Jost Hite was a native of Strasburg, in Alsace;[6] his sons-in-law, Bowman, Chrisman, and Froman, and his friend Peter Stephens, as well as most of the others in the Opequon settlement, were also Germans; but with these were a number of Scotch-Irish, among whom were Robert McKay, William Duff, and probably Robert Green.[7] It appears, indeed, that John Lewis, the Scotch-Irish pioneer of Augusta County, came from Pennsylvania to Virginia with Hite and his party in 1732; but, passing on up the Valley the same year, began his settlement near the site of Staunton.[8]

For many years Jost Hite enjoyed the distinction of being generally regarded as the first permanent settler in the Shenandoah Valley. He certainly was one of the most influential citizens of his day, west of the Blue Ridge; and he was doubtless the leader in permanent settlement in the section now embraced in Frederick County; therefore he has been given a prominent place in this narrative; but that he was the first settler in the Shenandoah Valley, taken as a whole, is now no longer claimed with serious intelligence. As was intimated in the beginning of this chapter, several permanent settlements are known to have been made as much as five or six years prior to 1732: these we shall now proceed to notice in some detail.

In the year 1726 or 1727, Morgan *ap* Morgan, a Welshman, removed from Pennsylvania to Virginia; settled within the present boundaries of Berkeley County, W. Va.; and erected, at the site of the village of Bunker Hill, what is said to have been, and probably was, the "first cabin on the

6. Hite usually, perhaps always, signed his name in German, but did not always spell it the same way. Hite, Heid, Heyd, Heydt, Hyte, are some of the various forms written by himself and others. Jost is equivalent to Just, Justus, Justin, etc., and appears in different forms: Joast, Joist, Yost, etc.

7. Kercheval's History of the Valley, p. 45.

8. Peyton's History of Augusta, p. 25; Waddell's Annals of Augusta, pp. 24, 25.

Virginia side of the Potomac, between the Blue Ridge and North Mountains."[9] Morgan also built, about 1740, near his place of residence, the first Episcopal church in the Valley. He died in 1799, leaving a son with the same name. The same year that Morgan Morgan settled at Bunker Hill, or the year following, a company of Germans crossed the Potomac a few miles above Harper's Ferry, at the old Pack-horse Ford; and, a mile above the crossing, founded a settlement in what is now Jefferson County, W. Va. This settlement soon developed into a village known as New Mecklenburg; later, at the time of its legal establishment in 1762, called Mecklenburg;[10] and, later still, called Shepherdstown after its founder, Thomas Shepherd.[11]

In the year 1726 or 1727, when Morgan Morgan was building his cabin in the lower Valley, a little band of German pioneers, far up on the Shenandoah River, were selecting a place to be called home. That they were there at so early a date will appear in full as we proceed. They were from Pennsylvania; and were possibly at first members of that large and enterprising class of pioneers known as "squatters"; but we shall see that they were ready, as soon as the legal forms and representatives of government penetrated the Valley, to comply fully with every requirement of legality and justice.

In order to get the case before us fully and authoritatively, several documents from Palmer's *Calendar of State Papers* and other sources are herewith presented.

To the Honble William Gooch Esqr Lieutenant Governor &c &c—

The petition of the Subscribers humbly shew—

That about four years past, they purchased five thousand acres of land, of one Jacob Stover, and paid him a great Sum of Money

9. Meade's Old Churches, Vol. II, p. 302; Howe's Antiquities of Virginia, p. 273; Waddell's Annals of Augusta, p. 28; Lewis' Handbook of West Virginia, p. 31.

10. Hening's Statutes, Vol. VII, p. 600.

11. Lewis' History of West Virginia, p. 41.

for the same, Amounting to Upwards of four hundred pounds: that yr: petitioners were informed & believed the sd: Stover had a good right & title in the said land—that immediately after the sd: * * * all their lands & sevll other things in the County of Lancaster & Province of Pensylvania, where they then lived, & came & seated on the land they had bought of the sd Stover; and cleared sevl Plantations & made great Improvements thereon—Since which, they have been Informed that the sd: land (known by the name of Massannutting) is Claimed by one Wm Beverly Gent—& that the sd: Beverly hath brought suit agst the sd: Stover for the same, in the Honble the Generall Court—Yr Petitioners further shew that should the sd: Beverley recover the sd: land, that he will turn yr: Petrs out of Doors, or oblige them to give much more for their lands & plantations than they are worth, Which will entirely ruin yr Petrs—And yor Petrs cannot recover anything of the sd Stover, to make them amends for the Loss of their sd: lands, plantations &c, he being very poor, and is Daily Expected to Run away. Wherefore yr Petitioners humbly hope that as they are not Privy to any fraud done by the sd: Stover in obtaining the sd: Land & yor petrs beihg Dutchmen & not acquainted with the laws here concerning lands & Imagined the sd: Stover's right to be good & have Run the hazard of their lives & estates in removing from Pensylvania to the sd: land, being above two hundred miles & at a time when there was very few Inhabitants in them parts of Shenando, & they frequently visited by the Indians. And at this time yr petrs have nine Plantations, fifty one people, old & young, thereon & Expect to have two more familys to seat on the sd: land this spring, (none of which are any of the persons the sd: Stover swore was on the sd: land when he obtained the sd: Patent as yr petrs have been informed) nor did yr petrs hear of the sd: Beverleys' claiming the said land 'til they had made plantations thereon—And yr petrs have also paid his Majesties Quit rents for the said land, ever since they bought the sd: land of the sd: Jacob Stover, that Your Honrs taking all & Singular, the premisses into yr: Consideration, will be pleased to make such order or Decree thereon, that yr: petrs may Quietly Injoy the said land,

And yr: petr will every pray &c
MILHART RANGDMANN

ABRAHAM ——
MATHEW FOLK

—— ——

—— ——

ADAM MULLER
M—— CRIMSART.[12]

This petition is not dated; but it is placed in the *Calendar*

12. Palmer's Calendar of State Papers, Vol. I, pp. 219, 220.

in the year 1733, which is proved by various circumstances to be the correct date.[13] Moreover, it was presented early in the year, as is shown in the paper itself by the reference, "this spring." The original petition is still in existence, on file in the State Library at Richmond; and the signatures, fully and correctly given, are as follows: Adam Mueller, Abram Strickler, Mathias Selzer, Philip Lang (Long), Paul Lung (Long), Michael Rinehart, Hans Rood, Michael Kaufman.[14]

The following letter, written November 28, 1733, refers to the German petitioners and their interests, and fits the circumstances already detailed:

Sir, This is to Inform you that I was at the great mountains & saw several dutchmen that Came from Pencelvania and they told me they had agreed with Stover for Land on Sherando, but since they came they heard that Col: Wm. Beverley was at Law for it, therefore they would not settle it, unless Stover could make them a right to it, which if he did they would settle it directly—Which is the needfull from

Sr yr Humble servt
To Commd
FRA: THORNTON.

To Mr. William Robertson,
at Williamsburg &c.[15]

To supplement the above documents and complete the evidence for the statements already made, the following paper is presented:

William Gooch Esqr. His Majesty's Lieutenant Governour and Commander in Chief of the Colony and Dominion of Virginia.

To all to whom these Presents Shall come Greeting.

Whereas by one Act of Assembly made at the Capitol the 23d October in the year 1705 for the better Settling and peopling this His Majesty's Colony and Dominion it is Enacted that it shall and may be Lawful for the Governour and Commander in Chief of this Colony and Dominion for the time being by a public Instrument or Letters Patents under the broad Seal thereof, to Declare any Alien or Aliens Foreigner or Foreigners being already Settled or Inhabit-

13. Virginia Magazine, Vol. XIII, No. 2, pp. 121, 122.

14. Idem, p. 121.

15. Palmer's Calendar of State Papers, Vol. I, p. 220.

ants of this Colony or which shall hereafter come to Settle Plant or Reside therein upon His or theirs taking the oaths therein prescribed and subscribing the Test to be to all entents and purposes fully and compleatly naturalized and that all persons having Such public Instruments or Letters Patents shall by virtue of this Act have and Enjoy to them and their Heirs the same Immunities and Rights of and unto the Laws and Priviledges of this Colony and Dominion as fully and amply as any of His Majesty's Natural Born Subjects have and Enjoy within the same an[d] as if the[y] had been born within any of His Majesty's Realms and Dominions Provided that nothing therein contained Shall be construed to Enable or Give power or Priviledge to any Foreigner to Do or Execute any manner of thing which by any of the Acts made in England concerning His Majesty's Plantations he is Disabled to Do or Execute.

And Adam Miller born at Shresoin[16] in Germany having Settled and Inhabited for fifteen years past on Shenandoa in this Colony and now made Application to me for the benefit of Naturalization and before me taken the oaths prescribed by Law and Subscribed the Test, I Do hereby pursuant to the said authority Declare the said Adam Miller to be to all intents and purposes, fully and compleatly Naturalized and to have and Enjoy to him and his Heirs the same Immunities and Rights of and unto the Laws and Priviledges of this Colony and Dominion as fully and amply as any of His Majesty's Natural Born Subjects have and Enjoy within the same, and as if he had been born within any of His Majesty's Realms and Dominions according to the aforesaid act saving always in such matters and things which by the Laws of England concerning the Plantation he is Disabled.

Given under my hand and the Seal of the Colony at Williamsburg this 13th day of March 1741-2 in the 15th year of the Reign of our Sovereign Lord King George the Second By the Grace of God King of Great Brittain &c.

WILLIAM GOOCH.[17]

By a very simple process we may now determine almost exactly the date of the first settlement at Massanutting. About four years prior to 1733, that is, about 1729,[18] the

16. Perhaps Scherstein.

17. The original of this paper is now in the possession of one of Adam Miller's descendants, Miss Elizabeth B. Miller, who lives on part of the land which he owned, near Elkton, Rockingham County, Va. A copy of the document may be found printed in the William and Mary College Quarterly, Vol. IX, No. 2, pp. 132, 133.

18. In 1730, more probably, as will appear a little further on.

German petitioners had bought their five thousand acres of land of Jacob Stover. In 1729, or thereabouts, there were not many—but there were a few—inhabitants in the valley of the Shenandoah, in the vicinity of Massanutting. That Adam Miller, one of the petitioners of 1733, was one of the few there in 1729, and that he had located in that district two or three years before 1729, are facts proved by his naturalization paper, which states that he had been an inhabitant there for fifteen years prior to 1741-2:[19] that is, as early as 1726-7. At this date, therefore, we may place the beginning of the Massanutten settlement; and Adam Miller must have been one of the first settlers, if not the very first.

Other facts confirm the above conclusions. On June 17, 1730, Jacob Stover, a native of Switzerland, obtained for himself and "divers Germans and Swiss Families, his Associates," from the Virginia Colonial Council a grant for 10,000 acres of land on the Shenandoah River, in such tracts as he should select, upon the condition that within two years he should settle upon it the required number of families. He succeeded, by methods fair or false,[20] in getting this grant confirmed to him by two deeds bearing date of December 15, 1733, each for 5000 acres.[21] Both of these 5000-acre tracts were on the Shenandoah River: one in the vicinity of Lynn-

19. The Gregorian calendar was not adopted in the British Empire until 1751, long after most other countries had been following it. In that year it was prescribed by an act of Parliament that the next year, 1752, should begin on January 1, instead of March 25; and that in the following September eleven days should be dropped, in order to adjust the Old Style to the New Style. Accordingly, the day following September 2 that year was written and known as September 14; and the loss of time has never been felt. Counting the year as ending March 25, it was near the close of the year 1741 when Adam Miller obtained his title to citizenship; but, as we now count time, it was early in the year 1742.

20. Something on the methods Stover is reported to have used will be given further on.

21. Virginia Magazine, Vol. XIII, No. 2, pp. 120-123.

wood and Lewiston, now in Rockingham County; the other southwest of Luray, now in Page County. It is likely that each was partly on both sides of the river; and each must have extended along the course of the river for several miles. The tract near Luray was doubtless identical with the 5000 acres purchased of Stover in 1729,—possibly before he actually obtained the grant,—or in 1730, the year in which the grant was obtained, by Adam Miller, Abram Strickler, Mathias Selzer, Philip Long, and the rest; for their purchase was called Massanutting, as they relate in their petition; and Stover's lower grant of 5000 acres was on Massanutting Creek,[22] and so must have included at least part of the little valley of the said creek, on the west side of the river, known as Massanutten to this day. A village and postoffice, bearing the same name, are on the east side of the river, opposite the said valley and creek.

The foregoing account of the Massanutten settlement, based upon original documents still in existence, is in substantial agreement with and confirms the following traditional account of Adam Miller, preserved by his descendants. Adam Miller, as a young man, came from Germany with his wife and an unmarried sister, and settled in Lancaster County, Pennsylvania. Later, he went down the Chesapeake Bay into Virginia, and near Williamsburg learned from some of the members of Spotswood's company of the wonderful land west of the Blue Ridge. He went to the Valley, following Spotswood's route, and was so well pleased with the lands along the Shenandoah that he at once brought his family thither from Pennsylvania. He also induced some of his Pennsylvania friends and neighbors to come to the Valley, and locate near him.[23]

The entire case before us may be briefly summarized as

22. Kercheval's History of the Valley, p. 45; Foote's Sketches, p. 15.

23. Virginia Magazine, Vol. X, No. 1, pp. 84, 85.

follows: In 1726 or 1727, Adam Miller located on the Shenandoah River, near Massanutting; with him or soon following him came his friends, Abram Strickler, Mathias Selser, Philip Long,[24] Paul Long, Michael Rinehart, John Rood. and Michael Kaufman. On June 17, 1730, Jacob Stover obtained his two grants on the Shenandoah River of 5000 acres each, the lower one of which included the holdings of Adam Miller and his friends. Either shortly before or shortly after June 17, 1730, Miller and his friends bought this 5000-acre tract (the Massanutting tract) of Stover for 400 pounds or more. On April 30, 1732, William Beverley wrote to a friend in Williamsburg, asking him to secure for him a grant of 15,000 acres on both sides of the "main River of Shenondore," including an "old field, called and known by ye name of Massanutting Town";[25] on May 5, 1732, Beverley was granted 15,000 acres on the northwest side of the river, "including a place called Massanutting Town, provided the same do not interfere with any of the Tracts already granted

24. Eight miles southwest of Luray, on the Price farm, near Massanutten, is a monument with the following inscription:

In memory of
Philip Long
founder of my paternal
ancestry in America,
born in Germany A. D.
1678, Died May 4, 1755.

Erected by Caroline V. Long Price
of Jefferson City, Mo.,
July 4, 1891.

Built Old Ft. Long
near the heart of land estate
granted him by the English Crown
in 1730.

For a copy of this inscription I am indebted to the kindness of Prof. John S. Flory, of Bridgewater, Va.

25. Palmer's Calendar of State Papers, Vol. I, pp. 217, 218.

in that part of the Colony."[26] In the early part of 1733, Miller, Strickler, Selzer, and the rest petitioned for a confirmation of their right through Stover, as against Beverly, who was trying to oust them, or upset their title; on December 12, 1733, Beverley's *caveat* against Stover was dismissed; Stover's grants were confirmed; and the deeds were issued to him three days later—December 15, 1733.[27]

Adam Miller, the pioneer of the Massanutten settlement and of the upper Valley, owned first the "uppermost of the Massanutten lots," as is shown by the Orange County records. This tract, now in the southwestern part of Page County, near the Rockingham line, he sold; and, in 1741, settled near Elkton, at Bear Lithia Spring.[28] Later he seems to have settled still nearer Elkton, upon a site that has been continuously occupied by his descendants to the present day. In religion he was a Lutheran; and that he was possessed of a generous measure of Christian charity, as well as of a good share of native caution, will appear from the following extract from the diary of Leonhard Schnell, a Moravian missionary:

On Sunday, December 3rd [1749], the young Franciscus went very early with us to show us the way to Matthias Schaub, who, immediately on my offer to preach for them, sent messengers through the neighborhood to announce my sermon. In a short time a considerable number of people assembled, to whom I preached. After the sermon I baptized the child of a Hollander. We stayed over night with Matthias Schaub. His wife told us that we were always welcome in their house. We should always come to them whenever we came into that district.

Towards evening a man from another district, Adam Mueller, passed. I told him that I would like to come to his house and preach there. He asked me if I were sent by God. I answered, yes. He said, if I were sent by God I would be welcome, but he said, there are at present so many kinds of people, that often one

26. Virginia Magazine, Vol. XIII, No. 2, p. 138.

27. Idem, pp. 120-122; No. 3, pp. 295-297.

28. My thanks are due at this point to Mr. Charles E. Kemper, of Washington City, for personal assistance.

does not know where they come from. I requested him to notify his neighbors that I would preach on the 5th, which he did.

On December 4th, we left Schaub's house, commending the whole family to God. We traveled through the rain across the South Shenandoah to Adam Mueller, who received us with much love. We stayed over night with him.

On December 5th, I preached at Adam Mueller's house on John 7: 'Whosoever thirsteth let him come to the water and drink.' A number of thirsty souls were present. Especially Adam Mueller took in every word and after the sermon declared himself well pleased. In the afternoon we traveled a short distance, staying over night with a Swiss.[29]

Adam Miller was a soldier in the French and Indian War, as is shown by the military schedule in *Hening's Statutes,* where his name appears along with those of others who received pay from the Colony for services, September, 1758.[30] He lived to an advanced age, dying about the close of the Revolution.

It may be profitable at this juncture to catalogue, in chronological order, some of the earliest grants of large tracts of land, west of the Blue Ridge; two or three of which have been already referred to. It will be observed that some of these grants were made to Germans and Scotch-Irish from Pennsylvania; one at least to Germans from the Spotswood colonies; and some to Englishmen from East Virginia.

In 1727, Robert Lewis, William Lynn, Robert Brooke, Jr., James Mills, William Lewis, and Beverly Robinson petitioned for 50,000 acres, "on the head branches of James River to the West and Northwestward of the Cow Pasture."[31] This tract lay beyond the Valley, in the present counties of Highland and Bath. Whether the grant was made or not seems unknown.

On October 28, 1728, Robert Carter, in behalf of the Proprietors of the Northern Neck, entered a *caveat* against grant-

29. Virginia Magazine, Vol. XI, No. 2, pp. 126, 127.
30. Hening's Statutes, Vol. VII, p. 186.
31. Palmer's Calendar, Vol. I, p. 214.

ing a patent for 10,000 acres on both sides of Happy Creek, "joining on the great Mountains, &c &c," to Larkin Chew and others.[32] This tract was evidently in the present county of Warren: Happy Creek flows out of the Blue Ridge, and into the Shenandoah River just below Front Royal. William Russell was probably one of the "others" to whom the contested grant was made; for he and "his partners" took up land in that locality in 1728.[33] This seems to have been the first legal attempt made by anyone to secure lands in the Shenandoah Valley.

In 1729 Colonel Robert Carter ("King Carter") secured a grant of 50,000 acres of land, probably from the Proprietors of the Northern Neck, in the lower Valley, on the west bank of the Shenandoah River.[34] This tract included part of the northeast end of Warren County and a considerable portion of Clarke County. This large grant, secured in this section by Robert Carter at this early date, will explain the fact that the people of Clarke County are chiefly English. Only a few Germans got into that section of the Valley.

On June 17, 1730, John Van Meter was assigned 10,000 acres in the fork of the Shenandoah, including the places called Cedar Lick and Stony Lick, and "twenty thousand acres of land not already taken up by Robert Carter & Mann Page, Esqrs., or any other lying in the fork between the Sd River Sherrando and the River, Cahongaroota, & extending thence to Opeckon & up the South Branch thereof," for "himself & eleven children, & also that divers of his Rela'cons & friends living in the Government of New York."[35] This was some of the land secured a little later by Jost Hite.

On the same date Isaac Van Meter, brother to John, obtained a grant of 10,000 acres lying between Carter's land,

32. Palmer's Calendar, Vol. I, p. 215.

33. Virginia Magazine, Vol. XIII, No. 4, pp. 354, 355.

34. Idem, No. 2, pp. 116, 117.

35. Idem, pp. 115-117.

the River, and the Opequon Creek.[36] Hite and his colony probably got this tract also.

On the same date (June 17, 1730) Jacob Stover, of Switzerland, got his first two grants, each of 5000 acres, one in the Massanutten district, the other farther up the Shenandoah River, in the present county of Rockingham.[37]

On October 28, 1730, Alexander Ross and Morgan Bryan, of Pennsylvania, were granted 100,000 acres in the vicinity of Winchester, between the Opequon Creek and the North Mountain (Alleghany), upon which they settled a colony of Friends.[38]

On June 10, 1731, William Beverley, Joseph Smith, Joseph Clapham, Thomas Watkins, and Simeon Jeffries obtained a grant of 20,000 acres on the western side of the lower Valley, in Frederick and Shenandoah County, between Cedar Creek and Lost River.[39]

On the same date, John Fishback, Jacob Holtzclow, Henry Settler, Jacob Sengaback, Peter Reid, Michael Shower, John Vandehouse, George Wolf, William Carpenter, and John Richlu, "in behalf of themselves and other German Protestants," obtained a grant of 50,000 acres between the Blue Ridge and the Shenandoah River, in the present counties of Warren and Page.[40] These men were from east of the Blue Ridge, and some belonged to the Germanna families.

On October 21, 1731, Robert McKay and "Joost Heyd," of Pennsylvania, were assigned 100,000 acres in several tracts. The order of the Council in full is given herewith:

On the peticon of Rob't McKay & Joost Heyd, of the Province of Pensilvania, setting forth that they & divers other Families to the number of one hundred are desirous to remove from thence & Seat

36. Idem, pp. 118, 119.

37. Virginia Magazine, Vol. XIII, No. 2, pp. 120-123.

38. Idem, pp. 127, 128.

39. Idem, pp. 130-132.

40. Idem, pp. 132, 133.

themselves on the back of the great Mountains within this Colony, & praying that one hundred thousand acres of Land lying between the Line of the Land granted to John Vanmeter, Jacob Stover, John Fishback & others may be assigned them, and that the Residue of the sd hundred thousand acres may be assigned upon & including the several Branches of Sherundo River, above the Land of the said Stover & Fishback and his Partners. The Governor, with the advice of the Council, is pleas'd to order, as it is hereby Ordered, that the petrs, in behalf of themselves & their Partners, have leave to take up the Sd Quantity of 100,000 acres of Land within the Limits above described, & that upon the above Number of Families coming to dwell there within two Years, Patents shall be granted them in such manner as they shall agree to divide the same.[41]

In the association of McKay with Hite we see the reason for the commingling of the Germans and Scotch-Irish in the lower Valley.[42]

On May 5, 1732, Francis Willis, John Lewis, and Francis Kirkley were granted 10,000 acres on both sides of the South Shenandoah, just above the mouth of the Hawksbill Creek.[43] This grant must have extended up to, probably into, Jacob Stover's lower tract of 5000 acres—the Massanutten tract. The John Lewis mentioned here does not appear to have been the Scotch-Irish pioneer of Augusta.

On October 27, 1732, William Russell was granted 20,000 acres in and about the forks of the Shenandoah, near Front Royal and Riverton, in lieu of what he had claimed from the Van Meter grants.[44]

On October 28, 1734, John Tayloe, Thomas Lee, and William Beverly obtained a grant of 60,000 acres on the Shenandoah River, adjoining above Jacob Stover's upper tract of 5000 acres.[45]

In 1736, or thereabouts, Benjamin Burden (Borden) was granted a tract of 100,000 acres—possibly 500,000 acres—

41. Virginia Magazine, Vol. XIII, No. 2, pp. 133, 134.

42. Lewis' History of West Virginia, p. 42; Foote's Sketches, etc.

43. Virginia Magazine, Vol. XIII, No. 2, p. 138.

44. Idem, No. 3, pp. 288, 289.

45. Idem, No. 4, pp. 360-362.

lying at present in Rockbridge County and the upper part of Augusta.[46]

Among the Germans who thus early obtained large grants of land, Jost Hite and Jacob Stover are the most prominent. Both have been spoken of repeatedly in the foregoing pages; yet it may be well at this juncture to present a few additional facts in regard to each of them.

The rather uncomplimentary suggestions made with reference to some of Stover's methods in securing his land grants, will be understood from the following story, related by Kercheval:

> On his application to the executive for his grant, he was refused unless he could give satisfactory assurance that he would have the land settled with the requisite number of families within a given time. Being unable to do this, he forthwith passed over to England, petitioned the King to direct his grant to be issued, and in order to insure success, had given human names to every horse, cow, hog and dog he owned, and which he represented as heads of families, ready to migrate and settle the land. By this disingenious trick he succeeded in obtaining directions from the King and Council for securing his grant; on obtaining which he immediately sold out his land in small divisions, at three pounds (equal to ten dollars) per hundred, and went off with the money.[47]

This story appears to be strengthened by several statements in the petition of 1733, of Adam Miller, Abram Strickler, and the rest; for they declare that none of their fifty-one inhabitants at Massanutting, or of the two other families soon expected, were "any of the persons the sd: Stover swore was on the sd: land when he obtained the sd: Patent as yr petrs have been informed."[48] They also assert that the said Stover is very poor, "and is Daily Expected to Run away." Kercheval's assertion, that he did run away, is, however, probably a mistake; for the public records show that he was

46. Withers' Chronicles, p. 50; Peyton's History of Augusta, p. 65; Early Deed Books of Orange, Augusta, and Frederick.

47. Kercheval's History of the Valley, p. 46.

48. Palmer's Calendar, Vol. I, p. 220.

in the country almost continuously until his death, which occurred about 1740.

The deeds received by Stover, December 15, 1733, for the two grants of 5000 acres each, obtained over three years before, are said to be the first crown patents issued for lands in Virginia west of the Blue Ridge.[49] By the time these patents were issued he seems to have had the required number of *bona fide* settlers on the lower tract, and possibly on the upper one also.

But it was not long until Stover either got back his Massanutten tract, or secured other tracts very close to it. On September 17, 1735, he sold to Christian Clemon 550 acres on the south side of the Shenandoah, adjoining the 'upper corner of his lower five thousand Tract.'[50] On November 10, 1735, he sold to George Boone two tracts, of 1000 acres and 500 acres respectively, situated on a 'small branch of Sharrando River'—part of 5000 acres laid out for him by the Virginia Council, June 17, 1730.[51] These 1500 acres sold to Boone were evidently part of the 5000-acre tract that the petitioners of 1733 had bought. The grant seems to have been capable of indefinite expansion. But more is to come. On December 15, 16, 1735, Stover sold to five men, Henry Sowter, Abraham Strickler, Ludwick Stone, John Brubaker, and Mathias Selser, ten tracts of land, aggregating 3400 acres. Sowter got 300 acres on the south side of the river, "near the mouth of Mesenuttin Creek"; Strickler got 1000 acres at "Mesenuttin on Gerundo"; Stone got three tracts of 400 acres, 400 acres, and 300 acres, respectively, "on Gerundo River"; Brubaker got two tracts, one of 300 acres, one of 200 acres, on the river—the larger tract adjoining Mathias Selser; Selser got three tracts, two of 200 acres each, one of 100 acres, "on Gerundo River."[52]

49. Virginia Magazine, Vol. XIII, No. 3, p. 297.

50. Orange County Deed Book No. 1, pp. 151-154.

51. Idem, pp. 184-188.

52. Idem, pp. 200-216.

The capacious extensions of "Massanutten" may be explained, perhaps, by recalling that the term was sometimes applied to the whole Page valley; but how shall we explain Stover's repeated possession of the original 5000-acre tract, or at least large parts of it? Observe, in addition to the above, the two following cases: On September 20, 21, 1736, Stover sold to Peter Bowman 400 acres on the west side of the river, part of the 5000 acres granted to Stover, and the part he then lived on[53]; and on March 20, 21, 1738, he sold to Christopher Franciscus 3000 acres, with the mansion house, the land adjoining Peter Bowman on the river, and being part of the 5000-acre tract patented by Jacob Stover, December 15, 1733.[54] Evidently, by purchase or otherwise, Stover must have come into a second possession of the greater part of the land sold to the petitioners of 1733. In 1737 and 1738 there was some litigation between Stover and Ludwig Stone and others, concerning land; and a complete record might explain much of the foregoing; but unfortunately some of the papers relating to these legal proceedings appear to be lost.[55]

On March 21, 1738, Jacob Stover and his wife Margaret gave their bond to Christopher Franciscus for £700; later in the same year they gave another bond for £1000; and, in security, mortgaged 5000 acres of land on both sides of the Shenandoah River.[56] This may have been the upper tract, obtained in 1730. On December 13, 1738, Stover got a grant of 800 acres on the Shenandoah, near or adjoining his upper tract of 5000 acres.[57] On June 25, 1740, he conveyed

53. Idem, pp. 353-356.

54. Orange County Deed Book No. 2, pp. 229-232.

55. See Orange County Records; also, Virginia Magazine, Vol. XIII, No. 2, pp. 120-123.

56. Orange County Deed Book No. 2, pp. 233, 234.

57. Augusta County Deed Book No. 4, pp. 58, 65, etc.

to Christopher Francisco, Sr., 3100 acres of land a few miles below Port Republic.[58] This was evidently part of the upper 5000-acre tract, and the conveyance was likely made to satisfy the mortgage of 1738. In 1751 Christopher Francisco, probably the younger, who had come into possession of at least 470 acres of the upper Stover tracts, sold that amount to Thomas Lewis;[59] and the same year (1751), *Jacob Strover*—probably Jacob Stover, Jr.—owned a 5000-acre tract on the upper Shenandoah.[60]

Jacob Stover, Sr., died near the end of 1740, or early in 1741. On March 22, 1741, Jacob Stover [Jr.], with Henry Downs and Jacob Castle, gave bond for administering the estate. The record of the sale shows that a considerable amount of personal property was to be disposed of; it also shows that Ludowick Francisco, John Bumgardner, Philip Long, and Jacob Castle were among the purchasers. Francisco bought most.[61]

A proportionate sketch from known facts of Jost Hite's career would be an almost endless task, and cannot be undertaken here; neither is there any real need for it, since the subject has so frequently been presented to the public.[62]

As has been intimated near the beginning of this chapter, Jost Hite was a man of influence and prominence in the public affairs of his day, both civil and military; and many of his descendants have been of almost equal prominence. On April 23, 1734, the Virginia Colonial Council, upon the petition of the inhabitants west of the Blue Ridge for the

58. Virginia Magazine, Vol. XIII, No. 2, p. 120; Orange County Records.

59. Augusta County Deed Book No. 4, p. 58.

60. Idem, No. 3, pp. 498-503.

61. Orange County Will Book No. 1, pp. 140, 204, 205.

62. One of the fullest accounts of Hite and his descendants may be found in the West Virginia Historical Magazine, for April, 1903. It is, however, in error in so far as it represents Hite as the first settler in the Valley.

establishment of some form of civil system, appointed Jost Hite, with Morgan Morgan, John Smith, Benjamin Bourden, and George Hobson, a magistrate, with authority to settle differences and punish offenders against the public welfare.[63] In 1748 Jacob Hite, Jost Hite's second son, was appointed sheriff for Frederick County, by Governor Gooch; he gave bond in the sum of £1000, with John Hite (his elder brother), Isaac Hite (his next younger brother), Thomas Swearingen, and Samuel Earle as sureties.[64] Abraham Hite, Jost's fourth son, was a leading man of affairs in Hampshire County, and represented it in the House of Burgesses; he was a captain in the Revolutionary War, and served as paymaster of the 8th Virginia (German) Regiment. Others of the family were members of the House of Burgesses from Berkeley County. Major Isaac Hite (1758-1836), son of Isaac and grandson of Jost, was aide to General Muhlenberg at the siege of Yorktown. Isaac Hite married James Madison's sister, Nelly. He seems to have been the first man elected to membership in the now world-famous Phi Beta Kappa Society, founded by John Heath and others at William and Mary College, December 5, 1776. In January, 1777, the charter members assembled and chose officers; on March 1, laws were adopted; and, at a called meeting on March 27, Hite was elected to membership. He was the only one elected at the time, and was evidently the first man chosen by the charter members. Bushrod Washington, John Marshall, and other men who won national eminence were among the early members of the society.[65]

Jost Hite's greatest public service was doubtless performed in aiding, directing, and stimulating the rapid settlement and

63. Virginia Magazine, Vol. XIII, No. 4, pp. 351, 352.

64. Frederick County Deed Book No. 1, p. 491.

65. William and Mary College Quarterly, Vol. X, pp. 120, 121.—For Hite's connection with the Phi Beta Kappa, see the same magazine for April, 1896.

development of the country. The county deed books of Orange, Frederick, and Augusta contain almost innumerable records of land sales by Jost Hite. At the beginning of his colonizing enterprises in the lower Valley he had associated with him, as we have seen, Robert McKay. Later, Hite and McKay seem to have entered into a partnership in the land business with William Duff and Robert Green—the last being from 1736 to 1740 a member of the Virginia Colonial Assembly from Orange County, and later sheriff.[66] One of the best known grants secured by Hite, McKay, Duff, and Green was obtained on March 26, 1739, and contained 7009 acres—a tract that embraced much of the fertile Linville Creek valley, now in Rockingham County.

Very early in his career in the Valley, Jost Hite came into conflict with Thomas Lord Fairfax. The latter claimed the land within Hite's early grants, and the case was in the law courts for fifty years. This contention over titles caused a good many of the Germans, and possibly the Scotch-Irish also, following Hite into the Valley, to pass by his section and seek an abode further up, where the lands were not claimed by two parties. This dispute, coupled with the fact that the Scotch-Irish early secured a foothold in the upper Valley, explains to a great extent the concentration of the German element in the section between Winchester and Staunton. The case was finally decided favorably to Hite in 1786, four years after Fairfax's death, and twenty-six years after the death of Hite.

In 1753, Colonel John Hite, Jost Hite's eldest son, erected a fine stone house, still standing and excellently preserved, at Springdale, Frederick County, where the Valley Pike crosses the Opequon Creek. This is probably the site of the pioneer's first dwelling. In 1783, John Hite, Jr., built a large stone mill on the Opequon, at Springdale. This mill, at the time it was built, was the largest and best in the Valley; and,

66. Colonial Virginia Register, pp. 109, 112.

with modern improvements, it is still running. In the south wing of the old mansion is a large fireplace, with a bake-oven built into the wall at the left-hand side. In the adjoining room is another fireplace, the back of which is composed of a large cast-iron plate. On this plate, cast in bold relief, is the figure of a coat-of-arms, occupying a space about eighteen inches square. The cast has been considerably defaced by fire and rust, so that it is not very easily identified; but the writer was informed, upon a visit to Springdale a few years ago, that the casting represents the coat-of-arms of Lord Fairfax. If this statement be correct, the fact is deemed rather singular, in view of the protracted legal contests between Fairfax and the Hites. It may be, however,—let us hope it is true,—that they were enemies only in court. Lord Fairfax and Colonel John Hite were in 1752 both vestrymen in the Episcopal church of Frederick County:[67] possibly they did not allow the matter of a land title to vie with Christian charity. Another explanation of the figure in the fireplace is possible: It may be the coat-of-arms of the Hites themselves. Jost Hite has been called "the old German Baron";[68] and his family is represented as entitled to a place in the roll of Virginia heraldry.[69]

Apart from Jost Hite, Jacob Stover, and a few others who took up large grants of land at a very early date, most of the German settlers in the Valley contented themselves with the purchase of small tracts, ranging usually from a hundred to four or five hundred acres. A small farm, well tilled, seemed to be the ideal of the majority. A few, however, purchased larger bodies of land, for the purpose, usually, of selling it in smaller parcels to later comers. Of this number may be mentioned the following: The Funks and Stephens, in the lower Valley; Peter Stover and Jacob Miller, in the

67. Meade's Old Churches, Vol. II, p. 281.

68. West Virginia Historical Magazine, Vol. 3, No. 2, p. 118.

69. Baltimore Sun, July 16, 23, 1905.

section now embraced in Shenandoah County; Ludwig Stone, the Stricklers, and the Ruffners, of Page County; and William Lenivell, George Bowman, Samuel Wilkins, and Christopher Franciscus, of Rockingham County. Several of these men—the Stephens, Peter Stover, and Jacob Miller—will appear again later in connection with the founding of the towns.

One of the largest of these landholders was Peter Ruffner. He was the first of the name in Virginia, and settled in 1739 at the large spring on the Hawksbill Creek, now close by the edge of the town of Luray. His wife was Mary Steinman, whose father gave them a large body of land extending up both sides of the Hawksbill a distance of eight miles from its mouth. Ruffner himself added to the estate, extending his possessions four miles further up the stream.

William Lenivell bought in 1746 of Hite, McKay, and Green, 1500 acres about the headwaters of the stream that evidently was named after him—Lenivell's Creek, now Linville Creek. In 1746 and 1749 George Bowman bought two tracts, aggregating over a thousand acres, on Linville Creek: the first tract he bought of William Lenivell; the second, of Jost Hite. Samuel Wilkins owned large bodies of land on Cook's Creek, about the present town of Dayton, and elsewhere.

One of the most interesting characters of the class and period under consideration is Christopher Franciscus, some of whose dealings with Jacob Stover have already been noticed. He, with other Germans and Swiss, located in Lancaster County, Pennsylvania, in the year 1709.[70] On March 21, 1738, he bought of Jacob Stover 3000 acres of land, with the mansion house, for £350 5s.; the same day he appears to have loaned Stover £700, and later the same year, £1000, to secure which he took a mortgage on 5000 acres of Stover's land. By these transactions he seems to have come into

70. Rupp's Thirty Thousand Names, p. 436.

possession of large estates within the present limits of both Page County and Rockingham. Most of his land appears to have been along the Shenandoah River between Elkton and Port Republic. On December 13, 1738, he bought of Jacob Stover in this vicinity 470 acres, which he sold in 1751 to Thomas Lewis, who was the eldest son of the pioneer, John Lewis, and a brother to Gen. Andrew and Col. Charles Lewis. The tract of 3100 acres below Port Republic, conveyed to Franciscus by Stover in 1740, was probably to satisfy the mortgage of 1738, securing the loan of £1700.

On November 20, 1747, Ludwick Francisco, a son of Christopher, bought of Henry Downs 470 acres on the south side of the Shenandoah River.[71] During the years 1749 and 1750, Christopher Franciscus sold land in Augusta (now Rockingham) County to various persons; among others, Jacob and Valentine Pence, John Craig, and Henry Dooley. On February 6, 7, 1750, "Christopher Franciscus, Senior, of Lancaster County, Pennsylvania, and Anna Margaret his wife" sold to Jacob Thomas for £25 5s., from a large tract of 3000 acres, 185 acres of land on "Shannandore river and Cubrun."[72] The witnesses to this transaction were Nicholas Null and Christopher Franciscus, Jr. The latter signed in German. His father and mother both made their marks.[73] On August 15, 1751, C. Franciscus, Sr., makes C. Franciscus, Jr., his lawful attorney for the sale of his 3100 acres of land in Augusta County, on the Shenandoah River.[74] During the years 1751 and 1752 Christopher and Ludwig Franciscus, attorneys, sell land in Augusta to Thomas Lewis, Gabriel Jones, Peter Hull, Patrick Wilson, Ludwig Franciscus,

71. Augusta County Deed Book No. 1, pp. 453, 454.

72. Cub Run heads between Harrisonburg and the Peaked Mountains, runs round the end of Peaked Mountain, and flows into the Shenandoah River near Almond P. O.

73. Augusta County Deed Book No. 2, pp. 715-718.

74. Idem, No. 3, pp. 469, 470.

Nicholas Null, Valentine Pence, Nicholas Trout, and Maurice Pound. In February of 1751, Henry Lanciscus (probably *Franciscus*), bought of James Wood, William Russell, and William Green 310 acres of land on the north and south forks of the South Branch of the Potomac—evidently near the present town of Moorefield, W. Va.[75] Henry was probably another son of Christopher Franciscus, Sr.

Whether these Franciscos were kinsmen to Peter Francisco,[76] the strong man of Charlotte County, Virginia, or not, the writer is unable to say; but it seems probable that they were not related. So far as I know, there is no one in Rockingham County at present bearing the name. In Craig County, Virginia, there is a postoffice called Francisco, and a Francisco Mill; and between 1830 and 1840 a prominent citizen of Bath County was Charles L. Francisco. It is possible that Christopher Francisco, Sr., never fixed his home in the Valley; but his sons appear to have been permanent residents. In 1749 the Moravian missionaries, Leonhard Schnell and John Brandmueller, were in the neighborhood between Port Republic and Elkton; and, on December 2, Schnell wrote in his diary as follows:

> We continued our journey the whole day, because we wished to be with the Germans on Sunday. Once we lost our way. But our desire to preach to-morrow strengthened us in our journey. In the evening we attempted to hire a man to go with us part of the way, but none was willing. We continued for a time down the Tschanator [Shenandoah] and arrived rather late at the house of the sons of the old Stopfel [Christopher] Franciscus, who kept us over night.
>
> On Sunday, December 3rd, the young Franciscus went very early with us to show us the way to Matthias Schaub, who, immediately on my offer to preach for them, sent messengers through the neighborhood to announce my sermon.[77]

75. Augusta County Deed Book No. 3, pp. 129-134.

76. Howe's Antiquities; Hening's Statutes, Vol. 13, pp. 220, 221; William and Mary College Quarterly, Vol. XIII, p. 213; Vol. XIV, pp. 107-112.

77. Virginia Magazine, Vol. XI, No. 2, p. 126.

CHAPTER V.

Counties and County Records.

It may be helpful, before proceeding to what shall follow, to give at this point a brief account of the formation of the several counties in the Shenandoah Valley.

From the erection of Spottsylvania County in 1720, the whole country west of the Blue Ridge was considered as embraced within its limits, until the formation of Orange County, in 1734. From this date the Valley sections and adjacent regions to the west continued a part of Orange till 1738, when the country west of the Blue Ridge was divided into Frederick and Augusta. The establishment of these two counties was provided for by an Act of Assembly of November, 1738; but the two districts were to remain parts of Orange County until the Governor and Council should decide that the number of inhabitants was sufficient to warrant the establishment of courts and the appointment of justices.[1] It will be recalled, however, that as early as 1734 Jost Hite and others had been appointed magistrates for the regulation of local questions west of the mountains. In 1739 a petition was presented to Governor Gooch from the lower Valley, setting forth the hardships of going all the way, in some cases as far as a hundred miles, to Orange Court House to transact legal business, and praying that "ye sd: County of Frederica may immediately take place."[2] To this petition was appended a list of fifty-two names.[3] But it was not

1. Hening's Statutes, Vol. 5, pp. 78, 79.

2. Palmer's Calendar, Vol. I, p. 233.

3. Possibly there were only 47 names. Palmer gives only two, those of Henry Funk and John Little, saying that there were fifty others. By the kindness of Dr. H. J. Eckenrode, Archivist, Virginia

until 1743 that the request of the petitioners was complied with: the first session of court being held in Frederick County on November 11, 1743.[4] Courts were established in Augusta County in 1745.

In September, 1744, an Act was passed providing for the surveying of the line between Frederick and Augusta, and for dividing the cost of the work between the citizens of the two districts.[5] Frederick embraced all that is now Shenandoah, with a part of Page; Warren, Clarke, Frederick; and the West Virginia counties of Jefferson, Berkeley, Hampshire, and a part of Hardy. Augusta embraced Rockingham, with parts of Hardy, Pendleton, and Page; as well as the counties of Rockbridge, Botetourt, and the great country

State Library, I am enabled to present the entire list of petitioners, excepting one or two, as follows:

Henry Funk
John Little
John Crowsson
Tho. Foster
Charles Baker
John Downton
Robert Mcfaison
Thomas Hankins
Robert Mackay, Junr.
John Branson
John Flemingway
John Willcocks
Jacob Funk
John Funk
John F. Funk, Jun.
Peter Stouffer
Jacob F. Funk, Jun.
Honny F. Funk, Jun.
Adem Funk
——— Dellinger
Frederick Dellinger
Geo. Dellinger, Jun.
Jacob Hackman
Peter Bowman
Jno. Hackman
Jacob Hackman, Jr.
John Denton
Richd Tidwe'l (?)
Christian Blank
Joseph Ballinger
Isaac Parkins
Wm. McMachen
John Hardin
Meredith ———
Lewis Neill
John Lintey
John Neill
Jonas Lum
John Bowker
John Vane
Charles Handgin
Isaac Foster
——— ———
——— Swearingen
Ralph Orefe (?)
——— ———
——— ———

4. West Virginia Historical Magazine, Vol. 2, No. 2, p. 20.

5. Hening's Statutes, Vol. 5, p. 275.

west, as far as anyone cared to venture. In November, 1753, an Act of Assembly provided for the erection of Hampshire County from Frederick and Augusta.[6] In February, 1772, Frederick County was further divided, and from it were erected the new counties of Berkeley and Dunmore, both of which were to be organized from May 15, 1772.[7] Owing to the disfavor that Lord Dunmore brought upon himself early in the Revolutionary struggle, the people of Dunmore County would no longer endure the name. By an Act of Assembly of October, 1777, the name was to be changed to "Shanando" from and after February 1, 1778.[8] "Shanando" came in time to be "Shenandoah." In October, 1777, Rockingham County and Parish were formed from Augusta; in October, 1785, Hardy was formed from Hampshire; and in October, 1787, Pendleton was formed from Augusta, Hardy, and Rockingham.[9] Although the counties of Hampshire, Hardy, and Pendleton are beyond the Shenandoah Valley, a notice of their formation is included here for the reason that by virtue of their adjacent position on the west of Frederick, Shenandoah, and Rockingham, they received a considerable influx of the German settlers of the Valley.

A number of abstracts from the county records of Orange, Frederick, and Augusta, for the years beginning with 1735 and ending with 1755, will now be presented in chronological order. These are deemed valuable in our study for different reasons, historical and genealogical. They have been prepared chiefly from the deed books, and will therefore not only supply the names of many of the German families that located and purchased lands in the various sections during the several years up to the French and Indian War, but will also furnish material for an economic study in the progress

6. Idem, Vol. 6, p. 376.

7. Idem, Vol. 8, pp. 597, 598.

8. Idem, Vol. 9, p. 424.

9. Idem, p. 420; Vol. 12, pp. 86, 87; 637, 638.

of land values during the period covered. It should be borne in mind, however, that the items here given are selected from a greater number, especially in the years immediately preceding and following 1740; and therefore do not afford a safe basis for comparing one year with another in respect to the rate of German immigration.

1735.

From Orange County Deed Book No. 1.

July 14, 15:[10]—Henry Willis sells to Jacob Funks for £100 5s.[11] 2030 A., commonly called Stony Lick, on Tumbling Run, on the N. side of the N. Branch of Sherando: granted to Henry Willis, Aug. 21, 1734.

Sept. 17:—Jacob Stover (his mark) sells to Christian Clemon for £28 5s. 550 A., on a small run, on the S. side of Gerundo River, adjoining the upper corner of Stover's lower 5000 A. tract.—Witnesses, G. Home (?), Thomas Hill, W. Russell.

Nov. 10, 11:—Jacob Stover (Stauber) sells for £29 5s., Pennsylvania money, to George Boone two tracts of land, 500 A. and 1000 A., 'situate near the end of the North Mountain, so-called, on a small branch of Sherrando River': part of 5000 A. laid out for Stauber by the Va. Council, June 17, 1730.—Witnesses, Mordecai Simon, S. Hughes.—Boone was from Oley, Pa. Boone's Run, which heads in Peaked Mt., runs east, and flows into the Shen. R. about 2 miles below Elkton, was probably named after him.

Dec. 15, 16:—Jacob Stover sells to Ludwick Stone for £84 5s. three tracts of land, 400 A., 400 A., 300 A., on Gerundo River.

10. The double dates are owing to the legal requirements of the time. Upon the first date the parcel of ground was leased, usually for a year; upon the next day the "release" was given, and "use" was transferred into "possession."

11. The sum of 5 shillings is in almost every case the "consideration" in the earlier instrument—the "lease."

Dec. 15, 16:—Jacob Stover sells to Mathias Selser for £41 5s. three tracts of land, 200 A., 200 A., 100 A., on Gerundo River.

Dec. 15, 16:—Jacob Stover sells to John Prupecker (Brubaker) of Pa., for £41 5s., two tracts of land: 300 A. on the N. side of Gerundo River, adjoining Mathias Selser; 200 A. on Gerundo River.—Witnesses, John Bramham, Gideon Marr, William Ferrell.

Dec. 15, 16:—Jacob Stover sells to Abraham Strickler of Pa., for £84 5s., 1000 A. at "Mesenuttin on Gerundo," apparently on the N. side of the river.

Dec. 15, 16:—Jacob Stover sells to Henry Sowter (?) for £15 5s. 300 A. on the S. side of Gerundo, near the mouth of Mesenuttin Creek.

1736.

From Orange County Deed Book No. 1.

Feb. 23, 24:—Ludwig Stein (Stone) sells to Michael Cryter of Pa., for £100 5s., three tracts of land, 217 A., 200 A., 100 A., on Gerundo R.—Witnesses, Gideon Marr (perhaps *More*), John Newport.—For the sake of the names of persons and places, the description of these lots is copied below:

Three parcels or tracts of land situate lying & being on Gerundo River. The first tract contains 200 acres & lies on the South side Gerundo between Matthias Selser & Michael Coffman. The other tract is the uppermost of the Mesenutten Lotts and joins at the upper side of Martin Coffman's upper tract and contains 200 acres. The other piece lies near Elk Lick on ye north Side Gerundo adjoining to Martin Coffman and John Prupecker.—(From the Lease.)

The next tract [the second] begins at the uppermost corner of Stover's survey and runeth from the river N 5 E 490 poles to ye uppermost corner at the mountain thence N 80 E 48 poles to two corner white oaks & ash thence S 7 E 540 poles to river thence up ye sd River to the beginning. The third tract is an hundred acre tract adjoining to Martin Coffman's tract at Elk Lick and Prupecker's lower tract.—(From the Release. There appear to be a few discrepancies in the statements of quantity.)

Feb. 23:—Ludowick Stein sells to Michael Coffman for

£40 5s. 217 A. on Gerundo R.: part of the land formerly granted to Jacob Stover.

Mar. 20, 21:—Jost Hite sells to Christian Niswanger for £16 435 A. on the W. side of Sherrendo: part of 3395 A. granted to Hite, June 12, 1734.

Mar. 23, 24:—Jost Hite sells to Stephen Hunsenbella for £14 5s. 450 A. on the W. side of Shen. R., on Opeckon Creek, near the head thereof: part of 5012 A. granted to Hite, Oct. 3, 1734.

Mar. 23:—Jost Hite sells to John Van Metre for £205 475 A. on Opeckon Creek: part of the tract "on which John Selbour [?] lives."

Mar. 25, 26:—Jost Hite, Gentleman, and Mary his wife sell to Robert Dwarfe for £7 15s. 300 A. on the W. side of Sherrendo R., on a branch of the said river running into the N. Branch thereof at a place called the Long Meadow: part of 2160 A. granted to Hite, Oct. 3, 1734.

Sept. 20, 21:[12]—Jacob Stover sells to Peter Bowman for £30 5s. 400 A. on the W. side of Sherundo R.: part of 5000 A. granted to Jacob Stover: likewise the part that the said Stover then lived on.—Witnesses, G. Lightfoot, Thomas Nicholls.

Sept. 25, 26:—Henry Sowter sells to Ludwig Stine for £25 5s. about 300 A. on the S. (?) side of Gerundo R.—This is likely the same tract that Sowter bought of Jacob Stover, Dec. 15, 1735, for £15 5s. If so, he sold at a gain of over 65 per cent. in less than a year.

1737.

From Orange County Deed Books 1 and 2.

Feb. 15, 16:—Jacob Funck sells to John Funck of Lancaster Co., Pa., for £18 5s., 180 A. on the N. W. side of

12. Hon. J. A. Waddell's statement, p. 28, Annals of Augusta, "The first allusion in the records of Orange to Valley people is under date of July 20, 1736," is evidently a mistake; since all the entries thus far are earlier than that date.

Shen. R., the N. Branch thereof, near a place called Stony Lick: part of a tract of 2030 A. granted to Henry Willis, Aug. 20, 1734, and sold to Jacob Funk.—Witnesses, John Smith, John Hite.—This item may belong to the year 1736. In the record the date appears to be written 1734; but this is evidently not correct, since Jacob Funk did not buy the tract of 2030 A. from Willis till July 14, 15, 1735.

Feb. 23, 24:—Ludwig Stein sells to Martin Coffman of Pa., for £200 5s., three tracts of land: 300 A. on the S. side of Shen. R.; 217 A. on the N. side; 100 A. on the N. side of Gerundo at Elk Lick, part of 200 A. granted to Stone by Jacob Stover.

Mar. 25, 26:—Jost and Mary Hite sell to Lewis Stussy (?) for £10 5s. 339 A. on the W. side of Shen. R., near the head of Crooked Run.

May 25, 26:—William Russell, Gent., sells to Christian Bowman, Farmer, for £47 10s., 675 A. on the S. side of the N. River Sherundore, at the mouth of a run.

Oct. 22:—Peter Bowman sells to Christian Redlicksberger for £30 5s. 400 A. on Shen. R.

1738.

From County Records of Orange and Augusta.

Feb. 22, 23:—William Russell sells to John Funks for £21 5s. 320 A. on the E. side of the N. River Shenandoare, adjoining Christian Bowman.—*Orange County Deed Book No.* 2, pp. 222-228 (*O C D B* 2—222-228.

Mar. 20, 21:—Jacob Stover sells to Christopher Franciski for £350 5s. 3000 A., with the mansion house, adjoining Peter Bowman on the river: part of 5000 A. patented to Jacob Stover, Dec. 15, 1733.—*O C D B* 2—229-232.

Mar. 21:—Jacob Stover and wife Margaret give bond to Christopher Franciski for £700. The same year they give Franciski another bond for £1000. They mortgage 5000 A. on both sides of Shen. R.—*O C D B* 2—233, 234.

Mar. 22, 23:—Ludwig Stein sells to Philip Long (who signs in German) for £100 5s. two tracts of land, 205 A. and 800 A., on Shen. R.—Witnesses, John Newport, Christian Kleman.—*O C D B* 2—260.

May 24, 25:—Jacob Funk sells to John Funk for £18 5s. 180 A.—*O C D B* 2—343.

Dec. 13:—Jacob Stover obtains a grant of 800 A.—*Augusta Co. Deed Book 4*, pp. 58, 65, etc.—This land was on the S. Shenandoah, below Port Republic, and was at least in part on the S. side of the river, opposite the "Great Island." This island, containing about 60 A., was bought of the Franciscos on Aug. 31, 1751, by Thomas Lewis. Two days earlier, Aug. 28, 1751, Lewis had bought of the Franciscos a tract of 470 A., on the S. side of the river, part of the 800 A. tract granted to Stover in 1738.—*A C D B* 4—58-62; etc.

1739.

Mar. 26:—Jost Hite, Robert McKay, William Duff, and Robert Green secure a grant of 7009 A. in the present county of Rockingham.—*A C D B* 1—103-106.

This was the year in which Peter Ruffner obtained, through his father-in-law Steinman, his large estate on the Hawksbill. When he settled there in 1739 some of the other Germans in the neighborhood were, the Stovers, Stricklers, Rollers, Heistands, and Beidlers.[13] The Ruffner name occurs frequently in the Frederick County records.

1740.

July 23, 24:—Mathias Elser (Selser) sells to Jacob Neglee 200 A. in the Massanutting tract.—*A C D B* 2—792-795.

1741.

Mar. 22:—Jacob Stover, Jr., with Henry Downs and Jacob Castle as sureties, gives bond and qualifies as administrator of the estate of Jacob Stover, dec'd.—*O C W B* 1—140.

13. West Virginia Historical Magazine, Vol. I, No. 2, pp. 31, 32.

1742.

Oct. 20, 21:—Jost Hite sells to John Painter 189 A. on the N. side of Shen. R.—*F C D B* 2—324.

1743.

Mar. 1:—Charles Baker,[14] Planter, sells to Samuel Earle for £5 25 A. on the E. side of Crooked Run in Frederick County: land bought by Baker of John Branson; by Branson of Jost Hite.—*F C D B* 1—42.

1744.

From Frederick County Deed Book No. 1.

Jan. 15, 16:—John Funk, Sr., sells to Martin Funk[15] for

14. Most of the well known Baker families of Frederick County are of German ancestry. Several generations ago the name was frequently written "Becker."

15. Martin Funk was probably the son of John Funk, Sr.; and the latter was likely a brother to Jacob Funk, Sr. (See F C D B 1 and F C W B 1.)

On November 14, 1906, the writer made what may perhaps be a discovery, in a small way, in the Mt. Hebron Cemetery at Winchester. Upon previous visits he had had the grave of George Becker (July 17, 1765-May —, 1790), son of Henrich Becker, pointed out to him as the oldest marked grave in the cemetery; but upon the above date he found, three feet to the east of Becker's grave, an older one—that of Martin Funk. Funk's grave is marked by a low, thick, dark stone, sunk low into the turf; and far down in the thick grass is this inscription:

Here
Lays the body of
Martin Funk
Who ended his Pil-
grim life Octo. 5
1777 old [?] 54 y.

This grave, therefore, is 13 years older than that of George Becker. If this Martin Funk was, as is likely, the one who bought the 170 acres of land in January, 1744, he was at that time about 21 years old. The graves of Funk and Becker lie close to the entrance lodge, and are about 60 yards southwest of the ruin of the old Lutheran church and the tomb of Christian Streit, the first Lutheran minister born in America.

—5

£80 5s. 170 A. in Frederick County, "on the River," near or adjoining Jacob Funk and Christian Bowman: part of 320 A. conveyed to John Funk by William Russell.—Witnesses, David Vance, John Hite, Robert Warth (?).

Apr. 5, 6:—Jost Hite sells to Joseph Vance for £5 5s. 150 A. in Frederick Co., "on both sides of a meadow called the Long Meadow."

Apr. 15:—Jacob Funk of Fred. Co. sells to William Tidwell for £20 5s. 100 A. on the N. side of Shen. R.—Witnesses, James Porteus, G. Jones, G. Johnstone.

July 13, 14:—Jacob Funk sells to Joseph Helms for £30 5s. 200 A. on the N. side of the N. River of Shenandoah: part of a greater tract patented to Jacob Funk.—Witnesses, Samuel Earle, John Newport, W. Russell.

Aug. 10, 11:—Josiah Ballinger of Opeckon sells to James Wright 194 A.: obtained in grant by Ballinger, Sept. 12, 1735.

Aug. 30, 31:—Giles Chapman sells to Ulrich Ruble for £10 7s. 2d. 150 A. near the head of Yorkshire-man's branch of Opeckon Creek.

1745.

June 18, 19:—John Richards sells to Benjamin Fry 500 A. on Cedar Creek.—*F C D B* 1—102.

Aug. 5, 6:—John Kountz of Fred. Co. sells to Lewis Stephens for £65 5s. 195 A., in Fred. Co., on the N. side of "Sedar Run." Kountz bought of John Branson, and the land was obtained in 1732 by Branson in a 1000 A. grant.—Witnesses, Thomas Rutherford, W. Russell, John Hardin.—*F C D B* 1—227.

1746.

From Augusta County Records.

Apr. 10, 11:—Peter Ruffner of "Orange Co." sells to Christopher Comber for £40 5s. about 271 A. on the Hawksbill: formerly belonging to Francis Thornton.—Witnesses,

John Newport, Richard Price, Isaac Strickler. The last signed in German.—In the four instruments made on this date by Ruffner to Comber and Daniel Stover, Ruffner's name is written "Peter Ruffnaugh" in the body of the papers; but Ruffner, signing in German, spells his name as follows: *Pether Ruffner* (twice); *Pether Ruffnerdt* (twice).

Apr. 10, 11:—Peter Ruffner sells to Daniel Stover for £10 5s. 196 A. on Sharando R., at the mouth of the Hawksbill Creek: part of 250 A. patented to John Landrum.—Witnesses, John Newport, Richard Price, Isaac Strickler.

Apr. 14:—Peter Ruffenough, with Mathias Selzer and John Lionberger as sureties, qualifies as administrator of the estate of Abraham Strickler, dec'd.[16]

Apr. 19:—Inventory made of estate of Abraham Strickler, late dec'd, by appraisers: Jer. Sutton, Paul Long, Rudolph Maag (Mauck?): valued at over £200.—The inventory was admitted to record June 18, 1746.

June 17, 18:—Hite, McKay & Green sell to William Lenivell for £62 10s. 1500 A. in Augusta Co.

June 17, 18:—Samuel Wilkins sells to Hite, McKay & Green for £126 13s. 11d. 1264 A. on the W. side of the Blue Ridge, in the vicinity of Naked Creek.—This land seems to have been transferred on the same dates, and for the same considerations, by Hite, McKay & Green to Wilkins.

June 18, 19:—Jost Hite and Robert Green sell to Robert McKay for £119 5s. 1190 A. on the W. side of the Blue Ridge.—The records of this period show numerous land sales by Hite and his partners.

Aug. 5, 6:—Thomas Lenivell (or Linwell) witnesses, with Valentine Sevier, indentures of Jost Hite and Robert McKay (McCoy) to Robert Green.

Aug. 14, 15:—William Lenivell sells to George Bowman

16. It will be recalled that Abram Strickler was one of the original settlers at Massanutting, and one of the petitioners of 1733.

for £100 5s. (Pa. money) 500 A. on "Lenivell Creek."[17]—This was likely part of the 1500 A. tract that Lenivell bought of Hite & Co. in the preceding June, for £62 10s. He must have sold the 500 A. to Bowman at a good profit, unless the money of Pennsylvania was of comparatively little value.—Lenivell and his wife Elinor both made their marks.—This 500 A. tract sold to Bowman touched a 500 A. tract sold a few days later to Joseph Bryan. Bowman's land probably lay about the head of Linville Creek, including the site of the later well known Bowman's Mill.

Aug. 19, 20:—William Lenivell sells to Joseph Bryan for £12 5s. 500 A. on Linvells Creek.—Lenivell here appears to be selling land below cost. Twelve pounds and five shillings for Bryan's 500 A., as against £100 5s. for Bowman's 500 A., seems to indicate that there was a considerable difference in value between the money of Virginia and that of Pennsylvania. There may have been some difference in the two tracts of land, also; and Lenivell may have owed Bryan a debt that is not mentioned in the land deed.

Aug. 20, 20:—William Lenivell sells to Thomas Lenivell for £12 5s. 500 A. on Linvells Creek.—This appears to be another sale parallel to the one to Bryan.

Nov. 13, 14:—Thomas Lenivell sells to Jacob Christman,[18] of Fred. Co., for £100 5s. 500 A. on or near Linville Creek.—This is a sale parallel to the one to George Bowman by William Lenivell, Aug. 14, 15, of the same year. Did Chrisman also make payment in Pennsylvania money?—Thomas Lin-

17. This appears to be the first use of the name "Lenivell (Linville) Creek." Since William Lenivell bought this land in a larger tract only two months before, and since in that transaction no name is applied to the stream, it is quite probable that the stream received its name at this time, and from William Lenivell.

18. Christman was probably the son of Jacob Chrisman, Jost Hite's son-in-law; and the progenitor of the well known Rockingham family. The land he bought of Lenivell was likely near the present village of Chrisman, in West Rockingham.

vell made his mark. His wife's name was Hannah, but she did not sign.

1747.

From the Records of Augusta and Frederick.

Jan. 6:—Thomas Lenivell gives a mortgage to Morgan Bryan on 3 cows and a lot of smith's tools to secure a loan of £16.—*A C D B* 1—188, 189.

May 4, 5:—Morgan Bryan of Aug. Co. sells to Andrew Bowman, Jr., of Fred. Co., 200 A.: part of 400 A. granted to Bryan in 1735.—*F C D B* 1—301.

Aug. 12, 13:—William Beverly sells to John Miller 210 A. in Beverly Manor.[19]—Whether Miller was a German or not does not appear. He seems to have been living in Beverly Manor at the time of this purchase.—*A C D B* 1—332-335.

Sept. 4, 5:—John Millar and Hannah his wife (both making their marks) sell to Francis Hughs, of Lancaster Co., Pa., for £60 5s. 200 A. on the N. Shen. R., adjoining Thomas Moore.—Witnesses, Peter Scholl,[20] Matthew Skean, Thomas Milsap (mark).—*A C D B* 2—11-15.

Sept. 28, 29:—James Woode of Fred. Co. sells to Ephraim Vause of Augusta for £30 5s. 245 A. on Goose Creek.—*A C D B* 1—455-457.

Oct. 18, 19:—John Frewbaker [Frubaker, *Brubaker* (?)] sells to Abraham Frewbaker for £50 5s. two tracts of land: 300 A. on Shanando R., adjoining Jacob Nahale; 200 A. on

19. The limits of Beverly Manor are not very clearly understood: possibly they were never very clearly defined. John Lewis Peyton says that Rockingham County, or at least the Linville Creek section, was originally in Beverly Manor.—Peyton's History of Augusta, p. 66. See Waddell's Annals of Augusta, p. 29.

20. Peter Scholl lived on Smith Creek, now in Rockingham County, and was a prominent figure in the early days. On Oct. 30, 1745, when the first magistrates for Augusta County were appointed, Scholl seems to have been the one German in the whole number—twenty-one. A man of the same name, probably the same man, was living in Kentucky in 1776, intimately associated with Daniel Boone.—Waddell's Annals of Augusta, pp. 47, 52.

Shen. R.—Witnesses, Samuel Newman, William Scholl, Mathias Selzer.—The original papers were delivered from the clerk's office in May, 1762, to Jacob Burner.—*A C D B* 1—422-426.

Nov. 20:—Henry Downs sells to Ludwick Francisco of Augusta 470 A. on the S. side of Shen. R.—*A C D B* 1—453, 454.

1748.

From the Records of Augusta and Frederick.

Feb. 18:—Daniel Holman and Peter Gartner, with Abraham Strickler and William Anderson, sureties, become guardians for Julia, George, and Elsie Brock, orphans of Rudolph Brock, dec'd.—*A C W B* 1—107.

June 7, 8:—Iost Dubs sells to Peter Tostee for £97 11s. 8d. 125 A. in Fred. Co.—*F C D B* 1—410.

July 28, 29:—Jacob Dye and Mary his wife (both making their marks) sell to Ephraim Love,[21] late of Lanc. Co., Pa., for £60 5s. 377 A. "on ye head Draughts of Muddy Creek under the North Mountain," adjoining Daniel Harrison.—Witnesses, Peter Scholl, William White, William Carroll (mark).—*A C D B* 2—15-19.

Aug. 5, 6:—George Forbush (farmer) and Olive his wife (both making their marks) sell to John Miller (weaver) for £110 5s. (Pa. money) 400 A. "lying & being in the County of Augusta on the North branch of Sherrendo in the Gap of the Mountains," at or near the mouth of "beaver Dam run."[22] —Witnesses, Peter Scholl, Samuel Newman, David Stuart.—*A C D B* 2—4-7.

Aug. 16, 17:—Adam Müller (signing in German) sells to

21. Ephraim Love lived in what is now Rockingham County. He was a captain in the French and Indian War, as is shown by the military schedule of 1758, in the 7th volume of Hening's Statutes. Peter Scholl, the first witness to this sale, had been appointed a captain of militia in 1742.

22. This tract was apparently in Brock's Gap, in northwestern Rockingham.

Jacob Miller for £20 5s. 200 A. on Shen. R.—Witnesses, William Burk, John Carmichell, Henry Downs.—The original papers were delivered from the clerk's office to Henry Miller, July 24, 1759.—*A C D B* 2—1-3.—Adam Müller was doubtless the pioneer of the upper Valley, who was at this time living near the site of Elkton.

Aug. 18, 19:—Andrew and Mary Mitchell (both marking) sell to James Miller for £46 5s. 112 A. in Beverly Manor.—*A C D B* 2—60-63.

Aug. 19, 20:—David Stuart sells to James Miller 57 A. in Beverly Manor, adjoining John Miller.—*A C D B* 2—70-73.

Sept. 6:—Morgan Bryan sells to Samuel Strode 100 A. on Opeckon Creek: part of 450 A. granted to Bryan Nov. 12, 1735.—*F C D B* 1—423.

1749.

From the Records of Augusta and Frederick.

Jan. 26:—John Hockman's will written for him in German, he making his mark: his wife Barbara to have the whole estate.—Witnesses, Henry Pfifer, Henry Gnochnaur, Christian Harnish, Ulrich Hochman (mark).—*A C W B* 1—95.

Feb. 15:—Daniel Stover, with Abraham Strickler and George Leith sureties, appointed guardian for John, Mary, and James, orphans of John Campbell, dec'd.—*A C W B* 1—106.

Feb. 27, 28:—Ephraim Vause sells to Joseph Love for £70 5s. 200 A. on Goose Creek, at or near the mouth of a large run, near to Wm. Bewes.—*A C D B* 2—407-409.

Feb. 27, 28:—Ephraim Vause sells to William McCurry 248 A. on the S. Branch of "Roanoke."—*A C D B* 2—502-505.

Feb. 27, 28:—Samuel Wilkins sells to Daniel Harrison for £15 5s. 100 A. near the head of Cooks Creek.—*A C D B* 2—581-584.

Feb. 27, 28:—Samuel Wilkins sells to Alexander Herrin for £80 5s. 365 A. on Cooks Creek, adjoining the land of Daniel Harris[on].—Witnesses, Daniel Harrison, William Lusk, Silas Hart.—*A C D B* 2—588-591.

May 1, 2:—Lewis Stephens sells to John Nisewanger 355 A. on Long Meadow, Fred. Co., part of 3395 A. granted to Jost Hite, Oct. 3, 1734: sold by Hite to Peter Nuttenhouse, and by N. to Lewis Stephens.—*F C D B* 2—3.

June 16:—Inventory made by Daniel Stover, Jacob Burner, and John Holdman of the estate of Martin Kauffman, dec'd: total amount of the invoice, £236 7s. 9d.—*A C W B* 1—195-197.—Kauffmann's will is recorded in the same book, p. 125.

Aug. 16:—George Bowman (mark) deeds for life use to his mother, Ann Bowman, widow of Cornelius Bowman, a negro man Harry, 2 cows, 2 yearling heifers, 1 horse, 1 mare, with some household goods.—Witnesses, Martin Shoemaker (mark), William Rogers.—*A C D B* 3—60.

Sept. 22, 23:—Heinrich Ayler (signing in German) and Christopher Danner (mark), of Culpeper Co., sell to Jacob Harman of Aug. for £40 5s. 400 A. of land.—Witnesses, Isaac Smith, Casper Vought, Jacob Harman, Jr. (mark).—*A C D B* 2—312-315.

Oct. 3, 4:—Yost Heid sells to George Bowman of Fred. Co. for £100 5s. 545 A. on Lenivells Creek.—Witnesses, G. Jones,[23] John Hite, James Porteus.—*A C D B* 2—368-371.

Oct. 3, 4:—Yost Heid sells to Paul Froman for £100 5s. 500 A. on or near Lenivells Creek.—*A C D B* 2—371-374.

Nov. 13, 14:—Yost Hite sells to John Painter for £24 5s.

23. Gabriel Jones was probably the most famous lawyer of his day in the Valley, if not in Virginia. He lived first in Frederick County; later, in Augusta. He was a member of the House of Burgesses from both counties, and was prominent in the public affairs of a large section. He died in 1806 on his farm near Port Republic,—land bought in 1751 of Christopher Francisco: part of Jacob Stover's upper grant of 5000 acres.—Waddell's Annals of Augusta, pp. 81-84.

125 A. in Fred. Co., adjoining or near Jonathan Seaman.—Witnesses, Jasper Measener, John Miller, Gabriel Jones.—*F C D B* 2—38.

Nov. 26, 27:—Christopher Franciscus, Jr., sells to Jacob and Valentine Pence for £28 5s. (Pa. money) 210 A. on Cub Run, adjoining Nicholas Null.—Witnesses, Nicholas Noll, Ch. Franciscus, Sr., Stofel Francisco: all making their marks.—*A C D B* 2—725-728.

1750.

From the Records of Augusta and Frederick.

Feb. 6, 7:—Christopher Franciscus, Sr., of Lanc. Co., Pa., and Anna Margaret his wife (both making their marks) sell to Jacob Thomas of Aug. Co., for £25 5s., 185 A. on "Shannadore river and Cubrun": part of Francisco's tract of 3000 A.—Witnesses, Nicholas Noll (mark) and *Christofer Frantziscus Der Yungr.*—*A C D B* 2—715-718.—The original papers were delivered from the clerk's office to Jacob Miller, February, 1753.

Feb. 24:—Joseph Langdon, John Cook, and Joseph Cokenour make an inventory of the estate of Christian Miller, dec'd.—*A C W B* 1—227.

Feb. 26:—Jacob Nicholas and Valentine Pence qualify as executors of the will of Mat Shaup,[24] dec'd.—The following day Jacob Nicholas gives bond, with Valentine Pence and Jacob Miller sureties, as executor of the will of John Lawrence, dec'd.—*A C W B* 1—312, 313.

Feb. 27:—Valentine Pence, with Wm. Williams and Jacob Nicholas sureties, gives bond as executor of the will of Jacob Pence, dec'd.—*A C W B* 1—305.

July 9, 10:—Thomas Branson of Fred. Co. sells to John

24. Leonhard Schnell, the Moravian, enters in his diary a notice of his preaching at the house of Matthias Schaub on Sunday, Dec. 3, 1749. Schaub lived near Elkton, and evidently died in a month or two after Schnell's visit. The present form of the name is likely Shope or Shoop.

Painter for £100 5s. 162½ A., part of 1370 A. patented to Branson, Oct. 3, 1734.—*F C D B* 2—125.

Aug. 9, 10:—John Näglee and Jacob Näglee, executors for Jacob Näglee, dec'd, late of Philadelphia, sell to Ludowick Hounsdone for £96 5s. (Pa. money) 200 A. in "Orange Co.," part of the tract of land called the Massanutting tract, on the River.—Jacob Neglee, dec'd, had bought the land of Mathias Elser (Selser?), July 23, 24, 1740.—Witnesses (Aug., 1750), Samuel Wilkins, Samuel Bähm, John Wilkins, John Reyley, Jacob Burner, Jacob Strickler.[25]—The original papers were delivered to Jacob Burner, Aug. 17, 1756.—*A C D B* 2—792-795.

Aug. 20:—William Burk sells to Nicholas Null of Lanc. Co., Pa., for £58 5s. 400 A. on the N. side of the S. Shen. R., between the said river and Peaked Mt., at Boons Run.—Witnesses, Andrew Scott, Wm. Williams, Jacob Nichols, John McGuiness.—*A C D B* 2—796.

Aug. 28, 29:—Hans Baumgartner sells to Patrick Frazier for £52 5s. 400 A. on the head spring of "Stony Lick Branches": the said land having been granted to Bumgardner, Sept. 25, 1746.[26]—*A C D B* 2—838.

Dec. 30, 31:—Samuel Wilkins sells to Alexander Herring for £15 5s. 133 A. "upon a branch of the North River of Shanando called Cooks Creek."—Witnesses, Morgan Bryan, Robert Rollstone, John Wilkins.—*A C D B* 3—116-120.

25. The records state that, at the proving of these indentures in open court, Aug. 28, 1750, Samuel and John Wilkins made oath, and Jacob Strickler "affirmed." This circumstance is explained by the fact that Strickler was a Mennonite—a Mennonite preacher: many of the early settlers in the Page valley were Mennonites: they and the Dunkers, as well as some other religious bodies, avoid the formal taking of oaths. Jacob Strickler was likely a son of Abram Strickler, one of the first Massanutten settlers.

26. This land of Bumgardner's was probably on the north side of the Shenandoah River, a few miles below Port Republic, opposite the "Great Island"; since he owned land there at some time prior to 1751.

1751.

From the Records of Augusta County.

Jan. 28:—Nicholas Null (mark) of Lanc. Co., Pa., sells to Jacob Miller for £80 5s. 400 A. "on the North Side of the South River of Shanadoe between the sd River and the peaked Mountain," on or near Boones Run.—Witnesses, Jacob Nicholas, Valentine Pence, Henry Dooley.—This appears to be the tract that Null bought of Wm. Burk the preceding August.

Mar. 13.—John Dabkin, Nicholas Seeharn, David Magit, and George Scheniman make an inventory of the estate of Michael Rinehart,[27] dec'd: total value of the invoice, £80 3s.

Mar. 22:—John Bumgarner makes his will, witnessed by Benjamin Barger, Ch. Buck, and George Shunamen. Bumgardner mentions his sons, John and Christian; his daughters Mary, Elizabeth, and Modley; his grandson, Jacob Burner; and names his two friends, Mathias Suleer (Shuler?) and Jacob Burner, for his executors.

Oct. 4, 5:—Wm. Williams sells to Henry Pirkey 550 A. adjoining Jacob Strover's 5000 A.—Witnesses, Jacob Nicholas, Filty Pence.

Nov. 24, 25:—John Peter Salling[28] and his wife Ann sell land to Henry Fuller on the E. side of the N. Branch of James R.

Dec. 19:—John Jacob Rothgab (of the Page Valley) makes his will, witnessed by John Spitler, John Taylor, and Martin Forclight. He disposes of 400 A. of land, on or near the S. Shen. R.; he mentions his sons, John George and Peter; his daughters, Elizabeth, Anna, Barbara, and Catherine; and his wife Anna. The will was written in "High Dutch"; was translated by How Dickins, upon oath; and was proved by

27. Michael Rinehart was one of the early settlers at Massanutting, and one of the petitioners of 1733.

28. Salling was a noted German explorer, going frequently in company with Thomas Marlin.—Wither's Chronicles, pp. 48, 66.

the oath of John Taylor. The widow, Anna Rothgab, and Peter Ruffner qualified as executors, although the testator had "prayed" for Paul Lung and Anna Rothgab in that capacity. The latter is called Anna Hollenback in the bond.

1752.

From the Records of Augusta County.

Feb. 4:—Christian Funkhousa and Christianah his wife and Henry Brock and Mary his wife sell to Jacob Bare for £60 400 A. in Aug. Co., "on ye south fork of the North River of Shanando above the gap in ye mountain" (likely Brock's Gap).—The Funkhousas and Brocks all make their marks.—The property sold is warranted specially against John P. Brock and his heirs.—Witnesses, Peter Scholl, Samuel Newman, John Bare.

May 15, 16:—Andrew Fought, yeoman, sells to Casper Fought for £20 5s. 112 A., the same that was deeded to Andrew Fought, June 1, 1750.—Witnesses, Robert Turk, Robert Mehan.

May 19, 20:—Samuel Wilkins sells to Edward and Robert Shankland 400 A., whereon the said Wilkins lately dwelt: part of the 1265 A. on Cook's Creek, sold to Wilkins by McKay *et al.*—Witnesses, Peter Scholl, William Brown, Andrew Erwin.

June 17:—Jacob Miller sells to Nicholas Null for £60 5s. 400 A. on the N. side of the S. Shen. R., between the said river and Peaked Mt., on Boones Run.—This appears to be the same tract that Null sold to Miller for £80, Jan. 28, 1751, and that Null had bought of Wm. Burk for £58, Aug. 20, 1750.

Aug. 14, 15:—Henry Purkey sells to Abraham Estes for £130 5s. 110 A. on the S. side of Shen. R., adjoining George Boon and James Barton.—Witnesses, Nicholas Trout, Nicholas Null.

Nov. 14, 15:—Timothy Crosthwait sells to George Zimmerman for £16 5s. 400 A. on the branches of Cub Run.—Original papers delivered to G. Zimmerman, June, 1754.

1753.

Feb. 22:—Peter Reed sells to Peter Haas for £200 (Pa. money) 680 A. (Lot. No. 1.) on the S. Fork of the Wappacomo, or Great S. Branch of the Potomack.—Witnesses, Hendrick Cartright, Peter Thom, Tobias Decker.—*A C D B* 5—134.

1754.

From the Records of Augusta and Frederick.

Jan. 12:—Peter Shaver sells to John Miller for £10 5s. 37 A. on the S. W. side of "the New river on the head of Mill Creek."—Shaver had apparently bought this tract Aug. 22, 1753.—*A C D B* 6—107.

Jan. 14, 15:—Garrett Zinn sells to Emanuel Eckerling[29] 125 A. on the W. side of Woods River.—*A C D B* 6—112.

July 29:—Timothy Crosthwait sells to Jeremiah Early of Culpeper for £25 400 A. on Elk Run, a branch of Shen. R.—Witnesses, Francis Kirtley, Jeremiah Early, John Early, Thomas Kirtley, Thomas Stanton.—*A C D B* 6—329.—This Elk Run is likely the one that enters the river near Elkton, in Rockingham County; although there is also an Elk Run in Augusta County.

Sept. 8, 9:—Jonah Friend sells to Simeon Rice for £100 5s. 66½ A. in Fred. Co., on the S. side of the Potomac: part of 300 A. granted to Israel Friend, Oct. 3, 1734: the part devised by will to Jonah Friend.—*F C D B* 3—372.

29. It is probable that Eckerling, possibly Peter Shaver and John Miller also, belonged to the community of Ephrata Brethren on New River. The Ephrata Brethren were a mystical sect, an early offshoot of the Dunkers, named from the central place of their activity in Pennsylvania.—See Sachse's German Sectarians, Vol. II; Brumbaugh's History of the Brethren; etc.

1755.

May 5, 6:—Wilhelm Hubers (Huber, Hoover) and Margaret his wife sell to Samuel Fry for £36 5s. 168 A. on the N. side of the N. River of Shen., adjoining the land of Charles Huddle.—Huber signs in German.—*F C D B* 3—471.

Dec. 29, 30:—Christian Funkhouser and Christinah his wife sell to Henry Mire (Meyer?) for £34 200 A. on Holmans Creek[30] "a Branch of the North River of Shanando"—the said 200 A. being part of 444 A. granted by Fairfax to Ch. Funkhouser, Mar. 2, 1752.—Witnesses, Abram Denton, Caleb Odell.—*F C D B* 4—83.

In order to carry the foregoing studies into a later period, as well as for the sake of preserving some facts that are more or less interesting in themselves, a few more abstracts from the public records are presented below. They are taken chiefly from the deed books of Frederick County, covering the period from 1760 to 1780; the few from the records of Augusta and Shenandoah are separately indicated.

1760.

May 3:—Lawrence Snapp buys of Lewis Stephens for £10 three lots: Lot No. 16, containing ½ A.; lots No. 68 and No. 97, of 5 A. each; all in the town of Stephensburgh. Lot 16 was on Fairfax and German Sts.; lot 68 was on Squirrel Lane; lot 97 was on Rabbit Lane. All were a part of a 424 A. tract obtained by Lewis Stephens from Peter Stephens, May 2, 3, 1755; the latter secured the land in a tract of 674 A. patented to him Oct. 3, 1734.

1761.

Apr. 24:—Frederick Conrod buys of Theobald and Barbara Posing (Boszing) for £23 Lot. No 14 (½ A.), on the

30. Holmans Creek is in the southwestern part of Shenandoah County, and flows into the North Shenandoah River near Quicksburg.

"run that Meanders through Winchester town joining the said Town in Frederick County aforesaid."—Witnesses, William Green, Wilhelm Mongor (?) Henrick Bender. The last two and the Posings signed in German.

Dec. 26:—Charles Moyer buys of Lewis Stephens for £10 Lots No. 5 (½ A.), No. 29 and No. 93 (each of 5 A.), in the town of Stephensburgh.

1762.

Jan. 20:—Frederick Conrod, tanner, of Fred. Co., for £8 paid to Patrick Hagan, farmer, receives as tanner apprentice Marmaduke Hagan, aged 11 7-12 years, till he shall be 21 years old; also, for another £8, Conrod and wife get Hagan's daughter Hannah, aged nearly 13, till she shall be 18. Hannah is to be taught to spin, sew, and do household work; to read the Old and New Testaments; etc.—Witnesses, Wm. Green, Peter Helphenstein. The latter and Conrad signed in German.

Apr. 26:—Peter Hoffman buys of Jacob and Barbara Miller for 20s. Lot No. 85 (½ A.) on King St. in Woodstock; the said Hoffman to erect a house with stone or brick chimney on or before May 1, 1763, and pay a yearly ground rent of 5s.

July 5:—John Lance (Lantz) buys of Alex. Boyd for £150 5s. two lots in Winchester.

July 26:—Philip Hoofman buys several lots of Peter Stover in Strasburg.

Sept. 8:—Henry Rinker and wife Mary sell to Casper Rinker for £50 5s. Lot No. 104 (½ A.) in Winchester.

Nov. 3:—Christly Bumbgardner buys of Peter Stover and Frainey his wife a lot in Strasburg.

1763.

June 7:—Nicholas Pittman buys of Lewis Stephens Lots No. 2, No. 32, No. 100 in Stephensburgh.

1764.

May 4, 5:—David Halsinger buys of Lewis Stephens for £10 5s. 100 A., part of 1384 A. granted by Fairfax to Stephens Aug. 5, 1750.

1765.

Sept. 30, Oct. 1:—Adam Kern buys of Robert Willson for £7 5s. 3½ A. on Hoggs (Hoge's) Run, near the site of the present Kernstown.—Adam Kern appears to have been the first of the name to locate in the vicinity; but the next year Michael Kern bought land on Hoge's Run, and Henry Kern (Oct. 3, 1766) bought land of Lawrence Stephens on German St. in Stephensburg. On June 29, 1767, John Kern bought land of Thomas and Elizabeth Shepherd, probably at Shepherdstown.—I have recently been informed (May 10, 1907) that the Kerns are of Dutch descent.

1768.

July 11, 12:—John Glick buys of Richard and Rebecca Campbell for £65 5s. 150 A. 'on the waters of the North River of Shenondoah'—the same that Campbell bought of George Nicholas: part of 402 A. granted to Nicholas by Fairfax.—Witnesses, John Skeen, Ingabo. Skeen, James Moore.

1769.

Apr. 3:—Henry Kagay buys of Samuel and Catherine Lusk for £350 5s. 404 A. "lying on Smith's Creek," adjoining Samuel Newman's land.—This tract is in Shenandoah County, near New Market. Kagay had come to Page county from Pennsylvania in 1768.

1772.

May 18, 19:—Henry Wetzell sells to Philip Blay for £70 5s. 313 A. on Cedar Creek in Dunmore Co.—*Shen. Co. Deed Book A, p. 10.*

Nov. 24:—Jacob Borden and Mary his wife, of Fred. Co., sell to George Adam Bowman of Lanc. Co., Pa., for £50 5s. 180 A. in Shen. Co. adjoining Chas. Huddle and John Boughman.—Borden's name was written partly in German.—*S C D B-A*—148.

1774.

May 4, 5:—Philip Huver buys of Ebenezer Parkins for £74 52½ A. near Kernstown, on both sides of "the great Waggon Road that Leaves from Winchester to Stephensburgh."

1777.

Feb. 24, 25:—Nicholas and Catherine Pittman sell to John Hockman for £150 5s. 100 A. on the North River of Shenandoah: land conveyed to Pittman by Christian Whitmore.—*S C D B-B*—436.

1778.

Feb. 24:—Anthony Kline buys of Lewis and Mary Stephens for £50 Lot No. 55 (½ A.) in Stephensburg, and two 5 A. lots joining the said town.—In May of 1779 Kline bought more land of Stephens. On Sept. 7, 1779, Adam Kline bought of George Wright 400 A. on a branch of Opeckon Creek.

1780.

June 5, 6:—Casper Rinker buys of John Stonebridge for £120 5s. 224½ A. on both sides of Back Creek on Raccoon Run, adjoining James Odall and John McCoole.

1782.

Apr. 5:—Lawrence Snapp makes his will: signs in German.—*S C W B-A*—420.

1790.

Apr. 1:—Francis Huff buys of Alex. St. Clair and Jane

his wife for £25 Lot No. 19 (¼ A.) in Staunton.—*A C D B* 1 *A*—9.

July 5:—Jacob Swoope made attorney of Kuhn and Risberg of Phil'a to sell a tract of land in Staunton.—*A C D B* 1 *A*—15.

Sept. 1:—Balser Bumgarner of Aug. Co. buys of Francis Erwin, Atty. for Alex. Curry of the District of Kentucky, for £40 two tracts of land in Aug. Co.: one of 40 A., the other of 130 A.: both on or near a branch of Naked Creek.

CHAPTER VI.

TOWNS AND TOWN FOUNDERS.

Up to the beginning of the French and Indian War the settlement and development of the Shenandoah Valley went steadily and, for the most part, peacefully on; for the Shawnees and other tribes of Indians claiming possessions in the Valley appear to have made no serious trouble prior to this period.[1] The reputation for benevolence, possessed by Penn's colony, seems to have followed the Germans and Scotch-Irish who came to Virginia, and to have served them well as a protecting influence for nearly a generation.

The earliest settlements of the German pioneers followed, as we have seen, the main branch of the Shenandoah River—that is, the south branch—up through the Page valley: the Massanutting country. But only a little later the tide of immigration came up the western side of the Massanutten mountain, along the north branch of the Shenandoah, also. It appears, however, that some of the earliest settlers along the river on that side were of English or Irish stock. Among the first were Bemjamin Allen, Riley Moore, and William White, who came from Maryland in 1734 and located on some of the magnificent lands near the present town of Mt. Jackson.[2] The Germans concentrated on lines a little further west, along what after awhile came to be the "Middle Road," through Timberville, Forestville, Rinkerton, Hamburg, and Lantz's Mill; and the "Back Road," through Moore's Store, Conicville, and Columbia Furnace. The main line of travel up and down the Valley was doubtless nearer the river, following, for the most part, what had been for centuries a famous Indian trail. This highway was evidently the chief thoroughfare for

1. Kercheval's History of the Valley, p. 49.

2. Idem, p. 45; Foote's Sketches, p. 15.

travelers at an early period. The Moravian missionaries refer to it in 1753 as the "great road";[3] and it doubtless followed closely the line of the present Valley Turnpike from Winchester, through Woodstock, Mt. Jackson, New Market, and Harrisonburg, to Staunton.

But other roads were being opened and put in order at an early period, as the records and statutes show; and ferries were being established for transportation across the rivers. One of the earliest of these was near the present town of Front Royal, in Warren County, provided for by the Virginia General Assembly in August, 1736. It was to be "on Sherrendo river, from the land of William Russel, next above the mouth of Happy's creek, in the county of Orange, across into the fork, the price for a man three pence, and for an horse three pence; on or across the main river, the same".[4]

For centuries the only crossing place along the Potomac had been the old Packhorse Ford, a mile below Shepherdstown; but in due time ferries were established. In May, 1755, Thomas Swearingen was authorized to conduct a ferry over the Potomac, somewhere in Frederick County.[5] In 1761 Robert Harper was given permission to establish what afterwards became the famous "Harper's Ferry." In 1765 a ferry was established over the Potomac from the land of Thomas Shepherd, in the town of Mecklenburg (Shepherdstown), to Maryland.[6] Other ferries in the same vicinity were established before the close of the Revolution.

In these various enterprises, looking towards the public welfare and convenience, the Germans took an active part. Their lack of familiarity with the English language and manners was against them for many years; but they went ahead, with a persistent energy and willingness, in the things they

3. Virginia Magazine, Vol. XII, No. 2, pp. 143, 146.

4. Hening's Statutes, Vol. IV, p. 531.

5. Idem, Vol. VI, p. 494.

6. Idem, Vol. VIII, pp. 446, 447.

knew. On the petitions for roads and the establishment of courts of justice, the German names appear in fair proportion. In the year 1745, Peter Mauk, a German, made the first application at Winchester for naturalization papers.[7] This was three or four years after Adam Miller, the pioneer of Augusta, had obtained his.

In no phase of the early development of the country were the Germans more helpful and prominent than in the founding and building up of the towns. Following is a brief chronological account of those towns in the Valley, in the founding and legal establishment of which the Germans took a leading or important part.

Staunton.—As early as 1748 an Act of Assembly was passed for the establishing of a town in Augusta, and for holding annual fairs therein; but this Act was for some reason repealed in 1752 by proclamation.[8] In November, 1761, however, Staunton was permanently established by law.[9] The Scotch-Irish were of course the leaders in Staunton from the beginning, as they are at the present time; but it is a rather significant fact that a number of Germans have been found among the enterprising and influential citizens of the town from very early times. When the place was incorporated by an Act of Assembly of December 23, 1801, and the voters met shortly afterwards to elect their town officers, Jacob Swoope, a German, was chosen as the first mayor; and on the first executive board of twelve men were at least two other Germans: Michael Garber, alderman; and Michael Harman, councilman. Jacob Lease, alderman, was likely another German.[10] These facts, as well as others that might be given, are rather eloquent in their testimony for both the Germans and Scotch-Irish, as regards their capacity for mutual friendship and fraternal coöperation.

7. Norris' History of the Lower Valley, p. 84.

8. Hening's Statutes, Vol. VI, p. 215.

9. Idem, Vol. VII, p. 473.

10. Waddell's Annals of Augusta, p. 376.

Winchester.—This town was made up in the early times chiefly of Germans and Irish, as Kercheval tells us, together with a few English and Scotch. Tradition assigns the place two houses in 1738. It was legally established as a town, with provision for the inevitable annual fairs, in February of 1752; and was incorporated in October, 1779.[11] James Woode laid out the town in 1752: twenty-six half-acre lots about the court house. To these were soon added 54 other lots of the same size. The village, called Fredericktown and "Old Town" at first, evidently grew with devouring rapidity. In September, 1758, the boundaries were again enlarged, and trustees for it and the new town of Stephensburg were appointed, as follows: Lord Fairfax, Thomas Bryan Martin, James Wood, Lewis Stephens, Gabriel Jones, John Hite, John Dooe, Isaac Parkins, Robert Rutherford, Philip Boush.[12] The next year the granted extension was made, as shown by a deed of September 3, 1759, from James Wood to Henry Rinker, part of which is herewith given:

> Whereas by an act of General Assembly made at the Capitol in the City of Williamsburgh in the said 32d year of his said Majesty's Reign Instituted an act for erecting a town on the land of Lewis Stephens and for Inlarging the Town of Winchester etc. among other things it is Enacted that one Hundred and six Acres of land Belonging to the said James [Wood] Contiguous to the said town of Winchester Surveyed and laid off in lots with convenient streets be added and made Part of the said Town and that the Freeholders and Inhabitants of the said Town of Winchester now enjoy.[13]

It appears that the same year (1759) 173 lots were added to the growing town by Lord Fairfax.[14]

Stephensburg.—The place first known as Stephensburg, later as New Town, and at present as Stephens City, was established by law in September, 1758. It was laid out on the land of the German, Lewis Stephens, and was settled almost

11. Hening's Statutes, Vol. VI, p. 268; Vol. X, pp. 172, 173, 176.

12. Hening's Statutes, Vol. VII, p. 236.

13. Fred. Co. Deed Book 5, p. 256.

14. Hening's Statutes, Vol. VII, p. 315.

exclusively by people of the same nationality.[15] The original founder of the town was Peter Stephens, father of Lewis, who came to Virginia in 1732 with Jost Hite. At the time of the legal establishment of Stephensburg (1758), the same trustees were appointed for both it and Winchester, as noted above; and, among the ten men, at least three, Lewis Stephens, John Hite, and Philip Boush, were Germans. The following abstract from the Frederick County records relates to the early days of Stephensburg, and may be of interest in this connection.

May 3, 1760, Nicholas Pittman[16] bought of Lewis and Mary Stephens for ten pounds three lots in the town of Stephensburg: Lot No. 1, of a half-acre, on German Street; Lot No. 85, of five acres; and Lot No. 141, of six acres. The three lots were part of a tract of 424 acres bought by Lewis Stephens of Peter Stephens, May 2, 3, 1755; the said 424 acres being part of a larger tract of 674 acres granted to Peter Stephens, October 3, 1734.

One of the present industries of Stephens City is the manufacture of lime. The farming lands immediately surrounding the town are some of the best in the Valley.

Strasburg.—This town was first called *Staufferstadt*, after its founder, Peter Stover; but when, in November, 1761, it was established by law, Stover had it called Strasburg, after

15. Howe's Antiquities, p. 272; Kercheval's History of the Valley, p. 179.

16. Nicholas Pittman was a man of prominence in his day, and is the ancestor of one of the best known Valley families. He came over from Bingen on the Rhine about the year 1740, with some of the Bakers and Conrads of Winchester. His son, Lawrence Pittman, built in the year 1802 the old brick mansion at Red Banks, beside the North Shenandoah River and the Valley Turnpike, about four miles below Mt. Jackson, Shenandoah County. In the days of staging through the Valley, Red Banks was one of the famous stopping places.—For most of the facts presented in this note the writer is indebted to the kindness of Miss Mary C. Pittman, of Fauquier County, Va.

his birthplace in the Fatherland. The ten trustees appointed for the town were the following gentlemen: William Miller, Matthew Harrison, Jacob Bowman, Valentine Smith, Charles Buck, Peter Stover, Isaac Hite, Leonard Baltice, John Funk, and Philip Huffman. In the Act, which also provided for the establishment of Staunton and New London, the following statement was made: "It shall not be lawful for any person whatsoever to erect or build, or cause to be erected or built, in either of the said towns, any wooden chimnies." All such already built were to be pulled down by the first of the following August.[17]

Woodstock.—This town was established on the land of Jacob Miller, and was first called after him, *Muellerstadt.* Of all the towns in the Valley, it was probably the most carefully and extensively laid out. Miller had come into the country sometime prior to the year 1752, and had settled near Narrow Passage, a few miles above the site of the town. He bought several large tracts of land, until finally he owned about 2000 acres. In 1761 he laid out upon a larger scale the village that likely was already called after him; and in March of that year the Virginia Assembly passed the Act of which the following is a part:

> Jacob Miller, of the county of Frederick, hath laid off twelve hundred acres into streets and lots, 96 acres of which are divided into lots of half an acre each, and the residue into streets and lots of five acres each, and (that) several persons are now settled there, and many others would soon purchase and reside there if the same was by law erected into a town: Be it therefore * * * & shall be called * * * Woodstock.[18]

The following gentlemen were appointed directors and trustees: Cornelius Riddel, John Skeen, Burr Harrison, Matthew Harrison, Joseph Langdon, Moses Striker, Adam Yeaker, Jacob Miller, and Peter Hainger.

17. Hening's Statutes, Vol. VII, pp. 473-475.

18. Idem, pp. 406, 407; W. Va. Historical Magazine, Vol. 2, No. 2, pp. 39, 40.

Shepherdstown.—This appears to be the oldest town in the Valley, having been settled by German immigrants about 1727. It was first called New Mecklenburg; later, Mecklenburg; and it is at present called after the name of its leading founder, Thomas Shepherd. On fifty acres of his land the town was legally established in November, 1762, and was called Mecklenburg. During the years immediately following, Thomas Shepherd and Elizabeth his wife sold a number of lots: Brown, Mays, Neally, Morgan, Bedinger, and others being among the purchasers. November, 1766, two annual fairs were provided for, to be held during two days each, one beginning on the second Wednesday in June; the other on the second Wednesday in October. [19]

Martinsburg.—This town was established by law, October, 1778, on 130 acres of land laid out by Adam Stephen, about the Berkeley County court house and sundry dwellings near it. The trustees appointed were, James McAlister, Anthony Noble, Joseph Mitchell, James Strode, Robert Carter Willis, William Patterson, and Philip Pendelton.[20]

Harrisonburg.—By the same Act that, in May, 1780, gave a legal existence to the town of Louisville, at the falls of the Ohio, in the county of Kentucky, the town of Harrisonburg, laid out upon 50 acres of land, by Thomas Harrison, in the county of Rockingham, was established;[21] and, although it has not quite kept pace with its rival on the Ohio, it is, nevertheless, one of the best kept and best equipped towns in the country, and is now rapidly approaching the proportions of a city. Harrisonburg is right in the midst of German communities; and, in consequence, many of its townspeople are of the same race. Of the twenty persons owning lots in the town in 1785, at least five—John Apler, Peter Conrad, Frederick Spangler, J. Shipman, and Anthony Sourbeer—were

19. Hening's Statutes, Vol. VII, p. 600; Vol. VIII, p. 255.

20. Idem, Vol. IX, p. 569.

21. Idem, Vol. X, pp. 293-295.

Germans.[22] One of the oldest streets is German Street. The German element has had a prominent place in the life and progress of the town from the beginning to the present.

New Market.—This town was established by law in the year 1784.[23] Numerous German families in and about the place—the Henkels, Zirkles, Raders, Olingers, Bushongs, Neffs, Rosenbergers, Koiners, and others—have contributed largely to its growth and character.

Front Royal.—In 1788 this town was established, in the county of Frederick (now Warren), on 50 acres of land—the property of Solomon Van Metre, James Moore, Robert Haines, William Cunningham, Peter Halley, John Smith, Allen Wiley, Original Wroe, George Chick, William Morris, and Henry Trout. The trustees appointed were the following gentlemen: Thomas Allen, Robert Russell, William Headly, William Jennings, John Hickman, Thomas Hand, and Thomas Buck.[24] Van Metre was likely a Dutchman; and, of the others named, Halley, Chick, Trout, and Hickman were probably Germans.

Keezletown.—Keezletown or, as it was first called, Keisell's-Town, was given a legal existence in October, 1791. From the Act of Assembly of that date the following is copied:

> That 100 acres of land, the property of George Keisell, in the county of Rockingham, as the same are now laid off into lots and streets, shall be established a town, by the name of Keisell's-Town; and that George Houston, George Carpinter, Martin Earhart, Peter Nicholass, John Snapp, John Swisher, and John Pierce, gentlemen, shall be, and they are hereby constituted trustees thereof.[25]

There is said to have been a sharp rivalry between Keezletown and Harrisonburg for the position of honor as county-seat; but the latter finally won the coveted distinction.

Passing from the list of the older towns of the Shenandoah

22. Rockingham Register, March 26, 1885.

23. Howe's Antiquities, p. 467.

24. Kercheval's History of the Valley, p. 185.

25. Hening's Statutes, Vol. XIII, p. 297.

Valley to those that have risen into prominence within the last century, many are found in which the Germans have played an essential part: few, indeed, there are in which their influence has not been a telling factor. Space forbids the presentation of detailed facts: only a few names may be mentioned. Waynesboro, Stuarts Draft, Weyers Cave, and Mt. Sidney, in Augusta County; Bridgewater, Dayton, Elkton, Broadway, and Timberville, in Rockingham; Mt Jackson, Quicksburg, and Edinburg, in Shenandoah; and Luray and Shenandoah in Page, are all thriving towns of wealth and importance. Every one of them is surrounded by German communities; and in every one of them is a strong element of German citizens.

In order to show still more completely how thoroughly the German settlers of a century and more ago took possession of certain sections of the Shenandoah Valley, a list of villages and post offices that bear German names in the several counties is appended. In this list none of the names of towns already mentioned are included.

Augusta County:—Avis, Clines Mills, Kiracofe, Koiners Store, Molers, Sangerville, Snyder, Stover, Swoope, Vanlear.

Berkeley County:—Bedington, Foltz, Van Clevesville.

Frederick County:—Heiskell, Hinckle, Kernstown (Dutch?), Neffstown, Rosenberger, Shockeysville, Siler.

Jefferson County:—Bakerton, Keller, Molers, Myerstown, Snyders Mills.

Page County:—Hamburg, Koontz, Long, Mauck, Printz Mill, Shuler, Spitler.

Rockingham County:—Bakers Mill, Bowmans Mill, Capbingers Store, Chrisman, Cootes Store, Criders, Fort Hoover, Friedens, Goods Mills, Harnsberger, Hollar, Hoover, Hupp, Karicofe, Kise, Linville, Meyerhoeffers Store, Ottobine, Stemphleytown, Suters, Wengers Mill, Whissens Mill, Wittigs, Zerkle Station.

Shenandoah County:—Bowmans, Getz, Hamburg, Harmans Mills, Hepners, Hottle, Hupps Shop, Jacobs Church, Kerns Spring, Koontz Mills, Lantz Mills, Maurertown, Pughs Run, Rinkerton, Rosendale, Rudes Hill, Saumsville, Smoots Mills, Smoots Store, Stickleys Quarry, Zepp.

Warren County:—Hamburg.[26]

Altogether by the above showing, counting towns, villages, postoffices, and places of business, whose names are listed in standard publications, there are in the Shenandoah Valley no less than eighty-two places with German names: there are possibly eighty-five. Of these, twenty-seven are in Rockingham County; twenty-two in Shenandoah; eleven in Augusta; eight in Frederick; seven in Page; six in Jefferson; three in Berkeley; and one in Warren. Thus far I have not been able to find any in Clarke.

26. These names have been copied from the U. S. Postal Guide and from Rand, McNally & Co.'s Map of Virginia and Shipper's Guide.

CHAPTER VII.

Proportion and Distribution of the German Element in the Valley.

The latter part of the preceding chapter, in which the towns and villages with German names in the several counties of the Shenandoah Valley have been enumerated, will serve as an introduction to this one.

It has already been observed that the large land grants obtained west of the lower Shenandoah River in 1729 and thereabouts, by Robert Carter, Mann Page, and other Englishmen from eastern Virginia, kept the Germans out of what is now Clarke County, as well as from adjacent sections, to a greater or less degree. Moreover, the immigrants were urged on still further south and west, in many cases, by the dispute between Lord Fairfax and Jost Hite. So they went in largest numbers beyond the English colonies on the lower Shenandoah, and beyond the debatable ground below the Massanutten Mountain, and thronged into what are now the counties of Shenandoah, Page, and Rockingham. They were checked before they reached the hills of Staunton by the strong lines of Scotch-Irish, rapidly forming and taking position in those quarters, in and after the year 1732. At a much later date many of the Germans out-flanked the defenders of Augusta and Rockbridge, and took advanced positions in what are now the counties of Botetourt, Roanoke, and Franklin; but with them we have not to do in this study.

Some of the earliest German settlements in the Valley were, as we have seen, in what are now Jefferson and Berkeley counties, West Virginia; but, upon the whole, the Germans have always been in the minority in the districts between Winchester and the Potomac. It is between Winchester and Staunton, therefore, in upper Frederick, western Warren, in Page, Shenandoah, Rockingham, and lower Augusta that we find the German strongholds. Woodstock, in early times, was doubtless very near the heart of the German communities; but in later times the center of population would likely be found further southwest, considerably nearer Harrisonburg. For, as time went on, the tide of immigration continued to roll slowly up the Valley. Many of the Scotch-Irish went further south and west; and the Germans steadily followed them. Says Mr. Waddell:

> The places of the emigrants [from Augusta westward] were taken by immigrants from Pennsylvania and the lower valley, generally people of German descent—the most thrifty of farmers—and thus the country suffered no loss in population.[1]

From the Valley counties of Frederick, Shenandoah, and Rockingham, the German pioneers soon spread across the mountains westward into the valleys of the South Branch of the Potomac, and helped to build up the counties of Hampshire, Hardy, and Pendleton, in West Virginia. Some of the family names borne by this contingent were, Strader, Bowman, Hite, Minear, Stump, Snyder, Woolford, and Brake.[2] On the eastern side of the Blue Ridge, home-seekers from Germanna and adjacent colonies came up along the Robinson River in Madison County, and took positions very near to their kinsmen just beyond the mountain range. Sometimes they must have reminded one another that they were neighbors; and occasionally the religious leaders of the eastern side crossed the rugged barrier of nature, and ministered to the shepherdless flocks along both branches of the Shenandoah. Among these early neighborly neighbors of Madison County were Yeagers, Utzs, Wielands, Huffmans, Zieglers, Zimmermans, Clores, Fleishmans, Kochs, Schmits, and Blanchenbuchters.[3]

At the present, one would be safe in saying that in the Valley

1. Annals of Augusta, p. 376.

2. Fast and Maxwell's History of West Virginia, p. 9.

3. Orange Co. Deed Book 2; Virginia Magazine, Vol. XIV, No. 2, pp. 136-170.

counties of Frederick, Warren, and Augusta, about one-half of the people are of direct German descent, and bear German names; and that in the counties of Shenandoah, Rockingham, and Page, from two-thirds to three-fourths are German. This does not mean, of course, that any considerable number of the people still use the German language, or that all of the German family names would at once be recognized as such; but the statements are held to be true, not only of the present, but of the last hundred and fifty years, except in the case of Augusta County. There, a century or more ago, would have been found a much smaller proportion of Germans than at the present.

Basing a calculation upon the figures supplied by the census of 1900, and assuming that 70 per cent. of the people in Page, Rockingham, and Shenandoah are of German descent; that in Augusta and Frederick the rate is 50 per cent.; in Warren, 40 per cent.; and, in Berkeley and Jefferson, 20 per cent., a total would be reached in these eight counties of about 90,000.

Partly in proof of the foregoing statements, and partly to show how these conclusions have been reached, a few particular facts and figures are herewith presented.

From the records of Frederick, Augusta, and Shenandoah counties, the names of persons whose wills were recorded during the period of the Revolution have been collated; and, from the records of Rockingham, the names of persons who sold land during the same period. The last list has been taken from the deed books, for the reason that the will books of Rockingham for the period under review were badly damaged by fire during the Civil War. These four lists of names, copied indiscriminately, have been used for the purposes of comparison. Of a list of 125 names from the records of Frederick County, from 1770 to 1783, about 45, or 36 per cent., are German; in a list of 92 from Augusta, from 1778 to 1786, about 12, or slightly over 13 per cent., are German; among 102 names from Rockingham, from the organization of the county in 1777 to 1793, about 52. or 51 per cent., are German;

and among 68 names from Shenandoah (then including most of Page), from the organization of the county in 1772 to 1784, about 48, or over 70 per cent., are German.[4] In the Shenandoah County Deed Book B, a volume of 544 pages, covering the period from 1774 to 1777, at least half of the signatures are recorded in German script.

In the year 1809, a list of the unclaimed letters, remaining in the Harrisonburg postoffice on September 30, was published in the Staunton German newspaper — *Der Deutsche Virginier Adler*—of November 18; and, among the 58 names of men and a few women, at least 34, or over 58 per cent., are German. On January 10, 1821, a similar list of letters in the Woodstock postoffice was published in the *Woodstock Herald;* and, of 78 names, at least 54, or over 69 per cent., are German.[5] The lower county, Shenandoah, still embracing most of what is now Page, is still ahead of Rockingham in German names; but the balance is becoming more nearly even, as the tide of humanity continues to push upward.

Other figures of a still later period show substantially equivalent results. In 1861, at the outbreak of the Civil War, the Tenth Regiment Virginia Volunteer Infantry, commanded successively by Colonels S. B. Gibbons, E. T. H. Warren, and D. H. Lee Martz, was composed of 671 men: five companies from Rockingham; two companies from Shenandoah; one company from Warren; and one company from Page. Of the 671 men in the regiment as a whole, at least 342, or nearly 51 per cent., bore German names. Among the 338 men composing the five companies from Rockingham, at least 175, or nearly 52 per cent., bore German names. Of the two Shenandoah companies, aggregating 152 men, no less than 95, or over 62 per cent., were Germans. Twenty-eight out of fifty-eight, or over 48 per cent., in the Warren company, and 44 out of 123, or nearly 36 per cent., in the Page company,

4. For the lists of names in question, see Appendixes C, D, E, F.

5. For the full lists in question here, see Appendixes A and B.

were Germans. The proportion of Germans from Rockingham, Shenandoah, and Page would doubtless have been much greater, had it not been for the fact that in these counties were large German communities of Dunkers and Mennonites, who, being opposed to war upon religious principle, of course did not volunteer. Comparing the particular companies of this regiment, Company F, the Muhlenberg Rifles, from Woodstock in Shenandoah County, had the largest proportion of German names: 54 in 76, or over 71 per cent.; while Company H, Chrisman's Infantry, from western Rockingham, came next in order, with 60 German names in 90, or 66⅔ per cent. Company H, 12th Virginia Cavalry, Ashby's Brigade, commanded first by Captain, later Colonel, Emanuel Sipe, was composed chiefly of men from eastern Rockingham; and had at least 84 German names among 124—nearly or quite 68 per cent.[6] In Hardesty's historical and biographical atlas of Rockingham County, published in 1884, are given biographical sketches of 86 prominent citizens—chiefly natives—of the county; and among the number are about 55, or 64 per cent., of German name and lineage.

If one should attempt to go beyond the number of families and individuals with German names, and make a census of all the people in the Shenandoah Valley who have a considerable infusion of German blood, it is likely that only a few—a very few—could prove their right to exclusion. But the impracticable and impossible shall not be attempted. Before leaving this phase of our subject, however, it is deemed appropriate to notice in some detail the transformations that many of our German names have undergone, and the consequent difficulty that one must experience in the effort to trace their proper origin. The ingenious disguises under which these names are often found, make it extremely probable that any enumeration of them, based chiefly upon their

6. These figures are based upon muster rolls given in Hardesty's Atlas of Rockingham County.

present forms, is apt to fall below their actual number. There have been many forces at work in America,—and it has been necessarily so from the very nature of things,—to change German names into English forms; such changes have come as naturally and inevitably as the change of language; but there have not been any appreciable forces tending to change English names and American common speech to German. While we may expect, therefore, to find many German families of to-day writing their names in English, Irish, and Scotch-Irish forms, we need not expect to find many English, Irish, or Scotch-Irish families hidden under German names. Furthermore, there seem to have been a few individuals among the early German immigrants that brought English-looking and English-sounding names with them.

In exemplification of the last statement, the instances immediately following are cited. In the seven years beginning with 1749 and ending with 1755, no less than ten of the German immigrants landing at Philadelphia—men for the most part over sixteen years of age—bore the family name of *Adam* or *Adams*: Jacob Adams, Hans Adam, Adam Adams, Johan Henrich Adam, Peter Adam, Johannes Adam Adam, Han[7] Jacob Adam, Ernst Christoph Adam, Jacob Adam, Friederich Adam.[8] In 1739 Jacob Allen signed the port register; and in 1751, Johann Adam Allan. In 1752, 1753, and 1754, five men with the name *Arnold*, twice wholly in its English form, were entered: Christoph Arnoldt, George Arnolt, Johannes Elias Arnoldt, Lorentz Arnold, Wilhelm Arnold. In three years, 1750-1752, there were at least thirteen *Browns*, with only two letters in spelling and nothing in pronunciation to change: Hans Braun, Johannes Jacob Braun, Johann Georg Braun, Andreas Braun, Johan Friederich Braun, Johan

7. Han may sometimes be a corruption of the French Jean, but is more frequently, perhaps, from the Dutch Jan or the German Hans.

8. These and the following illustrations in this chapter have been prepared from a study of Rupp's Thirty Thousand Names.

Georg Braun, Jacob Braun, Valentin Braun, Christian Braun, Johannes Braun, Johannes Braun, Jr., Jacob Braun, Jacob Braun, Sen. Christian Fisher was almost an Englishman upon his arrival in 1749. In 1750 Bernhart Gilbert, and in 1752 Johann Georg Gilbert and Andreas Gilbert, came to Pennsylvania: How long after their descendants learned English was their name recognized as German? Other examples under this head may be given in rapid succession: Jacob Daniel (1750); Henrich Hall (1751); Hans Hay, Johann Hay, both in 1751; Johann Conrad Hay (1752); Hans Georg Hay (1753); Andreas Linden (1753); Jacob Paule (1750); Nicklas Paul and Peter Paul (1754); Johan Valentin Ross (1751); Johann Jacob Ross (1753); Adam Samuel (1763); Jacob Stark (1750); J. Henry Tillman (1751); Johannes Tillman (1752); Baltzer White (1751). Other names not English, perhaps, yet at the same time not usually German, were: Paulus Christian (1750); Hans Georg Christein, Christian Christein, and Peter Christein, 1751; Johan Christian, Ludwig Christian, Frederick Christian, Joh. Wilhelm Christian, Johann Christian, and Johannes Christian, in 1753 and 1754; Johann Nicklaus Ker, Johann Georg Curr, and Henrich Curr, 1751; and Isaac Reno, in 1751. Most of the Herrings of the Valley are perhaps Scotch-Irish; yet there were a number of Germans in Pennsylvania bearing the same name. Within a period of four years, seven at least landed at Philadelphia: in 1751, Philip Hering, Johan Henrich Hering, Philip Wendel Höring, Johannes Höring, Johannes Hering, and Johann Friederich Hering; and, in 1753, Jacob Hering. It would not be strange if one or two of these men got up into the Shenandoah Valley.

Reverting from those German names that were occasionally introduced into America already clad in English or Scotch-Irish dress, to those whose German form was of such a sort as to be readily lost in another, we have an almost endless number of such as the following: Altrich; Bischoff;

Fuchs (Fox); Hamen; Henrich; Konig, König (King); Mohr;[9] Newman; Œllen (Allen); Pfuller; Preyss (Price); Reiss, Reys (Rice); Röller; Stauber, Stauffer, Stoever (Steffer, Stover); Stein (Stone); Von Weber, Weber (Weaver); Wilhelm (Williams); Yung (Young); Zimmermann (Carpenter).

No name looks less German, perhaps, than *McInturff;* and yet it is very probable that the well known Valley family bearing this name at present is not of Scotch descent. "McIntorf," "McEntorf," "Mackinturf," "Mackingturf," and "Macanturf" are some of the earlier forms in which the name has been written. The writer was informed several months ago by Colonel S. R. Millar, of Front Royal, Va., that he had been told the name was of German origin. Under date of October 24, 1906, Prof. J. B. McInturff, of Strasburg, Va., wrote the author as follows: "As to the origin of the name, I know nothing authoritatively. Otto Portner, an educated German, * * * told me more than once that he thought our name was originally the German 'Mugendorf.'" The probability here recognized is considerably strengthened by the following record, more than a century and a quarter old: On June 25, 1779, John Macanturf, Sr., made his will; and from it we learn his wife's name, Roseanah; the names of his daughters, Mary and Margaret; and the names of his six sons: John, Frederick, Daniel, David, Christopher, and "Gasper."[10] The names Frederick, Christopher, and "Gasper" sound exceedingly German. At any rate, it is hardly probable that the three would have been found in one Scotch family.

I am informed by Dr. O. B. Sears, of the University of

9. From 1749 to 1754 no less than ten Germans with this name landed at Philadelphia: Anthony Moor, Andreas Mohr, Peter Moore, Johann Michel Mohr, Andreas Mohr, Hans Martin Mohr, Johannes Mohr, Bastian Mohr, Johan Wilhelm Mohr, and Johan Jacob Mohr.—The founder of the well known town of Moorefield, W. Va., was evidently a German—Conrad Moore.—Hening's Statutes, Vol. 9, p. 425.

10. Shenandoah County Will Book A, p. 250.

Virginia, that there are now in this country persons of eight different nationalities bearing his name; and that one stock or family in this group has derived the present form of the name from the German-Swiss, "Zäher."

As curious examples of patronymical metamorphoses, the two names, Coyner and Grabill, are cited. The former has been written in at least fifteen forms, namely: Coiner, Coynant, Coyner, Kaeinath, Kainath, Keinath, Keinodt, Keinot, Keynot, Kiner, Koinath, Koiner, Konot, Koynat, Kyner; the latter has been transformed even more frequently, and has appeared with the following variations: Crabill, Creabill, Crebil, Crybile, Grabill, Graybill, Grebiel, Grebihl, Greebel, Gribel, Gribeler, Griebil, Gröbil, Krebil, Krebill, Kreble, Krebüll, Krehbiel, Kribel, Kriebel.

There have been, occasionally, deliberate efforts on the part of government authorities, as in Pennsylvania in the first quarter of the nineteenth century,[11] to oblige German immigrants to anglicize their family names; but such cases are likely rare; and the main causes for the disguising of German names are likely to be found elsewhere: in ignorance, both of the Germans themselves in reference to the English language, and of English officials in reference to German forms; in a natural desire on the part of the Germans for political privileges in the commonwealth, and for social recognition among their neighbors; and, finally, in a gradual and natural process of evolution, which seems to influence all nationalities in speech and literature: of which few individuals are conscious, and for which fewer still are responsible.

A pleasing contrast to these many changes is afforded by the fact that intelligent and persistent efforts have been made in some cases to preserve the ancient landmarks of speech and name. Not only is this true of certain families and individuals; but organizations of wide influence have made similar efforts. In 1820, the Lutheran Tennessee Synod, a body strongly represented in the Valley of Virginia counties,

11. Report of Commissioner of Education, 1901, Vol. I, p. 547.

passed a resolution directing that all the discussions of the body should be carried on in the German language; and that the printed reports should also be sent out in German.[12] Doubtless there was behind this action a cherished sentiment; but there was also the desire to avoid a confusion of tongues, and to promote uniformity and even-handed justice in ecclesiastical legislation. The Mennonities of Rockingham and adjacent sections, with perhaps one or two other religious bodies, also made a systematic endeavor to perpetuate the language of their fathers; and they appear to have succeeded for the most part in doing so until about the middle of the last century.[13]

But the old order has changed, and has very generally given place to the new. As one generation has succeeded another, the circles in which the German language and customs are preserved have steadily narrowed, until at the present time it is not probable that over five per cent. of the German families in the Valley still use the German language.[14] Most of these are to be found in the western sections of the counties of Rockingham and Shenandoah.[15] It may be in place to observe, moreover, what may readily be surmised, that this language is a sort of *patois*—a form of "Pennsylvania Dutch"—

12. Henkel's History of the Tennessee Synod, p. 25.

13. Hartzler and Kauffman's Mennonite Church History, p. 203.

14. Prof. Seidensticker puts the number of German newspapers published in Virginia in 1880 at only five; and it is doubtful whether any one of these was produced in the Shenandoah Valley. It is possible that some—a very few—of the older Germans in that section may have been subscribers to one or more of the 87 German papers that were printed at the same time in Pennsylvania.—Die Erste Deutsche Einwanderung in Amerika, p. 17.

15. The writer has been able to re-enforce his own observations on this point by information received through the kindness of the following gentlemen, all of whom have a wide acquaintance with the Valley people: Eld. Daniel Hays, Broadway, Va.; Eld. H. C. Early, Harrisonburg, Va.; Prof. J. Carson Miller, Moores Store, Va.; Eld. B. W. Neff, Quicksburg, Va.; Prof. E. T. Hildebrand, Roanoke, Va.; Rev. P. S. Thomas, Harrisonburg, Va.

and is limited almost without exception to the familiar intercourse of the home circle. Another generation or two will almost certainly witness its utter extinction. As the old dialect is going out, however, a better form is coming in. It has already been remarked that many of the present generation are taking up as an accomplishment what their forefathers long ago cast off as an impediment: many of the boys and girls in school are now studying German. This action on their part will not only enable them to know better who and what their fathers were; but it will also enable them to appropriate from the wealth of ancient treasures, in art and song and story, the best that their fathers knew.

CHAPTER VIII.

Religious Life and Organization.

Most of the Germans identified with the Shenandoah Valley have been pious, God-fearing people; and although it was probably a generation or more after the time of their first settlements until they had church houses and regular pastors, they nevertheless did not neglect the assembling of themselves together in the services of worship. These early meetings were doubtless held, for the most part, in family dwellings and in schoolhouses. It appears to be an established fact that the English and Scotch-Irish, particularly the latter, had regular church houses and settled pastors before the Germans. The Tuscarora meeting house, near Martinsburg in Berkeley County, and the Opequon church, about three miles south of Winchester, both erected about 1736, were probably the first buildings of the kind in the Valley. The old Stone Church, Fort Defiance, Augusta County, was erected in 1740; and shortly afterwards a church must have been built a few miles to the southeast, at Tinkling Spring.[1] All of these were Presbyterian churches.

There are, and have been from early times, five religious denominations in the Valley that may be regarded as German sects, to which most of the people of German descent in that section have been attached; but there are to this rule numerous and notable exceptions, which shall first be hastily reviewed.

A number of the prominent German pioneers of the lower Valley appear to have been identified with the Episcopal church. This condition is perhaps explained by the two facts, first, that the German sects were largely without efficient or-

1. Kercheval's History of the Valley, p. 59; Cooke's Virginia, pp. 322, 323; Foote's Sketches, p. 19; Peyton's History of Augusta, pp. 80, 81.

ganization and pastoral service until 1760 or later; and, second, that the Episcopal church had the influential support of the governing element of the colony. Thomas Shepherd, of Shepherdstown, was an Episcopalian, and erected the first Episcopal church at that place. Jost Hite is believed to have been a Lutheran or German Reformed; but his oldest son, John, was a vestryman of the Frederick parish; and Bishop Meade says that other descendants became active members or friends of the Episcopal church. Other Germans, who were vestrymen of the Frederick parish prior to 1769, were John Bowman, Isaac Hite, Thomas Swearingen, and John Funk. In 1772 Jacob Hite, Isaac Hite, and John Hite were members of a committee of ten appointed by the General Assembly for ascertaining the value of the churches and chapels in the parishes of Frederick, Norborne, and Beckford.[2] Van Swearingen, Philip Bush, Isaac Hite, Jr., and Frederick Conrad are other early Germans classed by Bishop Meade as Episcopalians; but Conrad, Bush, and some of the Shepherds appear later, in the work of the same author, as Lutherans. This fact lends credence to the opinion that some of the early German settlers entered the Episcopal communion only until the sects of their own nationality reached a better stage of organization.

The last observation suggests the protracted controversy regarding General Muhlenberg, as to whether he was an Episcopalian or a Lutheran. As a matter of fact, he seems to have been connected with both churches. By his antecedents, early training, and personal preference he was doubtless a Lutheran; yet he seems beyond question to have received Episcopal ordination; and he probably ministered occasionally to Episcopal congregations. His connection with the Church of England was probably sought in order that his work as a clergyman might receive the readier and fuller legal sanction.

2. Hening's Statutes, Vol. 8, pp. 415; 623-625.

Prominent among the later German Episcopalians were some of the Steenbergens, of Shenandoah County, and Daniel Sheffey, of Augusta.[3]

A few of the Valley Germans are at present members of the Presbyterian church; and the same thing has probably been uniformly true during the last century and a half. Some of the Engles and Molers, prominent families of the lower Valley, have been Presbyterians for several generations;[4] Dr. Henry Ruffner, a member of the noted Page family, and for many years president of Washington College, led his descendants into the same faith; Capt. Anthony Spengler, of Shenandoah County, was another early member of prominence; Rev. Dr. Conrad Speece (1776-c.1835), son of Conrad Speece of Germany, was the Presbyterian pastor for many years of the Augusta Stone Church.[5]

A fact generally lost sight of is that some—only a few, perhaps—of the early German settlers of Pennsylvania and Virginia were Catholics. About one-tenth of the German emigrants who flocked to London in Queen Anne's reign, seeking passage to the New World, were sent back to the Continent, for the reason, apparently, that they belonged to the church of Rome.[6] Nevertheless, a good many of the same faith got to America. On August 26, 1751, in a shipload of 236 German immigrants landing at Philadelphia, there were fifty Roman Catholics. This, however, was an unusually large proportion. From September 5, 1751, to November 7, 1754, ten different shiploads of immigrants, aggregating 2873 persons, included 78 Catholics: about 2¾ per cent. of the whole number, and an average of nearly eight individuals to each shipload.[7] How many German Catholics

3. Meade's Old Churches, Vol. II, p. 315; Waddell's Annals of Augusta, p. 439.

4. History of the Engle Family, pp. 19, 23, 34, etc.

5. Foote's Sketches, pp. 349, 486.

6. Pennsylvania Magazine, Vol. X, p. 381.

7. Rupp's Thirty Thousand Names, pp. 246-346.

got into the Shenandoah Valley in the early days, no one can tell; but there must have been a few. In 1743 and in 1749, Moravian missionaries found *N. Schmidt Stepfa,* or *Stephan Schmidt,* a Catholic, living on or near the Opequon Creek. Extracts from Leonard Schnell's diary, under date of November 20 and 21, 1743, are cited in point:

> At sunset we came to a German innkeeper, Jost Hayd, a rich man, well known in this region. He was the first settler there. He was very courteous when he heard that I was a minister. I asked him for the way to Carolina. He told me of one, which runs for 150 miles through Irish settlements, the district being known as the Irish tract. I had no desire to take this way, and as no one could tell me the right way I felt somewhat depressed. I asked the Lord to show me the right way, but slept little that night.
>
> On the 21st, immediately after arising, one of the servants came to me and told me that two miles from there a man lived, who could tell me the right way. I went to him. He was very kind and quite willing to tell me the way. His name is Stephan Schmidt, a Catholic, but hungry to hear the word of the cross. Many spiritually hungry people, of German nationality, live there, who have no minister.[8]

Six years later, Schnell and John Brandmueller were welcomed at Schmidt's house; but he assured them that the people of the surrounding country were generally hostile to them, owing to the warnings of Rev. Mr. Klug, the Lutheran minister of Madison County.[9]

A considerable number of the German families of the Valley belong to the Methodist church. Kercheval tells that in 1775, or thereabouts, two ministers of that denomination, John Hagerty and Richard Owens,—supposed to have been the first representatives of their faith in that part of the colony,—stopped over night at the home of Major Lewis Stephens, founder of Stephens City; and on the next day, Sunday, preached to the people of the neighborhood. A small church was soon built up, among the members of which were the following Germans: John Hite, Jr., and his sister, Mrs.

8. Virginia Magazine, Vol. XI, No. 4, pp. 373, 374.

9. Idem, No. 2, pp. 128, 129.

Hughes; Lewis Stephens, Sr., and wife; Lewis Stephens, Jr., and wife. Very cordial relations have always existed between the Methodists and the United Brethren; and this fact, coupled with a rather interesting circumstance in the transition from the German language to the English among the latter, was instrumental in adding to the former body a number of members of German descent in the early part of last century. For several years following 1809, these two denominations, in Rockingham and adjacent counties, seem to have labored much in common; indeed, there was a protracted effort for union between them; and, in consequence, while the older members of the United Brethren families still held tenaciously to the German language, many of the young people, who preferred the English, were advised to join the Methodist church.[10]

The Valley Germans have been represented among the Baptists, to a greater or less degree, for several generations. Michael Engle (1781-1829), of Jefferson County, seventh son of Philip and Mary Darke Engle (Mary Darke being a sister to Gen. William Darke), was such a devout Baptist that he made all the nails and spikes for Zoar Church, free of charge. Hon. Joseph Stover Spengler of Shenandoah and Warren, was a member of the Primitive Baptist church. In Page County, at the present day, a considerable number of the families of German descent belong to the same denomination.

For at least ten years, from about 1743 to 1753, the Moravians of Bethlehem, Nazareth, and other points in Pennsylvania, made occasional missionary tours through the valleys of the Shenandoah and the South Branch of the Potomac. In 1748, Brother M. G. Gottschalk made a list of the places in Virginia where Germans were found—eleven places in all, as follows: Patterson's Creek, South Branch, New-Found River, New River, Shenandoah, Massanutten, Cedar Creek,

10. Harrisonburg Daily News, March 21, 1905.

"The Upper Germans" [at or near Germanna], The Great Fork of the Rappahannock, the Little Fork of the Rappahannock, and Germantown [in Fauquier County]. But notwithstanding their frequent tours, unselfish labors, and patient endurance of hardships, the Moravians do not appear to have secured any permanent footholds. Here and there an individual or a family received them with kindness and gratitude. On October 22, 1753, a company of the brethren made record of the hospitality of the people in the neighborhood of the present town of Harrisonburg. But frequently they found conditions far otherwise. Prejudice and suspicion preceded them. Upon several occasions they felt constrained to note in their diaries the warnings that the Rev. Mr. Klug had given the people against them, upon his occasional visits to Massanutten and other points in the Valley. Moreover, the proclamation of Governor Gooch, made April 3, 1747, against "Itinerant Preachers—New Lights, Moravians, and Methodists," gave a legal sanction to religious bigotry.

A few of the early Germans of the Shenandoah settlements appear to have belonged to the society of Friends. Paul Froman, who married Elizabeth, daughter of Jost Hite, is said to have been a member of that fraternity.[11] Several generations ago there was a Quaker meeting house and graveyard near Quicksburg, Shenandoah County; and the Friends of Winchester and the vicinity still maintain a respectable place of worship in that city. It is not likely, however, that in either of these congregations the Germans have ever formed more than a minority.

In certain parts of the district under review, the organization known as Disciples of Christ, or Christians, simply, embraces within its membership considerable numbers of persons who represent families of German descent.

Within the last fifty years or less a number of German Jews have located in the Valley, and have erected two houses

11. West Virginia Historical Magazine, Vol. 3, No. 2, p. 109.

of worship: one in Staunton; one in Harrisonburg. The total membership of these and neighboring congregations numbers between 300 and 400.

If the testimony of the Moravians may be credited again, there were other sects, in addition to, or different from, those already mentioned and those to follow, that numbered at least a few adherents each among the early settlers along the Shenandoah; but then, evidently, as now, many creeds did not necessarily make many or charitable Christians. In 1748 Brethren Joseph Spangenberg and Matthew Reutz wrote of themselves, in the third person, as follows:

> On July 27th, they journeyed from this place [Adam Rader's, near Timberville] to Messinutty, where Germans of all kinds of denominations live—Mennonites, Lutherans, Separatists, and Inspirationists. Bro. Joseph spoke to some of them, but they are very bad people. It is a dead place where their testimony found no entrance.[12]

Warnings by religious leaders and the proclamation by Governor Gooch had evidently made Massanutten a poor mission field for the Moravians; or it may be that the number of sects already there was deemed amply sufficient.

The rest of this chapter will now be devoted to a brief presentation, in order, of the five denominations referred to near the beginning; namely, the Lutherans, the Mennonites, the German Reformed, the Dunkers, and the United Brethren. These sects, as already intimated, may all properly be regarded as German sects; and within their folds the majority of the German people of the Shenandoah Valley have always been found. As to which body was first in the field, may be a disputed question; but they probably came in in the order above indicated: the Lutherans, Mennonites, and Reformed near together at the first; the Dunkers and United Brethren nearly two generations later.

It is the opinion of Mr. T. K. Cartmell, of Winchester, a gentleman who for many years has made a careful study of early conditions in the Valley of Virginia, that the Lutherans

12. Virginia Magazine, Vol. XI, No. 3, p. 240.

of that section had no resident pastors until forty years or more after their first settlements. A somewhat extended investigation of the subject has led the writer to the same conclusion. If we count from the date of Adam Miller's settlement, that is, early in the year 1727, the time will be over forty years. Adam Miller was a Lutheran; but Muhlenberg, who located at Woodstock in 1772, appears to have been the first settled Lutheran pastor. After his service, covering about three years, the Valley congregations were again without a resident minister till 1785, when Christian Streit settled at Winchester.[13]

But the various communities were not without religious services during all these years. At a number of places congregations were organized; at some places churches were built; and at most places the forms of public worship were regularly conducted either by some layman of the congregation, or by one of the ministers of their own or some other denomination, who paid the settlements occasional visits. After 1750 or thereabouts, it is probable that Lutheran preachers from Pennsylvania and adjacent sections were among these occasional visitors; but the earliest of all likely came from east of the Blue Ridge. The Moravians, in their diaries of 1748 and 1749, make repeated references to the pastoral attentions of Rev. Georg Samuel Klug, of Madison County, among the Valley congregations. Mr. Klug, who was ordained at Danzig on August 30, 1736, was called to Virginia in 1738, while Rev. John Casper Stoever was making his collecting tour in Germany. Klug lived till 1761; and although he was accused of some things not becoming to his office, he was very strict and earnest among his people, and had some—perhaps much—influence with the Governor. His ministrations in the Valley were evidently not limited to the sections now embraced by the counties of Rockingham, Page, and

13. Idem, No. 2, p. 127; Gilbert's The Story of Our Fathers and Muhlenberg's Ministry in Virginia.

Shenandoah, but also extended, in influence at least, into Frederick County. In 1749 the Catholic, Stephan Schmidt, living on the Opequon, told Schnell and Brandmueller how the people of his neighborhood were incensed against the Moravians, owing to the warnings of Mr. Klug. The following paragraph, written in 1748 by Brother Gottschalk concerning the Massanutten settlement, now in Page County, will be of interest in this connection.

> Many Germans live there. Most of them are Mennisten [Mennonites], who are in a bad condition. Nearly all religious earnestness and zeal is extinguished among them. Besides them, a few church people live there, partly Lutheran, partly Reformed. The Rev. Mr. Klug visits them occasionally. It is, so to say, one of his branch congregations. He preaches and administers also the Lord's Supper to them. They do not want to hear the preaching of the brethren at this place.[14]

The Moravians state elsewhere that Mr. Klug visited the Shenandoah Germans "two or three times every year"; and that he had correspondence with Muhlenberg—doubtless the General's father, H. M. Muhlenberg, who came to Pennsylvania in 1742.

As already stated, some churches were built before any of the congregations had resident pastors. On May 15, 1753, Lord Fairfax gave the Lutherans of Winchester an acre of ground "for sacred uses"; and on April 16, 1764, the cornerstone was laid for a gray limestone church, which was finally completed in 1793. Less permanent quarters doubtless served as a place of worship for the congregation in the meantime. The front wall of this old church, which was destroyed by fire on the night of September 27, 1854, is still standing, and occupies a position in the beautiful Mt. Hebron Cemetery, about sixty yards northeast of the entrance lodge. A few feet to the east of the picturesque ruin is the grave of Rev. Christian Streit; and a few rods further on is the grave of Gen. Daniel

14. Virginia Magazine, Vol. XI, No. 3, p. 229.—See also No. 2, p. 129; and Vol. XII, No. 1, pp. 60, 61.

Morgan. The old church was 52½ feet long and 42 feet wide; the side walls were 23½ feet high, 2½ feet thick, and were built upon a foundation wall 3½ feet thick. The aisles were paved with square bricks.

In 1768 the Lutheran and Reformed congregations living in the vicinity of McGaheysville, Rockingham County, made a written agreement, still preserved, to build a union house, which was known as the Peaked Mountain church. The same year, or earlier, the Lutherans and Reformed erected jointly, about a mile west of Timberville, the first structure known as Rader's church. In 1769, St. Paul's church, at Strasburg in Shenandoah County, was founded; and about 1773 young Muhlenberg's congregation at Woodstock began building a regular house of worship. The Woodstock church occupied a position upon the south corner of the public square, near the site of the present Episcopal church. In June, 1777, St. Peter's church, where Adam Miller worshiped, and where he probably was buried, was dedicated. This old church is about six miles north of Elkton, and only a short distance, on the opposite side of the South River, from the town of Shenandoah. Some five miles southwest of Waynesboro, Koiner's church, the first Lutheran church erected within the present limits of Augusta County, was built about 1780. The first trustees and organizers of the congregation were Casper Koiner, Martin Bush, and Jacob Barger. The Rev. Adolph Spindle was probably the first pastor. Mt. Tabor, also in Augusta County, dates from about 1785. On March 30, 1790, Rev. Paul Henkel and family located at New Market, where a house of worship, known for fifty years as Davidsburg church, now as St. Matthew's, was erected within the next two years. This church was also held jointly for some time by the Reformed and Lutherans, but the latter have had exclusive ownership and control for many years. The Lutherans of Mecklenburg, now Shepherdstown, built in

1795 St. Peter's church, which has just recently (1906) been renewed for the second time. Among others of the old Lutheran churches, the following should be mentioned: in Shenandoah County, Zion, near Hamburg; St. Jacob's, near Conicville; Solomon's, near Forestville; and, in Rockingham County, Friedens, located about seven miles south of Harrisonburg. The last is a very old church, and has probably been held jointly, throughout its history, by the Lutherans and Reformed.

Some of the Lutheran ministers who have been identified with the Valley of Virginia churches, by nativity or service or both, have been men of national eminence. The three most distinguished were John Peter Gabriel Muhlenberg, Joseph A. Seiss, and Charles P. Krauth. The last was pastor at Winchester from 1848 to 1855; Dr. Seiss labored in the Valley from 1842 to 1847; and Muhlenberg was pastor at Woodstock from sometime in 1772 to January, 1776. He probably served congregations occasionally at other points also; namely, Winchester, Strasburg, and Rude's Hill. The last place is about three miles below New Market, and is the site of an old Lutheran church. Mr. Elon O. Henkel, of New Market, thinks that the famous war sermon was delivered at Rude's Hill, as well as at Woodstock.

Rude's Hill, rising from the southwest side of Meem's Bottoms, is a well-known feature in the scenery along the Valley turnpike. It was named after a Lutheran preacher, Dr. A. R. Rude, who lived at its foot for a number of years just prior to the Civil War.

Dr. D. M. Gilbert, in his sketch of the Lutheran church in Virginia, names five men whom he calls the fathers of the church in this State: Streit, Carpenter, Henkel, Flohr, Butler.

John George Butler (1754-1816) was born in Philadelphia and died in Cumberland, Md. His great work for Virginia Lutheranism was done from 1800 to 1805, when, with

Botetourt County as a center, he worked out into the pioneer fields of western Virginia and Tennessee. George Daniel Flohr was born in Germany in 1759. He was a student of medicine at Paris in 1793, and a witness of many of the crimes of blood committed there in the name of liberty. After coming to America he studied theology under Mr. Carpenter, in Madison County, Virginia; and, a year or two prior to 1799, entered upon a long term of ministerial and pastoral service in Wythe County and adjacent sections of southwest Virginia. He died in 1826. Paul Henkel was born in Rowan County, North Carolina, December 15, 1754. From 1790 to 1800 and from 1805 till his death in 1825, he lived in Virginia, and traveled far and wide from his places of residence at New Market, Staunton, and elsewhere, doing the work of an evangelist. From the pulpit in the home congregations, and through the medium of the Henkel press, he also accomplished a telling work. He was one of the founders and organizers of the Synods of North Carolina, Tennessee, and Ohio. His journal, wherein he records various experiences of his missionary tours into these States, as well as into western Virginia and Kentucky, reinforces the solemn interest of truth with the no less real circumstances of romance and adventure. In 1787, or thereabouts, William Carpenter (1762-1833) was licensed by the Synod of Pennsylvania, and entered upon the duties of the Christian ministry in the county of his nativity—Madison, Virginia,—where he labored twenty-six years, as both pastor and theological teacher. In 1813 he followed a colony of Madison Lutherans to Kentucky, where he died after twenty years more of service. Christian Streit did his great work in the Valley from 1785 to 1812, having his home at Winchester, where he is buried. His grave, just a few feet to the east of the stone ruin of the first Lutheran church in that city, has already been referred to; and the following lines, copied from his monument, will tell in brief the story of his life:

Christian Streit
Born in New Jersey
June 7th 1749
[N-W. Side.] Ordained to the
Gospel Ministry, 1769;
Died at Winchester, Va
March 10th 1812.

First Minister of the
[S-W. Side.] Evangelical Lutheran
Church Born in America

I have fought a good fight
[S-E. Side.] I have finished my course
I have kept the faith

Pastor at Winchester
[N-E. Side.] July 19th 1785
To March 10th 1812

The Henkel family of New Market, distinguished alike in theology, letters, and medicine, has several other names that ought to have a place upon the roll of Virginia Lutheran church fathers: namely, Philip (1779-1833), son of Paul; Ambrose (1786-1870), fourth son of Paul; David (1795-1831), son of Paul; Polycarp (1820-1889), oldest son of David; Socrates (1823-1901), son of David. The last two must be ranked among the greatest leaders that the Lutheran church has ever had in the Southern States.

Most of the Lutherans in the Shenandoah Valley belong to the Tennessee Synod (organized 1820) and the Virginia Synod (organized 1829). A few congregations, mostly in Shenandoah County, are members of the Ohio Lutheran Synod; while a few, one at least in Augusta County, belong to the Missouri Synod. A peculiar fact about the first named synod is that at present it has no members (congregations) in Tennessee; but it still holds its name from the place of its original organization. Most of these bodies coöperate in the United Synod of the Evangelical Lutheran Church in the South, the tenth convention of which was held at Dallas, N. C., July 10-15, 1906.

At present, according to the reports of the synods of 1906, the various Lutheran churches of the Shenandoah Valley own about 70 houses of worship, and have altogether between 6000 and 7000 communicant members. Of this number, nearly half, or upwards of 40 per cent., are found in Shenandoah County. The Tennessee Synod has in Rockingham County six churches and about 500 members; in Page County, five churches and about 300 members; in Shenandoah, 16 churches and about 1400 members. The Virginia Synod has in Rockingham four churches and about 225 members; in Page, two churches and about 120 members; in Shenandoah, 11 churches and about 1200 members; in Augusta, 10 churches and about 1000 members; in Frederick, eight churches and about 900 members; and in Jefferson two churches and about 330 members.[15] The largest Lutheran congregation in the Valley is the one worshiping at Grace Church, Winchester, with a membership of 421. The three next in numerical order are the following: Christ Church, Staunton, 207; St. Peter's, Shepherdstown, 204; and St. Paul's at Strasburg, 192.

It is probable that some of the very first settlers in the valley of the Shenandoah were members of the Mennonite church. If Adam Miller, the Lutheran, was the pioneer of the upper Valley, it is quite likely that, among those who followed him to Virginia in 1728 or 1729 and settled at Massanutten, there was at least one Mennonite. Jacob Strickler, a Mennonite preacher, is said to have located near the site of Luray about 1731. He was very probably the son of Abram Strickler, who died in the Page valley in 1746, and who, as one of the petitioners of 1733, stated that he had bought land of Jacob Stover at Massanutten about 1729. On December 15, 1735, Abram Strickler bought a thousand acres more, which may have been intended for his son; and the said Jacob

15. These figures may be subject to some corrections, inasmuch as some of the churches are near county lines, and the congregations thereof may live partly in one county, partly in another.

Strickler is reported to have had 1640 acres in two tracts. Again, some of the early Page Mennonites are known to have borne the name Kauffman; and the reader will possibly recall that Michael Kauffman was another one of the eight men who signed the petition of 1733. It is not at all improbable, therefore, that Abram Strickler and Michael Kauffman were both Mennonites.

At any rate, we do not have to proceed far in this matter until we find ground that is certain. In 1739 Peter Ruffner, the ancestor of a well-known early Mennonite family, settled on the Hawksbill; and in 1748 the Moravian brethren found more Mennonites than any other denomination among the many Germans then living at Massanutten. In 1754 a dozen or more additional families came from Lancaster and Franklin counties, Pennsylvania, and settled in what are now the counties of Page and Shenandoah, near the sites of Luray and Woodstock, respectively. Among these families were the names Allebaugh, Blosser, Branneman, Fauber, Funk, Graybill, Kauffman, Stauffer, Schenk, Swartz, Rhodes, and Wenger.[16] At a period still later more came, and joined one community or the other. The Pennybackers, the iron-workers, came in 1781, and settled on the Hawksbill. Kercheval, writing in the earlier half of last century, said: "In what is now Page county they [the Germans] were almost exclusively of the Mennonist persuasion; but few Lutherans or Calvinists settled among them."[17]

And yet, strange as it may seem, there are to-day less than a score of Mennonites in both Page and Shenandoah together. Since the Civil War the denomination has become almost extinct in these counties, while gaining correspondingly in the counties of Rockingham and Augusta.

During the first three-quarters of a century or more of their history in Virginia, the Mennonites do not appear to have had

16. H. and K.'s Mennonite Church History, p. 198.

17. History of the Valley, p. 56.

any house erected exclusively for public worship, although as early as 1780 they had over forty churches in Pennsylvania. In Virginia, until almost the beginning of the second quarter of the nineteenth century, the regular Sunday services were held at the residences of some of the wealthier members, in large rooms of the dwellings, specially provided and equipped for the purpose. In 1822, however, a church was built—the first in Virginia—four miles west of Broadway, in Rockingham County. Trissel's church, as it is still known, was at first 20x25 feet in size; but was enlarged in 1854-5; and, in 1900, it was rebuilt with dimensions 40x50 feet. The first settlers in the neighborhood were the Brannemans, Brunks, Burkholders, Funks, Fulks, Rhodeses, Shanks, Swanks, and Trissels. In 1825 another house of worship, known as Moyers's, was erected about two miles east of Dayton. This house was rebuilt upon an enlarged plan in 1878, and is now known as the Pike church—being located on the Valley Pike. A schoolhouse was also provided for at an early date, in connection with this church. Branneman's church, two miles west of Edom, was built in 1826; Burkholder's, later Weaver's, two miles west of Harrisonburg, in 1827. Each of these churches had provision from the beginning for a schoolhouse on the church lot. The first two churches in Augusta County were the following: Hall's, later Kendig's, now Springdale, five miles south of Waynesboro, built in 1825; and Hildebrand's, three miles west of Crimora, built in 1828.

The communicants of the Mennonite congregations in the Shenandoah Valley at the present number between 800 and 900, distributed as follows: In Rockingham County, 585, with about ten churches; Augusta, 183, with five churches; Frederick, 16, with one church; Shenandoah, 15; Page, 2. In the adjoining counties of West Virginia there are several congregations; and there are a few members in each of the eastern Virginia counties of Warwick and Fauquier. The largest congregation in the State is that at Weaver's church, Rockingham County, numbering 229.

The Mennonites have always been noted for their strict honesty, temperance, pure living, and conscientious devotion to their religious principles. At the same time, their habitual conservatism has in some instances made them more or less tenacious with regard to things the loss of which they now realize was not attended by any real injury. For example, up to the year 1840 their preaching and singing was exclusively in the German language. For the next forty years the two languages, German and English, contended for supremacy, with a steady gain on the part of the latter. Since 1880 no Virginia congregation has heard a discourse in German from a Virginia minister. Again, although the founders and early leaders of the church were educated men, higher education was for a long time sadly neglected by the majority of the membership. Within recent years, however, this condition has been rapidly undergoing a change. The sons and daughters of the church are being afforded better educational advantages, both in Mennonite schools, that are being developed, and in others. Forty years before Robert Raikes started his noted Sunday-school movement, the Mennonites had a school near Harrisburg, Pa., where their children received instruction in the three R's during the week, and in the Bible on Sunday.[18] Yet the Sunday-schools were allowed to languish for many years. It was as late as 1870 when the first one in Virginia was organized at Weaver's church. After three or four summer sessions it was discontinued, owing to serious objections urged against it by prominent members of the church. Similar schools at one or two other places were suspended also at about the same time; but in 1882 the Sunday-schools were widely and permanently revived, and they have ever since been growing in favor and power. In 1892 the Virginia conference authorized the es-

13. H. and K.'s Mennonite Church History, p. 358.

tablishment of a home mission board, which has already accomplished a good work. Within the last decade foreign missions have been inaugurated by the church at large; and only within the last half-year a devoted daughter of Rockingham died in the service in Turkey, almost as soon as she reached the field.

The Virginia Mennonites have never been without leaders of considerable ability. The present bishop in Rockingham is a man of education and culture, learned in several languages, and widely recognized as a skilled mathematician. The most famous leader, perhaps, was Peter Burkholder (1783-c. 1853). At the age of 21 years and two months he was ordained to the ministry—younger than any other man of his church in Virginia, before or since. About 1837 he was chosen bishop to succeed Henry Shank, the first who held the office in the State. Burkholder was a preacher of great power, and a writer of no mean accomplishments. Among his published works are the following: A Treatise on Baptism (1816); a Confession of Faith (1837); "Nine Reflections on the Holy Scriptures" (1837); and a Treatise on Predestination. His son, Martin Burkholder, also a Mennonite bishop, was scarcely less distinguished.

Besides the doctrines and practices held and observed in common by all Christians, there are certain principles that are more or less distinctive of the Mennonites and a few other denominations. Fashionable and gaudy attire, the swearing of formal oaths, and membership in secret societies, are among the things carefully avoided; while feet-washing (John 13; 1 Tim. 5: 10), anointing with oil (James 5: 14, 15), the kiss of charity (1 Pet. 5: 14; etc.), and non-resistance—the avoiding of personal combat as well as war—are observed with the same religious care.

Their strong desire to refrain from all participation in carnal warfare brought upon the Valley Mennonites manifold and intense sufferings during the late Civil War, when persistent efforts were made to press them into service; and their history from very early times has been marked by the same conscientious effort to maintain all peaceful relations, even at great cost. The statute books of Virginia bear witness. In July, 1775, an ordinance for raising troops indulged the Quakers and Mennonites, agreebly to certain Acts of the Assembly, by exempting them from serving in the militia. In May, 1776, they were ordered to be enlisted, but were not compelled to attend general or private musters; but in October, 1777, they were drafted; and, although exempted from personal service, substitutes were to be provided by equitable assessment in the whole society. The last requirement was reinforced in May, 1780; and, in October, 1782, the requirements were put in the following form: Quakers and Mennonites were to be drafted. though not compelled to serve in the army personally; but a substitute was to be provided at "his expense"; and if "he" were unable to pay the price, the amount was to be levied on the whole society.[19]

There were members of the German Reformed church in the ancient colony of Germanna, and in the surrounding colonies of eastern Virginia that were offshoots from it; and we may be almost certain that persons belonging to the same denomination were among the first settlers of the Shenandoah Valley. The Lutherans and Reformed went much together; and it is quite probable that the latter as well as the former had some representatives in the Valley shortly after 1730, if not before. In his records of March and April, 1748, the Moravian Gottschalk notes that there were Reformed among the Germans of Massanutten, as well as Lutherans and Mennonites;[20] and in May of the same year the Rev. Michael Schlatter, organizer of the Pennsylvania Reformed church, made a tour through the Shenandoah Valley, and visited congregations of his own people.[21] On May 15, 1753, Lord

19. Hening's Statutes, Vol. 9, pp. 34, 139, 345; Vol. 10, p. 261; Vol. 11, p. 175.

20. Virginia Magazine, Vol. XI, No. 3, p. 229.

21. Journal of the Presbyterian Historical Society, Vol. II, No. 3, p. 148.

Fairfax presented a lot at Winchester to the German Reformed congregation, which had been organized in the vicinity about twelve years before. I was recently informed, while at Winchester, that tombstones in the Reformed church graveyard at Shepherdstown, W. Va., bear dates going back to the 1760's. It is probable that the burying grounds at Friedens Church, in Rockingham County, are even older. The records of the Peaked Mountain church, east of Harrisonburg, still preserved in the original German, begin about 1760, and show that the Reformed and Lutherans worked and worshipped together there from an early date. From February, 1762, to December, 1763, Rev. I. C. Van Gemuenden, a Reformed minister, served the congregation.[22] In 1768 the two bodies agreed to build a union house of worship, as already noted. Early in 1768, the Reformed were worshipping with the Lutherans at Rader's church, near Timberville, a house that was used jointly by the two denominations till 1879.[23] Many, perhaps most, of the early churches used by one were also used and partly owned by the other. In 1827 the Lutherans and Reformed issued a "fusion hymnbook," which was probably continued in later editions.[24]

Among the early German Reformed ministers of the Valley, none was more prominent or influential than Rev. Dr. John Brown, who labored in Rockingham and Augusta from 1799 to 1850. He was not only a man of deep religious convictions and broad learning, but he was also endowed with a large measure of foresight and good judgment, and was fully alive to the important issues of the times in which he lived. He was a rather prolific writer, and published a number of volumes through the Wartmann press at Harrisonburg, one or two of which will be reviewed in a subsequent chapter. Rev. John C. Hensel, whose term of service extended from

22. William and Mary College Quarterly, Vol. XIII, p. 247.

23. Virginia Magazine, Vol. XI, No. 3, p. 239.

24. First Century of German Printing, p. vii.

1857 to 1879, was another prominent leader in the same section. In the lower Valley, Rev. Henry St. John Rinker was a well-known minister, whose career of active service extended over the latter half of the nineteenth century.

There are to-day in the Shenandoah Valley about 30 Reformed churches, with a total membership of about 2600, distributed as follows: In Augusta County, two churches and 234 members; Rockingham, 10 churches and 898 members; Shenandoah, 11 churches and 808 members; Frederick, two churches and 126 members; Berkeley, two churches and 363 members; Jefferson, three churches and 145 members. The largest single congregation is the one worshipping in Christ Church, Martinsburg, numbering 342.[25]

As already observed, representatives of the Lutherans, Mennonites, and Reformed were among the first Germans that settled in the Valley of Virginia; the Dunkers and United Brethren, on the other hand, do not appear until the last quarter of the eighteenth century.

As early as 1745 some members of the Ephrata Sabbatarian colony, of Pennsylvania, came into Virginia, stopping first at Strasburg, then pushing on and founding a more or less temporary settlement on New River, in the present counties of Montgomery and Pulaski. The ill-fated, so-called Dunker settlements of Dunker Creek and Dunker Bottom, now West Virginia, were also likely made up of some of the Ephrata Brethren. In 1752 Heinrich Sangmeister (Brother Ezekiel) and Anton Höllenthal (Brother Antonius) came to the Funks at Strasburg, and established a community which gradually increased in numbers for several years.

The Strasburg brethren kept as holy both the seventh and the first day of the week. They were law-abiding and industrious, and maintained themselves confortably and above reproach; yet an incident growing out of their religious zeal at

25. These figures have been compiled from the Virginia Classis report for 1906.

one time seemed to threaten their peace. Brother Ezekiel and Brother Antonius built a small cabin far up on the peak of the Massanutten Mountain, as a place for retirement and prayer. The little oratory had but a single small window, facing the east; but, by virtue of its eminent position, it commanded a view both wide and beautiful. But various mysterious reports of this mountain retreat came in time to the ears of the county authorities at Winchester, and the sheriff was sent out to investigate. When he came to Strasburg, and learned the real facts in the case, he had no word of objection or censure to offer; but the two brethren, meek enough for the blessed inheritance, hearing beforehand of the suspicions they were arousing, and being anxious to prove their law-abiding intentions and avoid all appearance of evil, had already demolished the sacred structure, and scattered its timbers upon the mountain-side. A hundred years later the armies of the South and the North seized the height, now one, now the other, and erected their signals of war upon the site of the little house of prayer.

Sangmeister and Höllenthal returned to Pennsylvania in 1764; but the Strasburg community appears to have been maintained until the period of the Revolution or later.[26]

The fact that the Ephrata Brethren, who were an early offshoot of the Dunkers, came to Virginia at the period above indicated, has given rise to various confusions and misunderstandings concerning the latter, as to both historical sequence and matters of practice and doctrine. The following account, regarding the settlement of the Dunkers, or German Baptist Brethren, in Virginia, I am enabled to give through the kindness of Elder Daniel Hays, of Broadway, Va.

The first of the Dunkers to settle in the Valley was John Garber, who came with his family about the year 1777. He had probably come alone and purchased land a year or two

26. Sachse's German Sectarians, Vol. II, pp. 331-359; First Century of German Printing, p. 225.

earlier. He located in the upper part of Shenandoah County, near the present village of Forestville and the site of the first church—Flat Rock. John Garber had seven sons, six of whom became ministers. Martin, one of the six, was elder of the first church in Virginia, which in territory extended from Harrisonburg to the Maryland line. Other Dunker families, notably the Myerses, Wines, Klines, Bowmans, Millers, Kageys, Wamplers, Ziglers, and Florys, moved up from Pennsylvania and settled in the counties of Shenandoah and Rockingham. The number increased so rapidly that the annual conference of the whole Brotherhood was held at Flat Rock in 1799. Local congregations began later to take definite form. Flat Rock, the original congregation, was divided and subdivided, and now comprises Flat Rock, Linville Creek, Greenmount, Brock's Gap, Lost River, Woodstock, Frederick, Powell's Fort, and Page,—nine congregations, or districts, with a membership of about 2000.

In the district next above Harrisonburg, Garber's Church, located about two miles west of the town, is the oldest place of worship. The building was erected about 1800; and some of the early preachers that often officiated there were the following: Benjamin Bowman, Peter Nead, John Kagey, and Daniel Garber.[27] The first church organization of the Dunkers in Augusta County began about 1790, under the supervision of Elder — Miller.

Only a few of the early leaders of the Dunkers in Virginia were educated men; but many of them were strong in Christian character and well furnished unto good works. One hesitates to mention names, for the reason that others just as worthy may be overlooked; but the writer has heard the following often spoken of as men who loved their fellow men and did much, often through great sacrifice, to serve them: In Augusta County, Daniel Yount and John A. Cline; in

27. For this information I am indebted to Eld. J. M. Kagey, of Dayton, Va.

Rockingham, Peter Nead, John Kline, Daniel Thomas, Solomon Garber, Isaac Long, John Flory, Frederick Wampler; in Shenandoah, John Kagey, Jacob Wine, John Neff, Abram Neff; in Frederick, Daniel Baker; in Page, Samuel Spitler. Concerning Nead, Kagey, and Kline, a few more words may be allowed.

The time and place of Eld. Peter Nead's birth are not known to the writer; neither is it at all certain that he should be identified with Rockingham County rather than with many other places. His labors extended far and wide, east and west of the Alleghanies. He appears to have been a man of some learning, and is perhaps best remembered by his rather extensive writings. I have before me an octavo volume of 472 pages, entitled "Theological Writings on Various Subjects; or, A Vindication of Primitive Christianity." By Peter Nead, V. D. M. The title page bears the Latin quotation, *"Veritas, a quocunque dicitur, a Deo est."* The book was printed in 1850, at Dayton, Ohio. John Kagey (1757-1845) lived near New Market, but his ministerial services were given freely to a large number of surrounding communities. Because of his unfailing charities to rich and poor, white and black, and his uniform and sterling honesty, he was familiarly known as the "Good Man." The last seven years of his life were passed in blindness, but he still followed, as well as he could, his tasks of mercy and love. Joseph Salyards, the poet and self-made scholar, whose widowed mother often received for her children's need from his benevolent hand, has done honor to his memory in an elegy that deserves to live as long as beauty and truth belong to poetry. Elder John Kline (c. 1800-June 15, 1864) was perhaps the most active and influential church worker the Valley of Virginia Dunkers have ever had among them. He lived near Broadway, but his labors extended west, north, and northwest, across the mountains and beyond the Potomac and the Ohio. During the thirty years of his ministry he traveled upwards of a hundred thousand miles, mostly on horseback. Owing to the fact that he did not cease his journeys north and west during the Civil War, but continued as usual to go where he heard the call of duty, he was met in the public highway near his home, and shot in cold blood, by men who should have been his neighbors. But he died as he had lived: with his face forward, and with neither fear nor hatred of man in his heart. His memory lives.

In doctrine and worship the Dunkers are orthodox and evangelical. They are neither mystics nor ascetics, as some have supposed. Yet, like the Mennonites, they are marked by certain features that are more or less distinctive and peculiar. They observe as religious ordinances the kiss of charity, feet-washing, and the apostolic love-feast (*agape*) in connection with the communion in the eucharist; they practise the rite of anointing with oil, in cases of severe illness, though they do not at all neglect medical and hygienic aids; they avoid the taking of oaths (holding their simple word as binding all their powers), going to law, membership in secret societies, and fashionable dress; and are unalterably opposed to war and easy divorce of husband and wife. In consequence of their non-resistant principles, they, like the Mennonites, have been accused of a lack of patriotism, and have at times suffered much in consequence of this and their refusal to bear arms. But they are not lacking in patriotism. They only believe that war is always wrong and debasing. They believe, as a thoughtful writer of history has said, that "there are few things, if any, more important to the steady growth of a free nation than the maintenance of domestic virtues and the sanctities of family life."[28] They believe in helping the State and the nation, not by means of war and great standing armies, but by the useful and productive industries of peace; by earning an honest living, paying just debts and equitable taxes, by avoiding strife and contention as far as possible, by

28. Frederick Seebohm, The Era of the Protestant Revolution, p. 223.

settling peaceably, man to man or by additional counsellors, such disputes as inevitably arise; and thus making almshouses, jails, law courts, asylums, many policemen, and the expense of maintaining all these, largely unnecessary. They would apply this principle of peaceable adjustment of differences upon a large scale, and have nations, as well as individuals, observe the golden rule in business and diplomacy, and settle all disputed points by honest reason and just arbitration before, rather than after, the battle.

The founders, organizers, and early leaders of the Dunker church were men of education and culture; and they too, like the early Mennonities, anticipated Robert Raikes in the matter of Sunday schools; yet for many years, in what may be termed the middle age of the church's history, higher education, Sunday schools, and foreign missions were largely neglected. But the revival has come, and come with tremendous energy, within the last thirty or forty years; and the Dunkers of the Valley of Virginia are by no means the last or least among their fellows in the great forward and upward movement.

The following statistics, gathered with much care within the last few months, are regarded as substantially correct. The communicant members of the Dunker church in the Shenandoah Valley number altogether almost exactly 5000, and are distributed in the several counties as follows: Augusta County, 1531, with 18 churches and 7 preaching stations; Rockingham, 2391, with 26 churches and 10 preaching stations; Shenandoah, 620, with 13 churches and 6 preaching stations; Frederick, about 50 members, with two churches and one preaching station; Page, 400 members, with four churches. In summary, according to the reports received, there are 63 churches, 24 preaching stations, and 4992 communicants. Of the last, it will be observed that nearly 48 per cent. are in Rockingham County. A thriving college, founded in 1880, is maintained at Bridgewater.

In 1885, at Maurertown in Shenandoah County, was begun the first organization in Virginia of the more liberal branch of the Dunkers, usually known as the Progressive Brethren; termed by themselves simply the Brethren Church. On most points of doctrine they follow the same interpretation as the main body of the church, but have rules differing somewhat upon matters of form and church government. At present this branch of the church has, in the Shenandoah Valley, northeast of Staunton, about 20 congregations and a membership aggregating upwards of 1000.[29]

Neither the Dunkers nor the Mennonites have thus far sought any appreciable share in public or political life, partly because of their avoidance of show and display, partly because of their religious convictions in regard to formal oaths, and partly because the holding of certain offices might require them to violate their peace principles.

Since 1889 the majority of the United Brethren in the Valley of Virginia have adopted the New Constitution of the church, which does not prohibit membership in secret societies and allows lay delegates to the general conference. The smaller number still adhere to the Old Constitution. The first formal conference of this denomination met in Baltimore in 1789, the church having been organized shortly before by the German Reformed, Philip William Otterbein, and the Mennonite, Martin Boehm. One or more representatives of the Lutherans were also found among the early leaders. The United Brethren are Arminian in creed, and similar to the Methodists in organization. They have frequently been termed "German Methodists." Their first annual conference met at Frederick, Md., in 1800.

In 1809, when the Baltimore Methodist Conference met for the second time in Harrisonburg, Christian Newcomer, who succeeded Otterbein and Boehm as bishop of the United

29. For these statistics I am indebted to the kindness of Eld. E. B. Shaver, Maurertown, Va.

Brethren, was present as a commissioner to arrange for the union of the two churches. He was warmly received by Bishop Asbury and the rest, and a joint committee was provided for to report at the next conference. The effort for union was continued for five years, without success as to the main object; but the two bodies in the meantime, as well as afterwards, enjoyed very intimate and cordial relations, so much so that they labored often in common, and extended to each other very generally the use of places of worship. Moreover, many of the young members of United Brethren families, who preferred the English language to the German, were advised to connect themselves with the Methodist church. Practically all of the preaching by the United Brethren up to the year 1820 was in German; and that language was clung to tenaciously by many of the older members of the church for a number of years following.

Like the Mennonites and Dunkers, the United Brethren were uncompromisingly opposed to slavery, not only upon social and economic grounds, but chiefly upon religious principle. Their attitude in regard to this question, together with their opposition to secret societies and their adherence to the German language, made the growth of the church slow in Virginia during the first half of the nineteenth century. When Glossbrenner, who became a prominent leader, entered the ministry in 1830, there were only three church houses in all Virginia. One of these was Whitesel's, in Rockingham County, which was the first erected in the State. By 1860 the total membership in the large territory of the Virginia Conference, then including Maryland, did not exceed 3000. The war period was a trying time. Only one church, Salem, a small house in western Rockingham, was erected within the time and territory of the Southern Confederacy. The well-known opposition of the United Brethren to slavery put them in a class, so far at least as public opinion was concerned, with the hated Abolitionists; and they were in consequence visited with more or less of persecution and other attendant hardships. Some of the ministers were imprisoned, some went north, while a few staid at their posts; but, in general, the pastors were driven away and the flocks were broken and scattered. So discouraging did conditions appear at the close of the war to Bishop Markwood, himself a Virginian, that he exclaimed, "There is no United Brethren church in Virginia."

But the breaches were finally repaired and the waste places reclaimed. Under the leadership of Rev. John W. Howe (Dec. 4, 1829—June 17, 1903), and to a great extent through his own untiring personal efforts, the old congregations were reorganized and new ones formed. In 1876 a church school was established at Dayton, in Rockingham County, and the success of this has contributed largely to the success of the church. The total membership of the Virginia Conference, New Constitution, is at present about 13,000; and of this number probably more than half are to be found in the Shenandoah Valley. I am informed by Prof. J. H. Ruebush, of Dayton, Va., that between 2700 and 2800 members live in Rockingham County, owning 30 churches. At the recent conference, held (March 13-18, 1907) in Edinburg, at least 22 pastors were assigned charges in the Valley counties: In Augusta, four; in Rockingham, seven; in Shenandoah, two; in Page, one; in Frederick, three; in Berkeley, three; and in the part of Morgan County, belonging naturally to the Valley, two. Each of these men likely has three or four different congregations in his charge; so that the total number of churches in the Valley is probably 70 or more.

I have not succeeded in obtaining many statistics in regard to the adherents of the Old Constitution; but the membership in this branch of the church is much smaller than in the other. In 1905 there were in Virginia only 27 congregations or societies.[30]

In concluding this chapter, it may be profitable to fix in

30. W. H. Clay, D. D., Huntington, Ind., in a letter of January 16, 1907.

concise form the leading geographical distribution of the five religious bodies just reviewed. Three of them, the Mennonites, Dunkers, and United Brethren, have their strongholds in Rockingham County; one, the Lutherans, in Shenandoah; and one, the Reformed, are almost equally balanced between Shenandoah and Rockingham. Each of the five denominations before us, therefore, each of which is still predominantly German, has its stronghold, so far as the Shenandoah Valley is concerned, in either Rockingham or Shenandoah County.

CHAPTER IX.

Politics and War.

In neither war nor politics have any great number of the Valley of Virginia Germans been eminent leaders. The bent of the people as a class has not been toward either of these forms of activity to any considerable degree, but rather toward the scholarly or financially profitable vocations of a peaceful life, and the fruitful seclusion of the rural community. The quiet virtues of home and the common duties of the simple citizen have seemed to charm their ambitions most. This is especially true during the first hundred years of their history, as will appear more fully as we proceed: the later generations have been thrusting out more and more into the deeper tides and the louder strifes.

The reasons for this protracted isolation in political life are not difficult to find; and when they are pointed out they will at once be seen to have sprung partly from the nature and habits of the Germans themselves, and partly from the conditions by which they were surrounded.

To begin with, the German people are probably endowed with a constitutional reserve, an habitual conservatism. Then in early Virginia their language was a barrier to any extensive acquaintance outside of their own communities, and their manners and customs were different from those in the older parts of the colony. Along with these things went the inevitable suspicion of race—of the one race concerning another: of the Germans regarding the English; of the English regarding the Germans. This race suspicion on the part of the English was soon accentuated, and in time raised almost to antipathy, by various things, specially by the fact that some of the soldiers in the British armies during the Revolutionary war were Germans—Hessians. As soon as this feeling against them was perceived by the Germans they naturally became more reserved. Some of them indignantly held themselves aloof from contact; while a few of the weaker ones endeavored to hide their nationality. The geographical location of the Valley of Virginia itself, hedged in as it is by high mountains, added the bulwarks of physical nature to the barriers of race and language, custom and feeling. Then there were at least two other reasons why the Valley Germans—particularly the older generations of them—held back from politics: Most of them could not hope for any wide support because of their well-known opposition to slavery; and many of them, as has been shown in the preceding chapter, conscientiously refrained from political complications, as well as from war, because of religious conviction.

To show how little the Germans entered, or were allowed to enter, into the political life of early Virginia—even of their own section—and at the same time to record some of the exceptions to the rule, the following instances are cited.

In 1734, when, upon the petition to the colonial council of the inhabitants west of the Blue Ridge, magistrates were appointed in that section to settle disputes and punish offenders, only one of the five appointees was a German—Jost Hite; though it is likely that at least half of the people then in the Valley were Germans. On December 9, 1745, the first magistrates for Augusta County entered upon their work; but among the nine of them only one—Peter Scholl[1]—appears to have been a German. On March 3, 1748, Jacob Hite, a son of Jost Hite, was appointed by Governor Gooch sheriff of Frederick County. His bondsmen, in the sum of one thousand pounds, were his brothers John and Isaac Hite and his friends Thomas Swearingen and Samuel Earle. Early in the year 1778, seventeen justices were appointed by Governor Patrick Henry for the new county of Rockingham—a county always predominantly German; but among the number only

1. Waddell's Annals of Augusta, p. 47; Peyton's History of Augusta, p. 32.—Scholl lived on Smith Creek, in what is now Rockingham County. He was appointed a captain of militia in 1742. He appears to have come to Pennsylvania in 1719. Late in life he probably went to Kentucky.—Waddell's Scotch-Irish of the Valley, p. 84; Rupp's Thirty Thousand Names, p. 438.

two, Isaac Henkle and Anthony Reader, appear to have belonged to that nationality.[2]

But as time went on the Germans began to forge more to the front in the affairs of city and state, as well as in all of the larger interests of society. Within the first half of the nineteenth century, a half-dozen men who appeared in the courts and councils of the land won for themselves a reputation that far exceeded local bounds. Daniel Sheffey and Jacob Swoope were for many years two leading figures in Augusta County. The latter, as has already been noted, was the first mayor of Staunton, being elected to that position in 1802. He had come to Staunton from Philadelphia in 1789. He spent the remainder of his life in the Valley, and acquired both wealth and prominence. In the Campaign of 1809 he was the local leader of the Federalists, and was elected to Congress over his competitor largely because, as Mr. Waddell records,[3] he could speak German. This enabled him to outdo his rival in the canvass among the German voters. He served in Congress only two years, declining a reëlection in 1811. Although many eminent men were citizens of Augusta County from the very beginning, yet up to the year 1841 only two, Jacob Swoope and A. H. H. Stuart, had ever sat in the national Congress.

Daniel Sheffey was one of the four great lawyers of Staunton in his day, the other three being Chapman Johnson, John H. Peyton, and Briscoe G. Baldwin. Sheffey was born in Frederick, Md., the son of a German shoemaker; and appears to have learned his father's trade, his mother in the meantime teaching him in books. Going to southwest Virginia and settling at Wytheville to pursue his trade, he attracted the interest of Judge Smyth, who let him read law in his office. In due time he was admitted to the bar, where he soon won distinction. Prior to the year 1810 he was elected to Congress, where he held his seat for several terms; later he lo-

2. Judge John Paul's Address of October 15, 1896, pp. 7, 8.

3. Annals of Augusta, p. 383.

cated at Staunton, and for awhile represented Augusta County in the State legislature. In appearance Major Sheffey, as he was called, was short, stout, very near-sighted, and spoke with a decided German accent; yet his ability as a lawyer and statesman was universally acknowledged.

Thomas Van Swearingen and Isaac Leffler were two other Valley Germans who held seats in Congress within this period, the former from 1819 to 1822, the latter from 1827 to 1829.

Two other men of the period under review were Green B. Samuels and Isaac Samuels Pennybacker, cousins, and both natives of the same neighborhood in Shenandoah County. Samuels was a representative in Congress from 1839 to 1841, and Pennybacker from 1837 to 1839. The latter was one of the most distinguished lawyers and politicians of his generation. He was born at Pine Forge, September 6, 1805, and died in Washington City, January 12, 1847. In addition to his service in the house of Representatives, he was judge of the U. S. District Court, a regent of the Smithsonian Institution, and, from 1845 to the time of his death, was a U. S. Senator from Virginia. It is said that he was offered the Attorney-Generalship of the United States by President Van Buren.

Within the second half of the century just closed there are to be found a still larger group of men of German name and blood—a number of whom are yet living—that have won distinction and honor in the service of the commonwealth. Judge John Paul of Rockingham, whose mother came of a German family, was a member of Congress and a jurist of recognized powers. Harrison Holt Riddleberger of Shenandoah, who was a member of the State legislature and, from 1883 to 1889, U. S. Senator from Virginia, was a man of ability and influence. If one may be allowed to speak of the living, there are many names that might be mentioned, and a few that can scarcely be passed over in this connection: Absalom Koiner and Marshall Hanger of Augusta, George

B. Keezell of Rockingham, and Holmes Conrad of Frederick, are all men that have won honor throughout many years of distinguished public service.

It was intimated near the beginning of this chapter that the later generations of the Valley Germans have largely, if not altogether, overcome the obstacles that barred their ancestors almost entirely from public life. This fact has doubtless already become sufficiently patent from the instances cited; however, an additional illustration may be allowed in the conclusion of this phase of the subject. This illustration is in the nature of a series of contrasts, and is of a general rather than a particular character. Its value, therefore, is regarded as considerable.

From the year 1742 to the year 1776, thirty-nine men from the Valley counties of Virginia sat in the House of Burgesses and in the Virginia Conventions of 1775 and 1776;[4] and of these thirty-nine men not more than six, or less than 15½ per cent., were Germans. Counting years of service, the latter have 13 in 137—only about 9½ per cent. From the year 1883 to the present (1907), 22 men from the Valley counties have sat in the Virginia Senate;[5] and, of these twenty-two men, at least eight, or over 36⅓ per cent., have borne German names. Counting years of service, the figures stand 43 in 103—over 41⅔ per cent. During the same period 68 men, of whom 26, or over 38 per cent., have been Germans, have sat in the House of Delegates.[6] In period of service the twenty-six have had 56 years in 200, or 28 per cent. Counting the men from Valley counties in both houses of the Virginia legislature since 1883, there have been 90; and among them 34, or nearly 38 per cent., have been of German lineage. These 90 men have served altogether 303 years, 99 of which, or 32⅔ per cent., belong to the credit of the 34 Germans.

The fact that one or two of the counties included in this

4. See Appendix G.

5. See Appendix H.

6. See Appendix I.

computation are almost wholly English, in connection with the fact that several others are largely made up of German religious sects that seek practically no share in politics, reduces the German percentage considerably; but the figures still serve to illustrate the point that the German element in the Valley is rapidly coming into its political inheritance, whether it be for the better or the worse.

In at least one of the counties practically all of the public officials are at present of German stock. In Rockingham, in the fall of 1903, the Democratic nominations for office were as follows: For the State Senate, George B. Keezell; for the House of Delegates, H. M. Rogers and C. L. Hedrick; for County Treasurer, E. W. Carpenter; for Commonwealth's Attorney, George N. Conrad; for Clerk of the District Court, D. H. Lee Martz; for Clerk of the County Court, J. S. Messerley; for Sheriff, John A. Switzer. The remarkable fact in the case is that all of these eight men are of German lineage except one—Dr. Rogers—and he confesses to a good portion of German blood. It may be remarked, finally, that all of these gentlemen were elected except one, and he was defeated by the small majority of twenty-five votes. It looks as if the people of Rockingham are trying to balance the old score with Governor Patrick Henry.

In military affairs, as in political life, the Valley Germans have made a steady advance into prominence. A few of them, with a small percentage of officers of their own nationality, were active in the early Indian wars. In the Revolution they took a much more conspicuous part; and in the Civil War they made up the mass of fighting men from their particular sections, and supplied a large number of the important officers. Those sects that are opposed to war upon religious principle, consistently and steadily refused to bear arms, with very few exceptions; but those who did not belong to the peace societies, while also, no doubt, generally adverse to war, nevertheless proved, when they were called upon to fight, that they could do it with terrible effect.

Before proceeding to an orderly examination of the records of the several periods, it may not be out of place to catalogue here the names of a few men who held important military positions prior to the beginning of the nineteenth century. Peter Scholl of Augusta, who was made captain of one of the militia companies organized in 1742, has already been mentioned. Col. Adam Stephen, of the lower Valley, was one of Washington's field officers in 1755. Later, he lived near Leetown, Jefferson County, and was a major-general in the Revolution. Col. Ebenezer Zane (1747-1811) was a native of Frederick County, who in 1770 made the first permanent settlement at Wheeling, building the blockhouse known later as Fort Henry. He owned the land upon which the city of Zanesville now stands, and assisted in laying out the original settlement there. Captains Henry and George M. Bedinger were Revolutionary soldiers from the lower Valley. Col. John Hite and Capt. John Funk were men prominent in the civil and military affairs of Frederick County prior to and during the Revolutionary period. Major Isaac Hite (1758-1836) was aide to Gen. Muhlenberg at the siege of Yorktown. In 1781 Col. Swearingen was County Lieutenant of Berkeley. In 1789 Col. Jacob Rinker held the same office in Shenandoah County. Col. David Shepherd, of Sheperdstown, and Gen. Isaac Zane, of Frederick County, were other prominent figures in the last quarter of the eighteenth century.

In one of the old deed books of Frederick County are some memoranda of a court martial held at Winchester on Tuesday, September 2, 1755; and following is a list of the officers present: The Right Honorable Thomas Lord Fairfax, County Lieutenant; George William Fairfax, Colonel; Thomas Bryan Martin, Lt.-Colonel; Merideth Helm, Major; Richard Morgin, John Funk, Jr., Jeremiah Smith, Samuel Odell, Jacob Funk, William Bethel, Isaac Parkin, Edward Rodgers, John Hardin, John Linsey, Cornelius Ruddell, William Vance, Lewis Stephen, and John Denton, Captains. Of the number at least three, the Funks and Stephen, were Germans.

The seventh volume of Hening's *Statutes* contains a military list for a number of the counties of Virginia, showing the names of the men serving in the French and Indian War, and the respective sums paid them up to September, 1758. The same schedule also shows what persons furnished provisions and horses for the army, carried baggage on the expeditions, etc. Of the 39 counties covered by the schedule, Augusta has by far the longest list. From this county 676 men were in the military service of the colony, and 257 persons were paid for labor, provisions, horse hire, etc. Of the 676 soldiers, only about 136,—slightly over 20 per cent.,—bore German names; and among the 257 persons paid for provisions, etc., only about 44, or not quite 18 per cent., were Germans. It looks as if the proportion of Germans in Augusta at that date was rather small. At any rate, they were evidently as forward to serve in the army as they were to make money at its expense. In the same schedule Frederick County ranks fourth in numerical order; and there are about 34 German names, nearly 23 per cent., on her list of 149 soldiers, and about four Germans, 25 per cent., among the 16 persons paid for produce, etc.

At the outbreak of the Revolution no class among the colonists was more prompt to rise in opposition to what was looked upon as British tyranny than the German element in Virginia. Their spirit was no doubt powerfully stimulated by a newspaper, in their own language, *Der Staatsbote,* published at Philadelphia. This journal is said to have had many readers in the Shenandoah Valley. Heinrich Ringer, at Winchester, and Jacob Nicholas, at Peaked Mountain, were agents for the paper. *Der Staatsbote* of March 19, 1776, contained a special appeal to its German readers, reminding them of their sufferings in Europe, and warning them that the British ministry and Parliament were aiming to establish similar or even worse conditions in America.[7] Nearly two years earlier, June 16, 1774, some of the leading citizens in the vicinity of Wood-

7. Schuricht's German Element, Vol. I, p. 127.

stock called a public meeting, which, presided over by Pastor Muhlenberg, adopted spirited and patriotic resolutions. A committee of safety and correspondence was also appointed, consisting of Muhlenberg, Francis Slaughter, Abraham Bird, Taverner Beale, John Tipton, and Abraham Bowman.[8] The last, shortly after the outbreak of the war, succeeded Muhlenberg in command of the famous German regiment.

Mr. Waddell, the historian of Augusta, says:

> When the war of the Revolution arose the people of the Valley almost to a man espoused the cause of the colonies. I have found only one instance of disloyalty at the beginning of the strife. The person implicated was an Irish Presbyterian ex-minister, who was summoned before the County Committee of Augusta on October 3, 1775. He was solemnly tried and found guilty, and the committee recommended that he should be boycotted by the good people of the county and colony 'till he repents of his past folly.'[9]

The writer has found no like instance whatever among the Germans of the Valley, but one somewhat similar—even more serious—occurred in the section just west of Woodstock, in Hampshire, now Hardy, County. An old German of considerable wealth, Jacob Brake by name, with some of his neighbors of the same nationality, following the advice of John Claypole, a Scotchman, refused to pay taxes and serve in the militia. Their opposition became so grave that General Morgan was sent to break up the insurrection with an armed force. Shortly afterward a petition, signed by Jacob Brake, Adam Rodebaugh, Jacob Hier, Jacob Yeazle, and others, was sent to the Governor praying for pardon, and reciting that what they did was done "through ignorance, and the persuasion of others."[10] It is said that some of the whilom insurrectionists afterward volunteered for the campaign against Cornwallis.

Among a list of nineteen names belonging to Gen. Morgan's Winchester rifle company in the Revolution, the follow-

8. Schuricht's German Element, Vol. I, pp. 117, 118.

9. Scotch-Irish of the Valley, p. 87.

10. Palmer's Calendar, Vol. II, p. 686.

ing are German: Adam Heiskell, George Heiskell, Frederick Kurtz, Adam Kurtz, Peter Lauck, Simon Lauck, John Schultz, Jacob Sperry.[11] Howe says that Peter Lauck and John Schultz outlived all the rest of the band. How long they survived is not known; but the Government records show that they were both living and drawing pensions in 1835.

In a roster of Capt. Thomas Buck's Shenandoah company, made at Woodstock and dated August and September, 1777, at least 23 German names, including that of Jacob Yost, second lieutenant, appear in a total of 45.[12]

The writer, after searching vainly through various lists of Revolutionary soldiers for a muster roll of the 8th Virginia, or German Regiment, commanded at the outbreak of the Revolution by Muhlenberg, has recently been informed by Hon. James Hay, member of the House Committee on Military Affairs, that no roll of this regiment is preserved. This loss is a matter for keen regret, since such a roll would doubtless preserve the names of the majority of the able-bodied Germans found in the Valley in 1775 and 1776; for the regiment that followed the priest turned soldier that January day in the year of Independence, was not composed by any means exclusively of men from Shenandoah County, but included within its ranks many a sturdy "Dutchman" from far southwest, west, east, and northeast. In December of 1775 the Virginia Assembly passed an Act providing for the raising of six additional regiments, each to be composed of 680 men —10 companies, 68 men in a company. One was to be called the *German Regiment,* and was to be made up of German and other officers and soldiers, as the military committees of the several counties of Augusta, West Augusta, Berkeley, Culpeper, Dunmore, Fincastle, Frederick, and Hampshire, should judge expedient.[13] It is related that to the call of Muhlenberg's drum and fife there came seven young men from near

11. Boogher's Gleanings, p. 171.

12. Idem, pp. 178, 179.

13. Hening's Statutes, Vol. 9, p. 76.

Harper's Ferry, three the sons and four the grandsons of old Friedrich Ladner, who had come from Würtemberg in 1751.

The history of the German Regiment needs no recital here. Its open record, south and north, till the siege of Yorktown, and its brilliant part there, are known well enough. A few facts less familiar may be noted. When Muhlenberg was made a general in 1777, Abraham Bowman of Frederick, a grandson of old Jost Hite, succeeded to the command. Capt. Abraham Hite of Hampshire, a son of Jost, was paymaster of the regiment from January 1, 1779, to May 12, 1780. Among the field officers was Maj. Peter Helfenstein, of the lower Valley.

On January 25, 1781, it was reported to the colonial government that the men in Berkeley County were unwilling to go to join Gen. George Rogers Clark, in his western campaigns; and in March following Clark himself made similar complaint of the militia of Frederick, Berkeley, and Hampshire.[14] How to explain such backwardness at this time is rather difficult, specially so in view of the heroic achievements of the men from the same section only two years before.

Considering the difficulties overcome and the magnitude and importance of the results accomplished, in view of the small number of men engaged in the enterprise, Clark's achievement in the capture of Kaskaskia and Vincennes and the conquest of the Northwest in 1778-1779, stands almost without a parrallel in the whole field of history. One may therefore be justified, perhaps, when writing of the Germans of the Shenandoah Valley, in pointing out with some detail the extent to which they entered into this campaign.

In Clark's little army was a company commanded by Leonard Helm of Fauquier, and another commanded by Joseph Bowman of Frederick. In the former company were likely a few Germans, while in the latter more than a third were of that nationality. Besides the Germans found in these two

14. Palmer's Calendar, Vol. I, pp. 461, 597.

companies, there were evidently a few others, chiefly from the Shenandoah Valley and adjoining sections. Following is a list of names, copied from English's Life of Clark, believed upon good evidence to be the pay-roll of Capt. Bowman's company. All the men whose names appear on this roll enlisted from January to May, 1778, and were discharged the following July and August, after the taking of Kaskaskia; but a number of them appear to have re-entered the service for the rest of the campaign.

Capt. Joseph Bowman
1st Lt. Isaac Bowman
2d Lt. Abram Kellar
Ser. Daniel Dust
Ser. Isaac Kellar
Ser. Jacob Speers
Michael Setzer
Abraham Miller
Wm. Slack
*Ligey Huste
*Thomas Perry
*Robt. McClanihan
*Barney Master
John Setser
John Bentley
Henry Honaker
Fred. Honaker
Henry Funk
Geo. Livistone
Henry Chrisman
Samuel Stroud
Edward Bulger
Abram James
Alex. McIntire
Philip Orben
Thomas Clifton
William Berrey [1]
Barnabay Walters
Wm. McGumrey
Jacob Cogar
Peter Cogar
Thos. H. Vance
James Bentley
*George Millar
Patrick Doran
Henry Traylar
Isaac McBride
Edward Murrey
Joseph Simson
Philip Long
George King
Joseph Pangrass
Francis Pangrass
Michael Pangrass
Charles McClock
*Nathan Cartmill
*James Gouday
*Samuel Dust
*William Berrey [2]
*Zebeniah Lee

*Deserted.

In this list of 49 names there are about 18—over 36 per cent.—that are borne by Virginia Germans, chiefly of the lower Valley.

For their services with Clark in the conquest of the Northwest, a large proportion of his soldiers were rewarded with allotments of land. In a list of 300 men who received land the 21 following names are found:

Maj. Joseph Bowman
Capt. Abraham Kellar
Lt. Isaac Bowman
Ensign Jacob Vanmeter
Ser. Isaac Kellar
Ser. Buckner Pittman
Ser. Wm. Rubey
Ser. Samuel Strode
Henry Funk
Henry Honaker
Peter Honaker
John Isaacs
Wm. Myers
John Peters
Wm. Ruby
Geo. Shepard
Peter Shepard
John Sitzer
Michael Sitzer
Van Swearingen
Isaac Vanmeter

A number of others who were officers and privates with Clark in some of his campaigns did not have their claims for land allowed. Among a large number of such were the following:

Ser. John Breeden
Ser. John Hant (killed)
Ser. Conrad Workman
Matross Philip Hupp
John Bender [Painter]
Lewis Bender (died)
Robert Bender
Christian Bowman
Peter Brazer
Richard Breeden
John Bush
Drewry Bush
Wm. Chick (killed)
John Conn [Kahn]
Christopher Coontz
Jacob Detering
Lewis Fache
James Hildebrand
Geo. Hite
Francis Holler
Fred. Sowers
Peter Veale
Thomas Vonshiner
Fred. Zimmerman[15]

15. English's Life of Clark, Vol. II, pp. 839-850; 1060-1066.

Practically all of the names in the two lists just given are borne by German or Dutch families that have been in the Valley for the last century and a half.

Before leaving this phase of our subject a word more should be said concerning Major Joseph Bowman. He was a son of George Bowman, who married Mary Hite, one of Jost Hite's daughters, and who was one of the original settlers with Hite in the lower Valley in 1732. He had three brothers: Col. Abram Bowman, who succeeded Muhlenberg in command of the German regiment; John; and Isaac, who was also an officer under Gen. Clark in the Illinois campaign. Maj. Joseph Bowman was second in command to Clark, and performed distinguished services; but he did not live to return from the expedition that has made him and his comrades famous. He died at Fort Sackville, August 15 or 18, 1779.

In 1835 there were living in the counties of Frederick, Page, Rockingham, and Shenandoah 172 men who had been soldiers in the Revolution, and who were drawing pensions. At least 69 of them, or upwards of 40 per cent., bore German names. The whole number were distributed in the several counties as follows: In Frederick, 86, of whom 29, nearly 34 per cent., were Germans; Page, 7, of whom 3 were Germans; Rockingham, 36, with at least 20 Germans—over 55 per cent.; Shenandoah, 43, with 17 Germans—nearly 40 per cent.[16]

Not very much information has been found regarding the Valley of Virginia men in the War of 1812; but a few names of prominent officers of the period are at hand. Capt. Abraham Lange and Capt. John C. Sowers, both from Staunton or its vicinity, were well-known leaders, the latter belonging to the artillery service. Henry Snyder served with Capt. Sowers, and was the chief drummer of Augusta County for many years. William Suthardt and George Orebaugh were his assistants. Col.—Koontz and Capt. John Link were also

16. See Appendixes L, M, N, O.

Augusta soldiers of the same period. In Rockingham, Col. Peter Roller, born in 1795, was a militia officer in the early part of last century. In Shenandoah County nearly all of the prominent civil and military leaders of the time appear to have been Germans, among whom were Col. Samuel Bare, Capt. George Shrum, Col. Philip Spengler, and Capt. Solomon Spengler.

In coming to the Civil War, I cannot introduce the Virginia German soldiers of the period better than by quoting the words of one who is a recognized authority on the subject.

> The men of Pennsylvania-German descent who fought in the Southern armies are not ashamed of the part we took in that war. We do not feel that we are any discredit to the race from which we spring, and it is affirmed with confidence, that when the history shall have been written of the part borne by the sons of the Pennsylvania-German element in the Confederate armies, there will be no brighter page in the records of this Society than that.
>
> In the famous Pickett's charge, his men were commanded by at least two brigadier generals, who were Virginia soldiers of German descent. The North Carolina troops were commanded in many instances by soldiers of the same stock. One family alone is said to have furnished as many as five general officers to the Southern Army. Another family furnished two or more, and there were other families of German blood, that furnished individual soldiers who were equally distinguished.[17]

Among the alumni of the Virginia Military Institute, who gaves their lives to Virginia in the struggle from '61 to '65, were the following men from Valley German families: Col. John F. Neff, Capt. Wm. Keiter, Capt. E. S. Trout, Capt. Ramsay Koontz, Lt. Thomas L. Harman, and Lt. Chas. E. Lauck.

It has already been shown in a preceding chapter that over 50 per cent. of the 671 men from Rockingham, Shenandoah, Warren, and Page, composing the Tenth Regiment Virginia Volunteer Infantry, bore German names; and that the same is true of nearly 68 per cent. of 124 men from Rock-

17. Gen. John E. Roller, in an address at Lebanon, Pa., Oct. 22, 1903, before the Pennsylvania-German Society.

ingham who formed one of the companies of Ashby's cavalry. And these are by no means exceptional instances, but they may be taken as fairly representing the other bodies of men from the same and adjacent sections. The Tenth Legion Artillery, commanded by Capt. M. M. Sibert, which was ordered to Charlestown in 1859 to attend the execution of John Brown, enrolled at least 20 German names in 41. Of 75 men, officers and privates, from New Market and vicinity, composing Co. B, 3d Regiment, 7th Brigade, C. S. A. Vol. Militia, no less than 50 were from German families. On September 7, 1906, there was held near New Market a reunion of Confederate veterans, which was attended by 185 men from Shenandoah and adjoining counties, representing various commands. Old soldiers who followed Jackson, Ashby, Mosby, Imboden, Rosser, and others were there, and their names were printed in the *Shenandoah Valley* of September 27, 1906. An inspection of the list shows that nearly 70 per cent. belong to such familiar German families as the following: Zirkle, Schaeffer, Henkel, Foltz, Bowman, Miller, Hoover, Bowers, Neff, Moomaw, Snapp, Zehring, Dellinger, etc.

The famous Stonewall Brigade may be termed, not inaptly, the Old Guard of the South. Its record is familiar to the world; but it may not be generally known that a large proportion of the men, from the Valley of Virginia and adjacent sections, who composed it, were of German lineage. The complete muster rolls have not been gone over; but, in view of the facts already presented, the proposition just advanced may be satisfactorily established by giving the names of some of the officers of the brigade, and showing that several of the regiments composing it were raised in sections of the Valley where the German element is strong.

The Stonewall Brigade was made up of the following bodies of men: The 2d, 4th, 5th, 27th and 33d Regiments, Virginia Infantry; the Rockbridge Artillery, and Carpenter's Battery. The 2d Regiment was composed of two companies (D and E) from Berkeley County; two (C and I) from Clarke County; one (F) from Winchester; and five (A, B, G, H, and K) from Jefferson County. The 4th Regiment was made up in the southwest Virginia counties of Wythe, Pulaski, Smyth, Montgomery, and Marion. The 5th Regiment was composed of companies from Augusta County and one (Co. K) from Winchester. The 27th Regiment was from the counties of Monroe, Grayson, Alleghany, and Rockbridge. The 33d Regiment was composed as follows: Co. A, from Hampshire County; Co. B, lower Shenandoah County; Co. C, Woodstock and vicinity; Co. D. western part of Frederick; Co. E, New Market and vicinity; Co. F, Hardy County; Co. G, Mt. Jackson and vicinity; Co. H, Page County; Co. I, Rockingham County; Co. K, Columbia Furnace and vicinity, in western Shenandoah. It will be observed, therefore, that the 33d Regiment was raised wholly in the heart of the German settlements; the 5th in Augusta and Frederick, where German families are numerous; and the 2d chiefly in Frederick, Berkeley, and Jefferson, where the German element is considerable. It is likely, moreover, that a few Germans were found in the other regiments, and in the artillery companies.

A glance at the names of some of the German officers in the Stonewall Brigade must conclude this particular division of our study. The fourth colonel in command of the 2d Regiment was J. Q. A. Nadenbousch. The 5th Regiment had upon its list of commanders Col. J. H. S. Funk and Col. Wm. H. Harman. Major Absalom Koiner, Adjutant James Bumgardner, and Adjutant C. J. Arnalt belonged to the same regiment. The commanders of the 33d Regiment were Cols. A. C. Cummings, John F. Neff,[18] F. W. M. Holliday, Edwin

18. Col. John Francis Neff, born Sept. 5, 1834, near Mt. Jackson, was the oldest son of Eld. John Neff, a prominent minister of the Dunker church. After graduating at V. M. I., young Neff studied law under Judge J. W. Brokenbrough. Admitted to the bar, he entered upon the practice of his profession in New Orleans; later at Baton Rouge; later still at Memphis, where he remained till the

G. Lee, and Abraham Spengler. Neff and Spengler were Germans, as was also Maj. Jacob B. Colliday. Among the captains of the same regiment were the following: John H. Grabill (Co. B); M. M. Sibert, George Bedinger, and Thomas E. Conn (Co. E); Abraham Spengler (Co. F); David B. Huffman (Co. G); and —Shuler (Co. H).[19] The names of the captains in the other regiments are not at hand.

It is said that the Pennybacker family, largely represented in the Valley, furnished more soldiers in the Civil War than any other family,—two major-generals being among the number. Not all of the soldiers bearing this name were from Virginia, however; and not all fought on one side. The Ladner incident of the Revolution is recalled and more than paralleled, at least in point of numbers, by the Engle family, from the same vicinity: thirteen Engles from the lower Valley served in the Confederate armies; one as a chaplain; two as captains of cavalry; two as quartermasters; two as infantry lieutenants; and six as troopers. The Pittmann family also, like many others that space forbids naming, have a military rec-

outbreak of the war. Then he came to Virginia, and was made Adjutant of the 33d Regiment. At the first battle of Manassas he won special distinction. In the spring of 1862 he succeeded Col. Cummings in command of the regiment, which he led after Jackson in the famous Valley campaign, winning particular notice at Port Republic. After the Seven Days' Battle around Richmond, while Jackson's corps was at Gordonsville, Gen. Winder, owing to a misunderstanding, put Col. Neff under arrest. In the battle of Cedar Mountain, shortly afterward, being still under arrest, he went into the thick of the battle without his sword. It was not long until he was acquitted of the charges against him, and was restored to his command. At the second battle of Manassas he was not well, and went to the front against the surgeon's advice. While leading his regiment in a charge, or in repulsing the countercharge, he was shot dead. He is said to have been the youngest regimental commander in the Stonewall Brigade.

19. For helpful information regarding the Stonewall Brigade, I gratefully acknowledge my indebtedness to Maj. R. W. Hunter, of Richmond.

ord, as the following concise statement, concluding this chapter, will show.

Lawrence Pittman had ten grandsons in the Confederate army. Philip Pittman, his oldest son, at the age of 16 served in the War of 1812; and, in 1861, at the age of 64, enlisted in the Confederate army, taking with him his youngest son, just 16 years old. The last year of the struggle his friends implored him to come home and be a candidate for the Virginia Senate. His reply was that the army had no soldiers to spare, but if they wished to elect him they could do so; but he would remain in the army until officially notified of his election. He was elected, but remained at his post until the Senate convened.[20]

20. Miss Mary C. Pittman, of The Plains, Va., in a letter of Nov. 6, 1902.

CHAPTER X.

Educational and Literary Activities.

That the Germans of the Shenandoah Valley of Virginia should be entirely unmindful of schools and of books, even during their early struggles as pioneers, could hardly be imagined in view of their antecedent training in Pennsylvania. Prior to 1697, Köster, a religious leader of provincial Pennsylvania, and his followers printed in "High Dutch" the first book published in the German language in America.[1] In 1728 Conrad Beissel, the mystic, issued his first volume through the German printer's art.[2] From 1738 to 1778—a period of forty years—the two Dunkers, Christopher Sower, Sr., and Christopher Sower, Jr., sent out from their publishing house at Germantown innumerable books, pamphlets, newspapers, and almanacs: the last having a circulation from New York to Georgia. In 1739 they started the first German newspaper in America—*Der Hoch-Deutsch Pennsylvanische Geschicht-Schreiber;* and in 1743 they sent out from their press the first Bible in a European tongue published in America.[3] The German Reformed and Lutherans of colonial Pennsylvania are said to have provided schools as soon as churches, and sometimes schoolmasters before regular pastors.[4]

Whether the immigrants called themselves Pietists, Mennonites, Dunkers, Moravians, German Quakers, members of the Reformed Church, Lutherans, or simply dissenters, and however great their differences of opinion in the interpretation of the Bible may have

1. Sachse's German Pietists, pp. 266, 276.

2. Seidensticker's First Century of German Printing, p. 6.

3. Brumbaugh's History of the Brethren, pp. 338-437; Kuhns' German and Swiss Settlements, pp. 115-152.

4. Kuhns' German and Swiss Settlements, pp. 143, 144.

been, on one point at least they were united. They all believed with Martin Luther:

"Burgomasters, princes, and nobles we can dispense with; schools can not be dispensed with, for they must govern the world."[5]

The great number of German books still to be found in the Valley of Virginia to-day—Sower Bibles, Testaments, Psalm books, hymn books, almanacs, etc.,—show that when the families moved to this section from Pennsylvania they brought books with them and had others, with current periodicals, to follow them. It was quite natural, therefore, that they should also establish schools, and educate their children. Men of wealth sometimes made provision during their lifetime or in their wills for the maintenance of schools. I am informed by Miss Sarah M. Spengler of Front Royal, Va., that Peter Stover, the founder of Strasburg, was one of this number. He donated a liberal amount of money, and also some land, for use in educational purposes in Strasburg.

As a case in evidence of the literacy of the early Germans of the Valley, Mr. Charles E. Kemper, of Washington City, cites the following instance: The records of the Peaked Mountain church, which was located in what is now Rockingham County, show an agreement made in 1768 between the Lutherans and German Reformed, to build a union house of worship; and, of the forty-eight men who signed this agreement, only four made their marks.[6]

The writer, in a rather extensive examination of the various county records, has found that a considerable number of the old German landholders could not write their names: at least they did not write them. It is likely, however, that some who made their marks did so not because they could not write, but because the indenture was written for them in English; and so, rather than sign in German to an English instrument,

5. Report of Commissioner of Education, 1901, Vol. I, p. 539. See also Rupp's Thirty Thousand Names, pp. 13, 14.

6. Virginia Magazine, Vol. XIII, No. 3, pp. 287, 288; William and Mary College Quarterly, Vol. XIII, pp. 248, 249.

they made their marks. It is probable that in the great majority of cases, when the instrument was drawn in German, it was also signed in German by the maker, without a mark. When all explanations are done, however, it will still doubtless be necessary to admit that some of our German great-grandfathers—and many more of our great-grandmothers—could not write. But the same is also true of at least a few of their English contemporaries. Their illiteracy was the fault of their day and generation, rather than of any individual, class, or nationality.

Granting, then, that some—a few—of the German pioneers were illiterate, we may still claim what appears to be the truth, that most of them could at least read and write. Some of them could do much more. All of them, with scarcely an exception, wanted to educate their children. And so they built schoolhouses as rapidly as, and often side by side with, their churches, and provided teachers. Indeed, they must often have had the schoolrooms in their dwelling houses, just as they often met for worship there, before they had either churches or schoolhouses.

Most of the education of those early days, however, doubtless was, as has been intimated, of an elementary sort: many of the pupils never got beyond a "speaking acquaintance" with the first three handmaids of knowledge; and very few reached the first stages of what would now be called higher education. This, too, was chiefly the fault of the time. Rather, it was an unwelcome necessity imposed by circumstances. When men and women undertake to conquer the wilderness and plant civilization in the face of savage enemies, they must forego for awhile many of the things that belong to civilization and make it desirable. Felling forests, grubbing stumps, ploughing virgin soil tightly tangled with roots, and preserving scalps in the place assigned them by nature, become duties of such strenuous and presistent sort as usually to crowd out the extensive reading and writing of books.

There have been other conditions, moreover, found in the later stages of the Valley settlements,—conditions not imposed by the hard necessities of pioneer life,—that retarded for a considerable period the full development of letters. Among certain of the religious bodies, particularly the Dunkers and Mennonites, higher education was long looked upon with more or less suspicion, and accordingly was either actually opposed or generally neglected. But these conditions, happily, during the last generation or two have been undergoing a change, as will appear more fully farther on; and both of these denominations seem now endeavoring to emulate their earliest leaders, most of whom were men of exact learning and broad culture.

The educational and literary activities of the Valley Germans will now be reviewed more specifically, in chronological order for the most part, under two heads: first, the establishment of schools, academies, and colleges; second, printing and publishing centers.

When and where the first school of advanced grade was established, is not known. The date, however, would certainly take us back more than a hundred years. In the year 1806 a school was begun at New Market, in Shenandoah County, by the German Lutherans and Reformed, in connection with the church. The scheme for the institution is reported to have embraced some of the higher branches of study, as well as the elementary grades and subjects. How long this school was continued is not known; but the project met with early opposition, and probably was soon abandoned. The difficulty seems to have arisen between the German and English elements in the congregation: the latter apparently objected to having part of the church lot given up to the use of a school that promised to be exclusively German. A school similar to the one at New Market was established at Harper's Ferry, probably at about the same period.[7]

7. Schuricht's German Element, Vol. II, p. 48.

On February 21, 1817, an Act was passed by the General Assembly of Virginia, incorporating Woodstock Academy, with the following thirteen gentlemen as trustees: Philip Miller, Jacob Ott, Joseph Irwin, Robert Gaw, Philip Williams, Martin Hupp, John S. Ball, George Fravell, Robert Turner, Michael Effinger, Joseph Arthur, Jacob Rinker, Jr., and James Allen. All of these men were prominent and influential in the important affairs of Shenandoah County, and six of them represented German families; but what success attended this educational enterprise has not been ascertained.

Upon the same date that Woodstock Academy was chartered, the Assembly also incorporated New Market Academy. The trustees named were, Samuel Coofman, Patrick McManus, Jacob D. Williamson, John Strayer, William Steenbergen, Solomon Henkel, Gilbert Meem, Samuel Huston, James Brown, Francis Sybert, Alexander Doyle, and John Morgan. Of the twelve, at least four, Coofman, Steenbergen, Henkel, and Sybert, were Germans.

Another early beginning in higher education—a movement of special significance—must be credited to New Market. In 1820 Rev. S. S. Schmucker, a young man of twenty-one, a graduate of Princeton Theological Seminary, became pastor of the Lutheran congregation, and continued in that capacity till 1825. During his pastorate he conceived the idea of founding a sort of pro-seminary; and, in 1823, he began his career as theological professor. The building in which he taught, though removed from its original site, is still standing; and some of his pupils became men of eminence and power in the church at large. Dr. Schmucker's New Market school, begun in 1823, gradually led to the founding of Gettysburg Seminary, in which he became the first professor.[8]

Only three years after Dr. Schmucker made his modest though fruitful beginning at New Market, a more pretentious movement was organized and put in operation a few miles

8. The Shenandoah Valley, Supplement, July 28, 1904.

west of the village. On February 18, 1826, an Act was passed by the General Assembly of Virginia, incorporating an institution known as Rockingham Academy, with the nine gentlemen whose names follow as trustees: Samuel Moffett, William McMahon, Samuel Newman, Andrew Moffett, Isaac Thomas, Peter Crim, John Hoover, Joseph Cline, and Samuel Hoover. The next year, 1827, or possibly the same in which the charter was granted, the school was put in operation, and it has continued, with occasional brief interruptions, until the present, though never at any time have the courses of study been more than partly devoted to advanced work. The site of the school is on the east side of the Little Shenandoah River, in Rockingham County, near the Shenandoah County line, and about midway between New Market and Timberville. The name "Rockingham Academy" has long been out of use, and the place is now called "The Plains." The original building was a log house, with a single room 22x28 feet. This structure was removed in 1857, and in its place was erected the present building—a double one-story house, one part of which is used for the school, the other as a church. The original trustees were members of the Primitive Baptist and the Dunker denominations; and their descendants still hold the property, though the number of trustees has been increased to thirteen, and most of them at present bear German names. About half of them belong to the Dunker church, several to the Lutheran, and probably one or more to other denominations; but the Primitive Baptist element has apparently been merged into other forms almost entirely. The church room of the building is free to all denominations; but the Mennonites and Dunkers are allowed precedence on the third and fourth Sundays, respectively, of each month. The present trustees of the one-time Rockingham Academy are the following gentlemen: John F. Driver, David J. Driver, S. H. Moffett West, David S. Roller, C. Newton Wine (lately deceased), Gilbert L. White, Henry M. Henkel, John

H. Hoover, Frank Alexander, Cornelius Driver, Samuel L. Hoover, B. F. A. Myers, and Jacob B. Garber.[9]

In 1837, March 22, an Act was passed chartering Front Royal Academy, in Warren County; and among the fourteen trustees were Edward B. Jacobs and Newman M. Jacobs, both probably of German descent.

In 1853 an institution was incorporated at Salem, Va., Roanoke County, as Roanoke College, and as successor to the Virginia Institute. This school, though within the bounds of the Valley of Virginia, is outside the geographical limits of the Shenandoah Valley; nevertheless a brief notice of it is included here for the reason that it is largely patronized by the German families in the valley of the Shenandoah. It is an institution under the direction of the Lutheran church; and naturally many—perhaps most—of the sons of Lutheran families, who attend college from the Shenandoah Valley, go to Roanoke. Moreover, its convenient nearness and the facility with which it may be approached, make it an institution of the section under review almost as much as if it were actually located therein. Roanoke College remained open during the Civil War, though without endowment. Within recent years a liberal endowment and a library of 22,000 volumes have been acquired, and the institution has had an encouraging developement. In addition to the regular college courses, which are partly elective, preparatory and commercial courses are offered. The attendance in 1906 was 202, representing 13 States and two foreign countries; and the faculty consists of 12 professors and instructors.[10] During the last ten years a gradually increasing number of women have been admitted as special students; so that at present the school may be termed co-educational. An appropriate and commendable attitude toward local history and biography is

9. For information regarding the later history of Rockingham Academy, I am indebted to Mr. John W. Grim, of Timberville, Va.

10. New International Encyclopedia, Vol. XV, p. 59; Fifty-third Annual Catalogue.

being manifested by the faculty, who occasionally assign to graduating students for discussion in theses such subjects as the German Immigration into Virginia, the German Element in the Valley, etc. At least two such subjects have been assigned within the last two or three years; but as yet the present writer has not enjoyed the privilege of seeing either of the resulting compositions.

On February 20 and April 7, 1858, the Virginia Assembly passed Acts granting corporate rights to John K. Booton, William C. Lauck, and A. C. Booton for establishing and maintaining a school in Page County, to be known as the Luray Institute. Mr. Lauck was evidently a German. The capital stock of the enterprise was not to exceed $25,000; and the school was to be a seminary for both men and women, and was empowered to grant diplomas, confer degrees, etc. The further history of the institution is not known.

In 1870, in Shenandoah County, was established a school for higher learning: the New Market Polytechnic Institute, which enjoyed a notable and influential career for twenty-six years. This institution was not founded or maintained exclusively by any particular sect or nationality; and yet one may doubtless assert with truth and justice that the German families of the town and community—specially the German Lutherans—did most to foster it and make possible its high development in scholastic fields. The most famous master of the school—probably the most distinguished teacher of the Shenandoah Valley—was the self-made man, scholar, teacher, and poet, Joseph Salyards (1808-1885), whose career as a teacher extended over more than half a century. Prior to the founding of the Polytechnic Institute, he had gained a wide reputation in the New Market Academy. Salyards was not a German, but he was affiliated mainly with the Valley Germans, and did a lasting work among them. Numerous and prominent among the disciples that sat at his feet, the friends that bore him to the grave, and the organization that raised a stone to mark his tomb, were men descended from that nationality.

Sometime prior to the year 1885, Rev. J. I. Miller, a Lutheran minister, organized at Staunton a female academy, which was maintained with excellent results to the Lutherans and others for a number of years, but which at the present is not in operation.

Three other educational institutions, founded, fostered, and successfully maintained through the initiative of three German religious bodies of the Shenandoah Valley, yet demand our notice under this head.

In 1875, at Dayton, Rockingham County, a school was organized by some leading spirits of the United Brethren denomination. From a small attendance and unpretentious claims the institution soon grew to larger proportions and wider influence. The second year (1876) property was purchased and the school was chartered as the Shenandoah Seminary; in 1879 it was rechartered and the name changed to Shenandoah Institute; since 1902 it has been known as the Shenandoah Collegiate Institute and School of Music. Although it is under the direction and control of the religious body above named, and draws its patronage largely if not chiefly from the same body, the institution endeavors to avoid sectarianism while inculcating Christian principles; and neither wealth nor social rank is allowed to antagonize the more essential qualities in the making of a man. The school is coeducational, and offers numerous and varied courses of study in letters, music, and commercial branches. Religious and athletic organizations have a prominent place. Three commodious buildings provide lecture rooms, literary society halls, offices, dormitories, etc. In 1906 the number of students in attendance from Virginia and other States was 192, and the faculty was made up of 13 professors and instructors.[11]

11. Thirtieth Annual Catalogue.

In the fall of 1880, Daniel C. Flory of Augusta County, Virginia, who had been a student at the University of Virginia from 1875 to 1878, started in Rockingham County a school known as the Spring Creek Normal School. The next year it was expanded into the Spring Creek Normal School and Collegiate Institute. In the autumn of 1882 the institution was moved to Bridgewater, and was called the Virginia Normal School; in April, 1889, the charter was so amended as to allow the name Bridgewater College to be assumed, and this name has remained unchanged to the present. The institution is coeducational, and is owned and chiefly supported by the German Baptist Brethren, or Dunkers; but endeavors to pursue an unprejudiced and liberal course in the promotion of broad scholarship and in the building of moral character; and it has in consequence always commanded a hearty confidence and generous support among the best families of the Valley, irrespective of religious affiliation. The school owns six good buildings, and is provided with one of the best athletic fields in the State. Special and varied opportunities for Bible study and spiritual development are afforded. In 1906 the number of students in attendance, representing seven States, was 201; and the number of teachers was fourteen.[12]

Massanutten Academy is located at the southwest approach to the historic old town of Woodstock; and the main building was formerly the residence of U. S. Senator H. H. Riddleberger. The school was chartered and opened to students in 1899, and is under the supervision of the Virginia Classis of the Potomac Synod of the Reformed Church, although one or two other religious denominations are represented on the board of trustees, and sectarian tendencies are studiously avoided. The faculty consists of nine professors and assistants; and the number of students in 1906 was 73, mainly from Virginia.[13]

12. Twenty-sixth Annual Catalogue; Bridgewater College, Its Past and Present, pp. 8-85.

13. Seventh Annual Catalogue.

From this sketch of the leading movements for higher learning, let us pass to a similar review of the chief publishing centers of the German element of the Valley.

Of the five places in Virginia, as catalogued by Prof. Oswald Seidensticker, where German printing was carried on prior to 1830, four—Winchester, New Market, Staunton, and Harrisonburg—are in the Shenandoah Valley. In 1805 a German almanac was issued from Winchester by Jacob D. Dietrich; in 1807 a newspaper was started at New Market; in 1808 one was started at Staunton; beginning a few years later, and continuing for nearly a generation, a series of German publications—books, pamphlets, etc.—came from the Wartmann press at Harrisonburg. In addition to these four early centers of German influence through the printing press, there have been in the Valley at least two others that shall receive due notice.

Dietrich's almanac, distributed from Winchester in 1805, was probably the first publication in the German language made in Virginia; though Seidensticker thinks it possible that this almanac was printed somewhere in Maryland. The next year, Ambrose Henkel established his printing office at New Market; and the year following (1807: not 1808, as Seidensticker says) he began the publication of the first German newspaper ever printed in Virginia.[14]

Ambrose Henkel, the fourth son of Rev. Paul Henkel and his wife Elizabeth, was born in Shenandoah County, Virginia, near Solomon's Church, 8 miles northwest of New Market, July 11, 1786. In 1802, at the age of 16, he set out, on foot, for Hagerstown, Md. There, with Gruber, the famous almanac man, and at Reading and Baltimore, he worked at the printing business for three or four years; then he purchased an outfit for himself: the bed and irons of a Ramage press and some old type: and in 1806, as above shown, he established the first printing office at New Market. He continued

14. Seidensticker's First Century of German Printing, p. 173; Schuricht's German Element, Vol. II, p. 13.

his work as printer and engraver till 1817, when he sold out the business to his brother Solomon. In 1823 he entered the Gospel ministry of the Lutheran church, wherein he labored till his death in 1870.[15] The Henkel press has continued in operation, and has remained in the Henkel family. Last year (1906) it rounded out a century of history; and, with increased facilities and modern equipment, it is to-day in the hands of two of Rev. Ambrose Henkel's great-nephews: Ambrose L. and Elon O. Henkel. By the kindness of these gentlemen the writer was recently enabled to examine a file of the old newspaper that was started by Ambrose Henkel in 1807. Inasmuch as it was the first of its kind in the Old Dominion, it has much interest and historical value, and hence a rather detailed account of it may be acceptable.

The title of the paper in question was, *Der Virginische Volksberichter, Und Neumarketer Wochenschrift*: translated by Rev. Socrates Henkel, D. D., as follows: *"Virginia and New Market Popular Instructor and Weekly News."*

It is made up in the ordinary four-page form, with three columns on a page; and each page is about ten inches wide, and about fifteen inches from top to bottom. At the top of the front page, above the title of the paper, is a cut of the American Eagle, keeping in his charge the American motto, *E Pluribus Unum.* Artistically disposed among the large lettering of the title, is found the following patriotic declaration: *Ich bin dem Patriot, Religion and Warheit treu; fänd ich auch weder Gold noch Brod noch Ehr dabey.* Mr. Henkel was at this time just twenty-one years old. For the preservation of chronological order and for the promotion of business conveniences, the following statements were also printed as part of the regular heading: *Ein Thaler des Yahrs.* * * * *Vier Cents Einzeln* * * * *Mitwochs, den 7ten October,* 1807. * * * *Neumarket, Schenandoah County, Virginien, alle Mitwoch herausgegeben von Ambrosias Henkel.*

15. Henkel's History of the Tennessee Synod, pp. 185, 186.

The first number seems to have been intended and used as a prospectus. It was dated, as just shown, October 7, 1807, and was labeled thus: *Band I, Num. o.* The first number of the weekly series, *Band I, Num. 1,* did not appear till ten weeks later, Dec. 16, 1807. From that date the *Volksberichter* seems to have been issued regularly at weekly intervals till June 7, 1809. At that time, or shortly afterward, the publication was suspended, chiefly for the want of advertising patronage. A rather pathetic sequel to that generous declaration of youthful enthusiasm, burning with a desire for the common welfare! There may be no occasion for mentioning in this connection a rather conspicuous fact, that, as early as the eighth number, issued February 3, 1808, the American Eagle is removed from the ornamental heading; and in his place is set the picture of a man on horseback, galloping, and blowing a horn from which proceed the words, *Ich bring das Neu's! So gut ich's weis!* These several cuts, as well as many others used from time to time in his work, were engraved by Henkel himself, a fact which bears strong testimony to the remarkable versatility of the man.

As in most of the weekly journals of the period, the contents of the *Volksberichter* were made up chiefly of general and foreign news. Along with the liberal quantities of such matter, appeared a few items with local reference; some meager advertisements; and a weekly poem. If more space had been given to local happenings and to local personages, the present historical value of the paper would be much greater; but this is a truth that only the present could well appreciate; and, even as the case stands, the ancient files of this pioneer publication are wellnigh invaluable, and should be carefully guarded from the destroying forces of time.

The *Volksberichter* of 1807 may be regarded as the progenitor of other weekly periodicals issued later from the Henkel press, and continued to the present. An important member of the series was the *Spirit of Democracy*. This paper was succeeded in 1868 by the *Shenandoah Valley,* which is to-day one of the best known weeklies of northern Virginia.

The year 1819 is the date of the last German publication credited to the Henkel press by Prof. Seidensticker;[16] but I am informed by Mr. Ambrose L. Henkel that numerous other German publications were issued up to the year 1830. Since that date most of the printing has been in English.[17]

In 1851, after a devoted labor of seven years, an English translation of the Christian Book of Concord, or Symbolical Books of the Evangelical Lutheran Church, was given to the public. A second edition appeared in 1854. The official sanction for this monumental work was given at a meeting of the Lutheran Tennessee Synod held at Zion Church, Shenandoah County, Va., October 6-9, 1845. The chief mover in the enterprise was Samuel Godfrey Henkel, M. D., who supervised the process of translation from the German and Latin, and had charge of the matter as it passed through the press. Valuable assistance was rendered by Rev. Ambrose Henkel, Joseph Salyards, M. A., Rev. Socrates Henkel, and others. The second edition, which was carefully and thoroughly revised with the assistance of many eminent scholars, was brought out under the supervision of Rev. Socrates Henkel, D. D. (1823-1901), a noted author and leader in his church, and the father of the two gentlemen at present constituting the chief members of the publishing firm of Henkel and Company.[18]

Apropos, the following is quoted from a letter of August 7, 1851, written to Dr. J. A. Seiss by Dr. Charles P. Krauth:

> The New Market men have finished their translation of the Symbols, and have actually passed it through the press. The Valley of

16. First Century of German Printing, pp. 208, 252.

17. For valuable lists of books, etc., issued from the Henkel press during the period from 1807 to 1830, see articles by Rev. A. Stapleton in the Pennsylvania-German of April, 1903, and April, 1904.

18. Henkel's History of the Tennessee Synod, pp. 111, 112; 126-132; Jenson's American Lutheran Biographies; Shenandoah Valley, Supplement, July 28, 1904.

Virginia will now have the credit of having produced the most important contribution to the Lutheran Theological Literature of this country, which has yet appeared. The thing, of course, is defective, but it is nevertheless highly honorable to them. It marks a distinct era in the history of our Church in this country. They have translated Muller's Introduction also, which adds very much to the value of the work.[19]

Another brief paragraph must conclude this account of the Henkel press. Rev. G. D. Bernheim, D. D., in his History of the German Settlements and the Lutheran Church in the Carolinas, has this to say:

The Lutheran Church in America has had its publication boards and societies in abundance which have doubtless accomplished a good work; but the oldest establishment of the kind is the one in New Market, Va., dating back to 1806. It was established by the Henkel family, and has continued under their management to this day, * * * and has issued more truly Lutheran Theological works in an English dress, than any similar institution in the world.

At about the same time that Ambrose Henkel was starting the *Volksberichter* at New Market, a weekly newspaper (distinguished also for its lack of local news) was being established at Staunton. It was known as the *Staunton Eagle,* and was continued for several years. The editor was our friend of the Winchester almanac enterprise of 1805, Jacob D. Dietrich. Occasional advertisements in the German language appeared in the columns of the *Eagle;* and sometime in 1808 the editor began the publication of another paper, printed wholly in German.[20] The title of this paper is given as the *Teutscher Virginischer Adler* by Seidensticker; and of it he has the following to say:

No copy of this paper has been discovered, its existence is surmised from an advertisement in the Cincinnati Liberty Hall, March 26, 1808, kindly copied and furnished by Mr. H. A. Rattermann. The first number of the paper was to appear in January, 1808. The advertisement calls for subscribers and makes the publication of the Adler contingent on sufficient encouragement.[21]

19. Spaeth's Life of Charles P. Krauth, Vol. I, p. 194.

20. Waddell's Annals of Augusta, pp. 381, 382.

21. First Century of German Printing, p. 174.

Herr Dietrich evidently believed in advertising. Cincinnati was far west in those days. In his endeavor to circulate the *Staunton Eagle* he had agents in nearly all the Valley counties of Virginia, and in the States of Pennsylvania, Maryland, Ohio, Kentucky, Tennessee, Georgia, and South Carolina.

Inasmuch as it is evident from Prof. Seidensticker's statement that copies of this early German paper are very rare, the writer deems himself rather fortunate in having discovered a copy within the past few months—the only copy extant, so far as is at present known. An extended examination of this copy has been made, and a description in some detail will follow. From this it will be observed that Prof. Seidensticker does not give the title exactly. It will also be observed that, unless a number of issues were omitted somewhere, the publication of the *Adler* did not begin until about November 12, 1808.

The *Adler* like the *Volksberichter,* was in the ordinary four-page form; but it had four columns to the page, and each page was ten inches wide and eighteen inches from top to bottom. The following simple diagram will give a fair idea of the first page of the issue examined. [See next page.]

The second page completes the account of the battle of Wagram, and begins a number of general and foreign news notes from various cities: (1) London, September 4, 6, 7; (2) Boston, October 18; (3) Philadelphia, November 7; (4) New York, November 1; (5) Foreign news, from New York; (6) Foreign News, from Boston, October 10, 14.

It was reported from Philadelphia that the U. S. war sloop *Wasp* had just arrived at New York from the Orient. There is also a note concerning the U. S. schooner *Enterprise,* at Amsterdam.

These news items end on page 3; then follow Editorial Notes, Advertisements, and a list of 62 unclaimed letters remaining in the Harrisonburg postoffice, September 30, 1809. They were to be kept until the 30th of December; then all still uncalled for were to be forwarded as dead letters to the

1809) (Numro 54.

Der Deutsche Virginier Adler

"Wo Freyheit bluhet, da ist mein Vaterland."

Samstag, den.. 18ten November.

Staunton, (Virginien.)

Gedruckt und herausgegeben von Jacob D. Dietrich.

Markt Preise.

Fur den Virginier Adler Wochentlich verbeszert.

Richmond.

....

....

....

Friderichsburg.

. ...

....

....

Baltimore.

....

....

....

Philadelphia.

....

....

....

Bedingungen
dieser Zeitung.

1. "Der Deutsche Virginier Adler" wird regelmaszig alle Samstag, auf einem ganzen Bogen Demey Papier, mit guten Schriften herausgegeben werden.

2. Der geringe Preisz von dieser Zeitung ist Ein Thaler und 50 Cents das Yahr.—Ein Thaler wird beym Empfang der ersten Nummer, und 50 Cents nach Verlauf des ersten halben Jahrs im voraus bezahlt.

3. ....

4. ....

5. ....

6. ....

7. ....

Auswartig.

Angabe
vom ostreichischen Territorium Besitz der Franzosen.

Ueber den Gegenstand eines Friedens zwischen Bonaparte und dem KaiserFranz, lauten die Geruchte noch immer widersprechend. ....

[End.]

Die Anrede

seiner Heiligkeit Pius der Siebente, an den Kaiser Bonaparte.

[End.]

Die Niederlage von Wagram hat unter den osterreichischen ......

Folgende Tagesordnung wurde am Morgen nach der Schlacht von Wagram offentlich bekant gemacht.

Tages Ordnung.
Goellersdorf,
den 7ten July.

In der gestrigen Schlacht haben die Truppen des linken Flugels keinesweges die Erwartung vollfuhrt,.. ....

[A long and interesting account, pointing out the conditions that led to the defeat.

This official paper is signed, "Karl, Generalissimus."

The account runs into the second page.]

general postoffice.[22] About one-third of page 4 is devoted to poetry and anecdotes; the rest to advertisements, two book notices, and items concerning property lost and found. The books advertised were Thomas à Kempis' "Imitation of Christ" and a Life of Heinrich Stilling. The former was for sale at Lancaster, Pa., by Hamilton & Ehrenfried; the latter at Lebanon by Heinrich Sage. Another advertiser was Henrich Speck, Saddler, of Waynesboro, Va. The two notices following were put in his paper by the publisher, Mr. Dietrich, and are given here to show that his business must have been growing.

An Drucker.

Ein Drucker Geselle wird in dieser Druckerey verlangt.

Ein solche, welcher ein guter Arbeiter und willig ist, am Kasten und an der Presse zu Arbeiten, wird guten Lohn und bestandige Arbeit bekommen. Ein solcher der Bucharbeit versteht, und der englischen und deutschen Sprache machtig ist, wird den Vorzug haben. Briefe die mit der Post geshickt werden, und worauf das Postgeld bezahlt ist, sollen sogleich besorgt werden.[23]

An Buchbinder.

Ein Buchbinder, Geselle, welcher sein Geschaft versteht, nuchtern und fleissig ist, wird den hochsten Lohn und bestandige Arbeit erhalten, wenn er sich in dieser Druckerey personnlich oder schriftlich (Briefe Postfrey) meldet.

Staunton, Octb. 7, 1809.

Upon the margin of the first page of this copy of the *Adler* is written a name, illegible now, but doubtless that of the subscriber of a hundred years ago. This rare old print is at present in the possession of Prof. F. W. Walter, of Staunton; and it was through his painstaking and generous kindness that the writer was enabled to prepare the foregoing description.

Sometime during the first or second decade of last century,

22. The names of the persons to whom these letters were addressed are given in Appendix A.

23. Postage in those days was a considerable item. This fact will doubtless account in some measure for the large number of unclaimed letters in the postoffices.

Laurentz R. Wartmann established a printing house at Harrisonburg, Va. Beginning as early as 1816—perhaps earlier —a number of German books and pamphlets, religious publications for the most part, were issued at frequent intervals from this press. Elder Peter Burkholder, the Mennonite, Elder Peter Bowman, the Dunker, and Rev. John Brown, the German Reformed, were among the authors of these works. Several of their publications will be found listed in the appended bibliography. Brown's important volume of 1818 has already been referred to in the chapter on religious activities, and will be noticed again in the following chapter, in connection with the subject of slavery.

In the summer of 1822 Wartmann founded a weekly newspaper, which, although it was printed in English from the beginning, deserves a prominent notice here; inasmuch as it was founded by a German publisher, has been in charge during the greater part of its history of German editors, and has always had a large patronage among the German people of Rockingham and adjoining counties. The periodical referred to is the well-known *Rockingham Register*; which, like the *Shenandoah Valley* (New Market), the *Shenandoah Herald* (Woodstock), the *Spirit of the Valley* (Harrisonburg), and the *Staunton Spectator,* has come deservedly into the honors of old age without losing any of the vigor of youth; and throughout its long and busy career has done much to collect, preserve, and disseminate the history of the Valley people, irrespective of race or creed. The *Register* remained in the hands of the Wartmann family for about fifty years; then it was purchased by Giles Devier and others, who conducted it until the spring of 1900, when it came into the possession of Mr. A. H. Snyder. In the spring of 1903 it became a semi-weekly, published by the News-Register Company, Harrisburg. Mr. Snyder has been the efficient editor of the *Register* since 1889. It has been published continuously since 1822, excepting brief periods of interruption during the Civil War.

Two more important publishing centers of the Valley Germans, both in Rockingham County, must receive attention in this review: the one at Singer's Glen, conducted by the Funks; the other at Dayton, directed by the Ruebush-Kieffer Company.

The little village of Singer's Glen, or Mountain Valley, as it was known in earlier days, situated in the western part of Rockingham, was for nearly half a century the source of authority and inspiration in the practice and theory of vocal music, not only for the great majority of the people in the Shenandoah Valley, but also for many beyond its borders. In addition to their achievements in music, the teachers of Singer's Glen were more or less eminent in religious literature. Joseph Funk, the leader in these activities, was born in Berks County, Pa., in 1778. He came to Rockingham County at an early age, and lived there till his death in 1862. In 1837 he translated from the German into English an important work of his church, the Mennonite Confession of Faith, with nine Reflections written by Eld. Peter Burkholder. This translation, with an extended and valuable historical introduction, written by himself, he published the same year in a volume of 460 pages. Ten years later (1847), he founded a printing establishment at Singer's Glen, which was the first Mennonite printing office in America. From this press, which was operated later by the firm of Joseph Funk's Sons, were issued numerous volumes, chiefly music books, written by the Funks themselves. Their most famous work was the "Harmonia Sacra," a large collection of sacred songs, with accompanying music, published first in 1832, and still used, in connection with a hymn book also published by the Funks, by some Mennonite congregations to-day. The "Harmonia Sacra," was first printed at Winchester; afterwards at Singer's Glen. One edition followed another till the later 70's. By that time seventeen editions, aggregating many thousands of copies, had been put forth.

In the meantime Joseph Funk and his sons, Joseph, Timothy,[24] Solomon, and Benjamin, were traveling literally all over the Shenandoah Valley, as well as throughout many sections of Piedmont Virginia, teaching: making a specialty of vocal music, but also giving instruction in other branches of study. Pupils also came to Singer's Glen, and went away with new stores of knowledge and inspiration. Joseph Funk did in his day, considering the obscure hamlet in which he lived and the limitations of his time, a work no less remarkable and no less telling than that of his illustrious kinsman[25] of the present day, who has, by reason of modern science, the powers of the sea and earth and air at his command.

In 1865 Aldine Stillman Kieffer (1840-1904), a grandson of Joseph Funk, came back from the wars and Northern prisons to the girlhood home of his mother, and joined with his uncles at Singer's Glen in building up again what the four years of storm and fire had wellnigh ruined. In a year or two was published a little yellow, paper-backed book, containing hymns and music, and called the "Christian Harp." A worn copy is before me as I write. There are only 112 pages, four and a half inches by six. Young Kieffer, poet and musician, was the editor. The book had a phenomenal sale, more then a hundred thousand copies going out within a comparatively brief period. About ten years later, Mr. Kieffer published another one of his numerous books—the best known of all—the "Temple Star." This is still being printed, and over a quarter of a million copies have been sold.

In 1878 the printing establishment of Singer's Glen was moved some ten miles south to Dayton; and Mr. Ephraim Ruebush, who in 1861 had married a sister to Kieffer, joined

24. On January 26, 1907, an "old-time singing" was held at Singer's Glen, in celebration of Mr. Timothy Funk's birthday, upon the completion of his 83d year. The old "Harmonia Sacra" was used; the old songs were sung; and the old singers were there—some, perhaps, for the last time.—See Harrisonburg Daily News, January 28, 1907.

25. Rev. Isaac K. Funk, D. D., LL. D., senior member of the firm of Funk & Wagnalls.—See Funk Family History, pp. 289, 290; 712; 758-760.

with the latter in organizing the publishing house of Ruebush, Kieffer & Company—at present well known as the Ruebush-Kieffer Company. Mr. Ruebush had been associated with Mr. Kieffer and the rest at Singer's Glen for several years prior to the removal to Dayton; so that the two publishing centers must be closely associated in thought, as they actually have been in fact: the one being the outgrowth or development of the other.

The work begun at Singer's Glen is now going on and still growing at Dayton. On January 1, 1870, Mr. Kieffer established at the former place a monthly journal called the *Musical Million;* this is now published at Dayton, with a circulation of 10,000 copies, distributed mostly in Virginia and the Southern States; and is believed to be the oldest music journal in the country. The *Musical Million* was preceded at no great interval by the *Musical Advocate,* which was published at Singer's Glen, beginning in 1858.

Inasmuch as the publishing activities at both Singer's Glen and Dayton have always been powerfully stimulated by religious interests, it may be well at this point to note succinctly the several prevailing tendencies of this sort. Joseph Funk, the elder, was a Mennonite, as we have seen; and his work, with the rights to certain of his publications, may be regarded as having been transmitted, through individuals bearing his own family name, to the present Mennonite Publishing Company of Elkhart, Ind. Several of Joseph Funk's sons, who conducted the later publishing work at Singer's Glen, have been ministers and influential leaders in the Baptist denomination. The present Ruebush-Kieffer Company is controlled mainly by members of the United Brethren church.

It has been observed already that Aldine Kieffer was not only a musician, but also a poet. In the latter capacity he is probably the leading representative of the Valley Germans; and of his talent they may justly be proud. Many of his lyrics, as, for example, "Olden Memories" and "Grave on the Green Hill Side," have touched thousands of hearts; and in his collection of poems, "Hours of Fancy: or, Vigil and Vision," are many more songs that have a music of their own.

Before closing this sketch of the educational and literary activities of the Valley of Virginia Germans, two significant facts, whose relation to the subject in hand has been intimate, and whose influence has been necessarily potent, must be mentioned.

In his able presentation of the historical development of German instruction in American schools, Hon. L. Viereck has this to say:

> The second epoch [1825-1876] begins with the appointment of a German professor [Blaettermann] to the chair of modern languages in the newly founded University of Virginia and the important step of permitting Prof. Charles Follen to teach his mother tongue at Harvard.[26]

At the opening of the University of Virginia in 1825, sixty-four of the 116 students took German from the beginning. Dr. Blaettermann held his position for some fifteen years. In 1844, Dr. M. Schele de Vere, another German, on his mother's side, was elected to the same chair, and was a prominent figure in the University's life for about half a century. In 1854-5 the department of modern languages enrolled 200 men.[27] During all these years, three-quarters of a century or more, many students from the Shenandoah Valley, a goodly number of them of German blood, must have sat at the feet of Blaettermann and De Vere; and they doubtless carried back to their homes west of the Blue Ridge a subtle something that enabled them the better to stimulate and direct the thought and sentiment of their own people.

The second fact of significance to be mentioned here—a fact that bears a double relation, both resultant and causal, to this particular phase of our subject—is this: The first Virginia State Superintendent of Public Instruction was Dr. William

26. Report of Commissioner of Education, 1901, Vol. I, p. 538.

27. Idem, p. 552.

H. Ruffner, a member of one of the oldest German families of the Shenandoah Valley. Dr. Ruffner was elected to this important and trying position in 1870, over numerous competitors; and during the twelve years of his public service in this capacity did a work that also deserves to be called epoch-making.

Mr. Ruffner's father, Dr. Henry Ruffner, was born in 1790 on the Hawksbill Creek, a mile from the present town of Luray, near the site where his ancestor, Peter Ruffner, had settled in 1739. Dr. Henry Ruffner was for nearly a generation officially connected with Washington College, now Washington and Lee University; and was for a number of years its president. He was a man of unusual powers: a skilled executive, a convincing orator, and an author of remarkable force and versatility. His novel, "Judith Bensaddi," went through several editions;[28] and his pamphlet of 1847 on slavery is a classic in its field. Dr. William H. Ruffner, now a venerable citizen of Lexington, Va., must have inherited many of his father's powers. The work he has done for public schools will tell for generations all over Virginia. He has been called, no doubt justly, the "Horace Mann of the South."[29] Of his own stock, the Valley Germans, he has said: "They are the leaders in popular education [in Virginia]. They have in fact a great future before them."[30]

28. Washington and Lee Historical Papers, No. 6, p. 107.

29. U. S. Educational Report, 1895-6, Vol. I, p. 270.

30. Schuricht's German Element, Vol. II, p. 134.

CHAPTER XI.

Rum and Slavery.

A writer in the *Pennsylvania Magazine of History and Biography,* Vol. X, page 390, asserts that, of all the nationalities of the Middle Colonies, the early Germans were least addicted to the use of rum and malt liquor. This statement has a rather odd sound in ears accustomed to hear much concerning the bibulous institutions and habits of modern Germans. Perhaps it may be, however, that much beer is by some feat of the imagination transformable into little liquor. But whatever may be the real state of affairs among the German race as a whole to day, or whatever may have been the condition in the Middle Colonies a century or two ago, it is the writer's opinion that the German element of the Shenandoah Valley may justly be regarded as a people who have always been somewhat above the average in the practice of temperance. This conclusion has been reached in a full consciousness of the painful exceptions afforded in numerous individual cases; and it may be that a census of our cities and larger towns might appear to disprove the statement; for many Germans would be found who keep saloons, and many more who patronize them immoderately; but if the census were made to include the smaller towns, villages, and rural districts, results strikingly different would likely be obtained. It would doubtless be possible to name at the present time a half dozen or more towns, whose population would average a thousand, in which no liquor is publicly sold; in some of which there has been no saloon for a generation; and in one or two of which there has never been one.

Another proposition is now ventured forth. If it be true that the Valley Germans have been somewhat above the average in temperance, it is the writer's opinion that the fact is not so because they came from Pennsylvania or some other middle colony, or even because they are Germans; but because of the strong and persistent influence of definite moral and religious teaching. The people of the Valley of Virginia have not enjoyed any universal immunity in respect to that particular and decided craving called thirst; if, therefore, they have done any better in subduing or disregarding it than others have done, it has been accomplished by means of hard struggle and fixed purpose. Traffic and traffickers in rum sought early and even illegal entrance, and have never ceased their troubling even yet. As early as 1745 Jacob Chrisman, a German, and a son-in-law of Jost Hite, was fined 2000 pounds of tobacco for keeping a tippling house and for retailing liquors without a license.[1]

In support of the statement that the any more than usual degree of temperance which may have existed or may exist among the Valley Germans is due mainly to religious influences, attention is called to the fact that several religious bodies, whose membership is found chiefly in communities prevailingly German, and at the same time prevailingly temperate, have always maintained a decided attitude against rum in all forms. The converse is also believed to be true: that the most intemperate communities are not only the ones least in touch with these anti-liquor sects, but also least under the influence of any religious denomination.

Of the several religious bodies largely represented in the Valley, the Mennonites and Dunkers have perhaps maintained the most uncompromising attitude in regard to the liquor traffic and other aids to intemperance. So far as can be ascertained, no Mennonite in the State of Virginia has ever been a saloon keeper or a distiller. Instances are reported in which, in the "earlier days," distillers were patronized by members of the church in the way of hauling to them surplus stores of apples; but the practice was always unusual; and,

1. Norris' History of the Lower Valley, p. 84.

upon protest from the Conference, it has long since been abandoned altogether.[2]

The German Baptist Brethren, or Dunkers, have been no less decided in this matter. As appears from the records of the annual meetings, some trouble was experienced by the Brotherhood in Maryland and Pennsylvania, during the period of the Revolution, due to attempts upon the part of some members of the church to run distilleries. At that early period, however, the body put in the form of definite declarations the rules of conduct long before regarded as obligatory, and has enforced them with general consistency ever since. By specific regulation from time to time, members of the church have not only been enjoined against intemperate indulgence in liquors and against their manufacture or sale, but they have also been forbidden to keep a tavern, if that would put them in the way of temptation; to work in distilleries for wages; to chop in their mills grain to be used in distilleries; to sell fruit or grain to distillers; to go security for dealers in liquor.[3]

It might be supposed that so much legislation would defeat its own aim; but it has been supported by such a strong moral and religious conviction that the cases of transgression in these particulars by members of the fraternity have been very rare. The church regards itself as unqualifiedly pledged to temperance by virtue of its religious profession; and hence has never regarded the organization of special temperance societies by its members as necessary or advisable. A similar attitude, less decided, is maintained respecting the use and handling of tobacco.

As a general rule, the Germans of the Shenandoah Valley were opposed to slavery. It would be possible to enumerate many instances in which individuals among them owned slaves, but such cases were exceptional. Moreover, some of the principals in these cases had had the practice thrust upon

2. From a letter of Nov. 4, 1906, from Bishop L. J. Heatwole.

3. Revised Minutes of Annual Meetings, pp. 158-162.

them largely by the force of circumstances, and endured it unwillingly. They no doubt realized in time the unpopularity of such an attitude, and the small opportunities they would accordingly enjoy for preferment in the larger political life of the State; but they nevertheless never became in any great numbers zealous advocates of the institution. Many of them, as we have seen, fought valiantly in the Southern armies when the civil strife came on; but not many of them fought to perpetuate slavery, we may well believe.

If we seek the reasons for this antagonism to slavery, they are found easily enough in certain small circles; but it is more difficult to determine why the Germans as a race assumed this attitude; for such opposition does appear to have been so general among them that we may almost say it amounted to a national sentiment. Wherever in the land the German element was strongest, there was found the strongest anti-slavery feeling. At the time that American independence was achieved, and even before, opposition to slavery was wellnigh universal in the colonies; but it was in Pennsylvania, the home of the Germans, that the crusade centered;[4] and the slavery existing there at the time is said to have been of a very mild form.[5] The German immigrants of later times, specially those of 1848, were opposed to slavery almost to a man.[6] Many of them fought in the Northern armies chiefly for the reason that they opposed the institution; while but few among their race-fellows under the Southern flag fought for it. There must have been something in the Teutonic temperament, deep-seated and ineradicable, that revolted at the sight or thought of human chattels. It may be that the persecution and oppression that drove many of them out of Europe had left a smoldering fire within them that blazed up anew in the presence of chains.

4. Hurst's Short History of the Church in the United States, p. 96.
5. Pennsylvania-German Society Publications, Vol. V, p. 26.
6. Report of Commissioner of Education, 1901, Vol. I, p. 562.

If we confine our attention to the Germans of the Shenandoah Valley, we may more readily enumerate causes for the conditions already remarked upon. In the first place, the Germans in that locality had the sentiment or whatever it was that seemed to belong to the race. In the second place, they had come from Pennsylvania, most of them, and consequently had their prejudices strengthened by that circumstance. Again, most of them, at least in the early days, were skilled workmen, small farmers, or tradesmen with limited business, and did not need help beyond that available in their own families. A few of them were doubtless able to judge of the social and economic effects of slavery, and hence to supply themselves with a fourth reason for opposing it. Finally, and perhaps most potent of all, there was the teaching of the churches. There was scarcely one denomination with any considerable membership among the Valley Germans that did not at some time make official protest against the buying and selling of negroes; and on the part of several of these religious bodies the measures were most persistent and decided.

As early as 1688 the Mennonites in Pennsylvania appear to have joined with the Quakers in a formal protest against the traffic in slaves.[7] They looked upon the owning of slaves and the trading in them as a breach upon their creed and discipline; and even the hiring of a slave was forbidden by their general conference.[8] The early United Brethren were exceedingly strict on the same subject. No member of the church was allowed to hold slaves. Bishop Glossbrenner, in enforcing this rule, is said to have expelled from membership his own father-in-law, one of the best citizens of Augusta County.[9]

In the year 1818, Rev. John Brown, who was for many

7. Hartzler and Kauffman's Mennonite Church History, pp. 396-398; Seidensticker's Die Erste Deutsche Einwanderung, pp. 80-84; Hurst's Short History of the Church, pp. 95, 96.

8. From a letter of Nov. 4, 1906, by Bishop L. J. Heatwole.

9. Harrisonburg Daily News, March 21, 1905.

years a leader of the German Reformed church in Rockingham and Augusta, published a well bound volume, already referred to, of 419 pages; and in it he devotes a section of 95 pages to the institution of slavery, favoring its abolition. He admits that he can find no ground of condemnation in the institution itself; nevertheless he thinks it hinders the spirit of Christianity, and enquires whether Christians, therefore, can in good conscience hold slaves. In the fourth place he discusses ways and means of liberating slaves, calling attention to propositions advanced on the subject by St. George Tucker and Thomas Jefferson. While he does not apparently commit himself to any specific method of procedure, he seems to recommend a selection and combination of the approved features in the various plans, so as to accomplish the end gradually and appropriately.[10]

The Dunkers were no less opposed to slavery, upon religious principle, than the Mennonites and United Brethren; and they no less consistently adhered to a practical enforcement of their beliefs. The Lutheran Tennessee Synod, a body having a strong constituency in the Valley of Virginia, put itself upon record in 1822, as follows: When a member present asked the question, "Is slavery to be considered an evil?" the Synod in reply resolved, "That it is to be regarded as a great evil in our land, and it desires the government, if it be possible, to devise some way by which this evil can be removed." The Synod also advised every minister to admonish every master to treat his slaves properly, and to exercise his Christian duties towards them.[11]

But the Germans, while taking an advanced and decided position against slavery, were not wholly without support upon the side of their neighbors, the Scotch-Irish, who appear to have been tolerant of it rather than its adherents. Mr. Waddell says: "The institution of slavery never had a strong hold upon the people of Augusta. The Scotch-Irish race had

10. Brown's Circular, pp. 278-373.

11. Henkel's History of the Tennessee Synod, p. 52.

no love for it, and the German people were generally adverse to it. Most farmers cultivated their own lands with the assistance of their sons."[12] In 1831-2 several petitions praying for the abolition of slavery, one signed by 215 ladies, were sent up to the State legislature from Augusta County.[13]

Of all the protests or arguments against slavery, made from the standpoint of the statesman and political economist, none was more able or convincing than the one presented to the people of western Virginia in 1847 by Dr. Henry Ruffner. Dr. Ruffner, as has been noted in the preceding chapter, was born of German parentage in what is now Page County, Virginia. His ancestors, at least on his mother's side, were Mennonites; but he had entered the communion and ministry of the Presbyterian church, and was at this time president of Washington College, at Lexington, Va. In a public debate in Lexington, Dr. Ruffner had given expression to anti-slavery views, though he was himself a slaveholder. Shortly afterwards he was requested by a number of leading citizens to publish his arguments.[14] This request was formally presented in writing on September 1, 1847, and was signed by the following gentlemen: S. McD. Moore, John Letcher, David P. Curry, James G. Hamilton, George A. Baker, J. H. Lacy, John Echols, James R. Jordan, Jacob Fuller, Jr., D. E. Moore, and John W. Fuller. Three days later Dr. Ruffner replied, agreeing to do as requested, and proposing some amplifications and revisions. With these improvements, the address was published in a forty-page pamphlet before the end of the year.

Dr. Ruffner, as already noted, himself held slaves; moreover, he detested the newly-risen fanatics called Abolitionists; yet he argued strongly against slavery upon the following propositions: (1) That it was driving away immigration; (2) that it was driving out white laborers; (3) that it was

12. Annals of Augusta, pp. 414, 415.

13. Ibid.

14. Of the population of Rockbridge County in 1840, 3510 in 14,284, or slightly over 24½ per cent., were slaves.

crippling agriculture, commerce, and manufactures; (4) that it was detrimental to common schools and popular education; and (5) that it was imposing hurtful social ideals upon the people.

He did not wish to interfere with slavery in eastern Virginia, if the majority of the people there preferred it; but he wanted to eliminate it from the section west of the Blue Ridge. The best way to reach all desirable ends he thought to be the division of the State along the Blue Ridge line; but thought it not impossible to obtain the desired results in a rational and political way without the division of the State. He planned for gradual emancipation; for deportation and colonization.

Basing his statements chiefly upon the U. S. Census of 1840, Dr. Ruffner declared that the slave population of eastern Virginia, dividing on the crest of the Blue Ridge, was eight times as large as that west of the line. In western Virginia at large, he said, the slaves were only one-eighth of the population, and the slave-holding population less than one-eighth of the whites.

Following is the outline of his plan for getting gradually rid of slavery in the western section of the State.

1. Let the farther importation of slaves into West Virginia be prohibited by law.

2. Let the exportation of slaves be freely permitted, as heretofore; but with this restriction, that children of slaves, born after a certain day, shall not be exported at all after they are five years old, nor those under that age, unless the slaves of the same negro family be exported with them.

3. Let the existing generation of slaves remain in their present condition, but let their offspring, born after a certain day, be emancipated at an age not exceeding 25 years.

4. Let masters be required to have the heirs of emancipation taught reading, writing and arithmetic: and let churches and benevolent people attend to their religious instruction.

5. Let the emancipated be colonized. [The freedmen were to labor in advance for the funds necessary for their transportation.]

6. The law might authorize the people of any county, by some very large majority, or by consent of a majority of the slaveholders,

to decree the removal or emancipation of all the slaves of the county, within a certain term of years, seven, ten or fifteen, according to the number of slaves.[15]

Ruffner's plan bears a close resemblance in many respects to one proposed by Henry Clay, and certainly would have been a wise and practicable measure; but the passions of the time were rising, and soon they clouded men's better judgment.

To illustrate further the status of slavery in the Valley counties, and to confirm certain foregoing statements as to the anti-slavery influence of the Germans, the following figures, prepared from the census of 1840, are presented.

Name of County.	Total Population.	Number of Slaves.	Percentage of Slaves.
Clarke	6,353	3,325	c. 52⅓
Jefferson	14,082	4,157	c. 29½
Percentage of Slaves of Clarke and Jefferson, about 36½.			
Augusta	19,628	4,145	c. 21
Berkeley	10,972	1,919	c. 17½
Frederick	14,242	2,302	c. 16 1-6
Warren	5,627	1,434	c. 25½
Percentage of Slaves in these Four Counties, about 19½.			
Page	6,194	781	c. 12½
Rockingham	17,344	1,899	c. 11
Shenandoah	11,618	1,033	c. 9
Percentage of Slaves in these Three Counties, about 10½.			

It will be observed that in the counties of Clarke and Jefferson, which have always been prevailingly English, the percentage of slaves was very high. In the counties of Augusta, Berkeley, Frederick, and Warren, in three of which the German element has been estimated to approach or to equal one-half of the white population, the percentage of slaves was much lower; and in Page, Rockingham, and Shenandoah, where the white population was probably three-fourths German, the percentage of slaves was very low.

A few additional comparisons may be interesting. In the

15. Ruffner's Pamphlet, pp. 38-40.—Copies of this once famous publication are now very rare. The only one known to be extant is in the possession of Dr. W. H. Ruffner, of Lexington; and it was through his generous kindness that access to it was secured.

seven Valley counties of Augusta, Berkeley, Frederick, Page, Rockingham, Shenandoah, and Warren—excluding Clarke and Jefferson—the percentage of slaves in 1840 was about 15¾. In the four counties, Albemarle, Orange, Madison, and Culpeper, lying just east of the Blue Ridge, the percentage was over 57. In the three partly German counties of Hampshire, Hardy, and Pendleton, lying just west of the Valley, the percentage of slaves was about 11 1-6; while in the six counties of Rockbridge, Greenbrier, Alleghany, Kanawha, Mason, and Monroe—some of them lying far west—the percentage was nearly 17½.

How have these conditions affected the Shenandoah Valley? In many ways; but in no way, perhaps, has the effect been shown more strikingly than in the rapid and complete recovery of the section from the protracted devastation of the Civil War. The Valley was a highway of marching armies and an almost constant battlefield, from the beginning to the end. When the end came conditions may not have been quite so bad as some of its enemies desired: a crow could perhaps have found a few pickings here and there, especially if he had been of the vulture species; but the ruin was certainly complete enough. On October 7, 1864, Sheridan at Woodstock reported to Grant that he had destroyed over 2000 barns filled with wheat, hay, and farming implements; over 70 mills, filled with wheat and flour; that four herds of cattle had been driven away before the army; that no less than 3000 sheep had been killed and issued to the troops; and that a large number of horses had been secured. Near Dayton and Harrisonburg he had burned all the houses in an area of five miles.[16]

No wonder some of the people had to go out of the country, or from one locality to another, for a time, to keep from starving. And yet, in less than a generation afterward, a native of Rockingham, who had returned to his boyhood

16. Peyton's History of Augusta, p. 239.

home, and had climbed to the top of Peaked Mountain to get a wide horizon, could write as follows:

> As I stood aloft gazing down on this prosperous valley, with its winding waterways and fertile meadow lands dotted thickly over with comfortable farmhouses and massive barns, with here and there a thriving town or village, I could but call up in contrast the devastated wastes left lying here on my departure in 1869. * * * Time and industry have prevailed; and, looking upon the present scenes of plenty and happy prosperity, without a knowledge of what has been, one would never dream of any time other than a thriving and peaceful one for the great Valley of Virginia.[17]

This remarkable and rapid recovery of the Shenandoah Valley has doubtless been due in large measure to the fact that the bulk of the losses that the people suffered during the war, aside from the long death-roll, was in property other than slaves; and to the fact that, apart from such material losses and sadly depleted numbers, they came out of the conflict much as they had entered it: taught in the habits of economy and with hands hardened to labor.

17. From the Tuscola (Ill.) Review, December 6, 1895.

CHAPTER XII.

Home Life and Industrial Habits.

A great deal of more or less interest might be written under this head; but inasmuch as the subject has already been treated at length in other publications,[1] the present writer feels somewhat relieved from the responsibility of an extended discussion, and shall therefore confine himself chiefly to those phases of the question that may be less familiar than others. Moreover, most of the accounts referred to deal with conditions as they existed a century or more ago; so that this discussion may be allowed the more freely to extend into the present time.

It has already appeared with sufficient clearness that the German pioneers followed the chief watercourses of the Shenandoah Valley, and fixed their settlements for the most part on or near the fertile bottom lands along the larger streams. In these localities the soil was most productive and most easily worked; and the lay of the land was generally most desirable. At many places there would be a wide bottom on one side of the river, sweeping out in an almost level expanse for a mile or more, even though on the opposite side of the stream, at that particular point, there might be an abrupt bluff. Frequently, too, there was but little timber to clear away on these broad levels. Along the banks of the stream there were always trees of a larger or smaller growth; but it is quite probable that many of the best lowlands were still largely prairie. After the bottom lands along the rivers were all taken up, the

1. For a comparison of life, several generations ago, in western Virginia with life in eastern Virginia, see Howe's Antiquities, pp. 152-160. For an interesting sketch of the manners and customs of the Pennsylvania farmers in the 18th century, see Kuhns' German and Swiss Settlements, pp. 83-114. For the best and fullest discussion of primitive home life in the Shenandoah Valley, see Kercheval's History of the Valley, pp. 151-155; 266-286.

settlers of course pushed out and selected the best of what remained; and here again they were often able to get rich tracts, bordering on the smaller streams. The great majority of the early dwellings were built within easy reach of running water. Besides other advantages, such a location was most convenient for watering the farmer's horses, hogs, cattle, sheep,[2] and poultry. In nearly every case the house of the early settler was built near a spring. This circumstance, when explained, will afford very satisfactory reasons why so few of the old houses were built on hills, and why nearly all of them were erected in hollows or on the low grounds near the streams. It may be that this habit of building near a spring was in part an ancient inheritance; for Tacitus wrote of their fathers, many centuries ago, as follows:

> The Germans do not dwell in cities, and do not build their houses close together. They dwell apart and separate, where a spring or patch of level ground or a grove may attract them. Their villages are not built compactly, as ours are, but each house is surrounded by a clear space.

But there were more modern reasons for building near a spring. The pioneers no doubt feared trouble with the Indians from the beginning; and it was not long till the fear was realized. When a house or fort—and many of the houses were built for forts or in connection with a blockhouse—was attacked, or laid under seige, it was very necessary to be able to get water easily and abundantly. And therefore many of the houses were built, not only near to springs and streams, but often right over them. The oldest house standing in Harrisonburg to-day,—a limestone structure built before the Revolution,—has under it a fine spring. If a house was not built actually over a spring, it was frequently connected with one by a covered or underground passage. Recently in excavating for the foundation of a building, not far from the old stone house just mentioned, such an under-

2. The writer is quite familiar with the popular superstition that sheep do not need any water to speak of; but he also knows quite well that they do drink frequently if they have the opportunity.

ground way was found. The old Burtner house at Dayton, which was used in early times as a fort, was connected in this manner with a spring near by; and both the house and spring are within a few rods of Cook's Creek. If there had been no other reason, the thrifty German would likely have built his house near a spring merely in order to save the labor and expense of digging a well.

In the construction of their houses the early settlers usually followed a style that was more or less uniform in all essential features, allowing for some variety in minor particulars. Most of the first dwellings were doubtless mere cabins, log huts, of one or two rooms on the ground floor and a bare loft overhead; but it was not long till larger and better structures —occasionally of limestone, but generally of logs—were erected; and of this class a few still remain. In building with logs, the timbers, usually of yellow pine and frequently huge boles a foot and a half in diameter, were cut in proper lengths and hewn flat with a broad-axe on two opposite sides. They were then built up into the desired structure, and held in place by great notches, fitting from one log to another in a sort of dovetail fashion, at the corners of the building. The spaces between the round edges of the logs would be filled with blocks and mortar. Sometimes, however, the logs would be hewn square, so as to fit down solidly one upon another. In such cases but little mortar was needed to close every crevice.

Usually but few openings for windows and doors were cut through the massive walls, and such as were made were generally small and at some distance above the ground. The joists supporting the floors and the rafters supporting the roof were also hewn out of the durable yellow pine, and were often heavy and strong enough to support a railroad train. In shape, the house was a simple rectangle in nearly every case: not many unnecessary corners were made. Frequently a kitchen of one story was built adjacent to one side or end of the dwelling. Usually in the center of the main structure was a great stone chimney, often eight or ten feet in diameter at the bottom, and big enough on the garret to hide an ox. Into the lower parts of this huge chimney would be built wide fire-places, and sometimes a cavernous bake-oven.

But the early German farmers did not expend all their resources on their houses. In fact, these were often rather badly neglected until substantial outbuildings—particularly a barn—had been provided. These barns were generally built of hewn timbers, and were often immense structures, even in very early times. At a later period more of them came to be built of stone and brick, as well as of sawed timber; but the size of them has constantly increased rather than diminished. It is likely that most of the earliest barns were built up solidly, with both the side walls straight from the ground to the eaves, like many of more recent times; but it was probably not long after the assured settlement of the country until some were built in the style that now prevails almost universally, and that has been generally in use for several generations. The particular style referred to is known as the "Switzer" or "Swisher" barn. In no part of the country can more of these be seen at the present than in the German communities in the Valley counties of Shenandoah, Rockingham, and Augusta, unless it be in the German sections of Maryland and Pennsylvania. These barns are rectangular structures from 30 to 60 feet wide, and from 40 to 120 feet long. They may be said to consist usually of three stories. The building site is generally chosen on a hillside sloping toward the east or southeast, where a sort of cellar is first excavated: the one side toward the hill being four or five feet deep, the other coming out flush with the downward slope. Inside of three sides of this excavation a strong wall, about six or seven feet high, is next erected: but the wall on the fourth side—the one facing down the hill—is built only a few inches or a foot above the ground. Upon this low side wall a heavy sill is laid, and upon it are set stout vertical timbers reaching up to the level of the higher walls. Thus far we have what may be called the first story of the barn: the place for the stables of horses, cattle, and sheep, with long passage ways for feeding the stock. Upon the short upright timbers is laid another long, heavy sill, reaching from one end of the building to the other. This sill, together with the end walls and the wall at the other side, affords a strong and steady foundation for the superstructure, which protrudes over the first story, towards the lower side of the slope, some six or eight feet. This extension is called the "overshoot." It projects over a part of the barnyard, and shelters the entrances to the stables in the first story, or basement. We see the reason now for the strong timbers in the substructure on the side toward the barnyard: this side of the foundation has to be an actual fulcrum for the long beams that lie across it and extend beyond it to support the overshoot.

The second or main floor, above the stables and extending over the barnyard the width of the overshoot, is divided into three sections: a wide mow for hay or grain at either end, and a threshing-floor, single or double, in the center. With a little filling in of stones and earth on the side of the barn towards the hill, an approach or driveway is easily made into the barn floors. Upon these floors heavy wagons loaded with hay or grain, and drawn frequently by four or more horses, are driven. At the threshing season the machine is rolled upon the barn floors, and connected by a long belt with the engine outside. Before the days of threshing machines, the grain was spread upon the floors and beaten out with flails, or tramped out by driving a number of horses round and round upon it. A granary is frequently built in one of the mows, at one side of the barn floor. Sometimes, in large barns, there is a granary at each side of the floor. When barns were smaller and fewer, and enemies more frequent, some of the old Germans had granaries in their attics.

The third story of the Switzer barn is frequently made by laying joists from sill to sill across the center floors, and thus making an overhead mow for storing hay or grain. The great side mows go clear up to the peak of the roof, with as few obstructing timbers as possible; and woe unto the poor swain whose lot it is to pack the hay or wheat up against the rafters and scorching roof on some sultry day in July or August! But the modern hay fork, with its endless ropes and numerous pulleys, has lightened his task decidedly.

The habits of thrift and industry among the early Germans of the Valley, especially in the rural districts, were regular and often more or less rigorous, but generally wholesome and invigorating; and many of the country families, not only those of German descent, but doubtless many also of other nationalities, have preserved many of the ancestral customs, with slight modifications, to the present. The family would usually retire very early in the evening, especially in the spring, summer, and early autumn. Half-past eight or nine o'clock was late enough. But the German farmer and his household were consistent: if they went to bed early, they also got up early. Four o'clock—earlier sometimes, never later—was considered a good time. During the winter months five o'clock was sometimes accepted as a compromise with the elements, if there was not too much to do. This would still enable the girls to help with the breakfast, the boys to feed the stock, and all to travel a mile or two to school in ample time for "books" at nine or half-past eight. In the summer time daylight came much earlier, so that four o'clock or even half-past three was not too early for the farmer and his help to be stirring. The horses would have to be brought in from the far pasture, and be fed, curried, and harnessed. It was sometimes no easy task to find them, especially if a heavy fog increased the darkness, as was often the case. If there was any newly ploughed ground accessible anywhere, the beasts would be sure to have rolled in the fresh dirt; and then currying them was no small job. By the time this task was finished and the harness on, breakfast would be called. Having washed in a copious supply of water, cold from the spring or pump, and having eaten his breakfast by the sputtering flame of a tallow dip or a lard lamp, the farmer boy would have to move quickly to hitch up and get out into the field or upon the road by daylight or sunrise.

Many of the young fellows on the farm used to go barefooted in summer. Sometimes in the early morning, when one would be picking his way out to the barn, the air would carry up the meadow a strong suspicion of frost, and the boy without shoes would become keenly aware of it. What did he do? go back and put on his shoes? Not he. He would go into the barnyard, chase up one of the sleepy cows, step quickly upon the spot of steaming ground where she had lain, warm his feet for two minutes, and then proceed about his business. The writer is not at all certain that this procedure can be claimed as an exclusively German trick.

Very early in the history of the Valley numerous mills for the grinding of wheat, corn, and other grains were built. The famous mill of the Hites, on Opequon Creek, has already been mentioned. George Bowman, one of Jost Hite's sons-in-law, erected a mill on Cedar Creek at a much earlier date. Many of the Germans who settled on watercourses built mills, large or small, and harnessed the streams for power. To these mills the farmer would haul his grain, specially his wheat; and it was by the sale of his surplus flour that most of his money was obtained. The flour was accordingly put up in barrels—not imported ones—and loaded on the farmer's wagon. This great wagon, with its capacious body, and his strong team of sleek horses, were the "Dutchman's" pride. With his load of flour, supplemented oftentimes with several hundredweight of bacon, the master of the farm would mount his saddle-horse and drive off to market: sixty miles, eighty miles, or more than a hundred, through great forests and over unbridged streams to the nearest point on the James River; to Falmouth or Fredericksburg; to Alexandria; or to Washington. There were certain luxuries—save the mark!—there were certain necessities of life that could be obtained no nearer.

But most of the things really needful to the people of a new country, the German farmer and his family—he usually had a large family—provided in some way themselves. They raised cattle and tanned their hides, or had them tanned by a neighbor, and thus got leather for their shoes and harness. The itinerant shoemaker or harness-maker came around once or twice a year, made new shoes and harness, and repaired the old; or else one of the sons of the family learned the arts and saved thenceforth much trouble and expense in those lines. In nearly every family the father or one of his sons was blacksmith enough to forge a nail and shoe a horse. The men raised sheep, clipped the wool, carded it or had it carded in the neighborhood,—and neighborhoods also were large in those days,—and the women spun it into yarn, dyed it, knitted it into gloves, suspenders, and stockings, and wove it into cloth: coarse cloth, perhaps, but good and warm. They grew flax, and turned it into linen. They raised geese, and plucked their feathers for beds and pillows. The housewives, by some magic touch, transformed old wornout clothes into new carpets, and stores of old meat rinds and grease, with a box of fresh wood ashes, into blocks of excellent soap. The health of the family was usually good; but, when one was sick, the mother with her teas and domestic poultices, and the father with his lancet to let blood or his formula of words, could often bridge over the need of a physician.

A word in more detail must be said in regard to the spinning and weaving of the olden days. Many of the ancient spinning wheels and looms can yet be found in garrets and obscure corners; and a few are still kept in the fuller light. It was during the winter months, especially, that the wheels and looms might be heard busily humming and thumping. In the larger households, where there were several daughters of working age, both of those useful implements might be kept in rapid motion from daybreak or before till after nightfall, the workers relieving one another in turn.

Inasmuch as some of my readers may never have been

initiated into the mysteries of making rag carpet, a brief outline of the process may be pardoned here. Old clothes, beyond redemption by patching, were washed, ripped apart, and the better pieces cut into strips about half an inch in width. These strips were sewed together into one continuous string, and then reeled into convenient skeins. The rags in skeins, frequently dyed with walnut hulls, hickory bark, or some other domestic coloring matter, were then wound on balls of a pound or less in weight. These balls were easily handled by the lady of the loom, who unwound them upon her smooth wooden shuttles, drove the shuttles back and forth by hand between the gaping warp-threads, or "chain," stretched upon the massive frames, and lo, at the other side of the loom came slowly out the completed fabric, rolled upon a long wooden cylinder, with its variegated stripes in warp and woof shining with no mean beauty.

But carpets and rugs, jeans, linen, and linsey-woolsey were not the only products of the home weaver's skill: the climax was probably reached in the exquisite coverlets and counterpanes that were often veritable works of art, and that are to-day sought out by connoisseurs and bought at fancy prices.

It may be interesting, and at the same time a matter occasioning surprise, to know that much hand weaving, upon the ancient wooden looms, especially of rugs and carpets, is still done in some parts of the Valley to-day. A few young ladies have learned the art of their grandmothers; but only a few. Most of the work of this kind is done by those who were taught in a generation older than the present one.

It is asserted in the preceding chapter that the Valley Germans have been a people somewhat above the average in temperance. This is believed to be strictly true in respect to their use of strong drink; but if we should apply a similar test to their cupboards and tables—to the amount of things they usually eat and have to eat—the result might be slightly different. The land in which they live has been wonderfully blessed with plenty; and, so far as the writer knows, the people have never been disposed to lessen their shadows, or the shadows of their guests, by too much fasting. Often, from time to time, the generous housewives had occasion, or made it, to feast a score or two of neighbors; and the bottom of the flour bins and krout tubs would never be touched or dreamed of. The better side of this quality, therefore, was a hearty and unstinted hospitality, for which the district in question has been justly noted. And this hospitality was extended not only to those who bore the name of neighbor or claimed the due to friend, but also to the shoeless tramp upon the highway and the stranger without the gates. In the hurry-day of our modern life, which has dawned also upon this fair land between the mountains, this oldtime virtue may be losing ground; but it is believed that even now the doors are very few that would close in the face of want and hunger, and the firesides as few whose warmth would be denied to the homeless wayfarer.

An account of the methods and implements of cookery, including the processes of development from the spit and Dutch oven to the complications of the modern steel range, would be impossible and interminable; but a few particulars may be allowable concerning what used to be one of the most important and conspicuous pieces of the housewife's equipment: the bake oven. A number of these were still in use in the writer's own neighborhood during the earlier periods within his recollection. Let it be understood at once that the bake oven was quite different from the Dutch oven. The latter was a sort of heavy, oblong iron kettle, rather shallow and flat in the bottom, having a cover upon which coals of fire could be heaped. It was used in various processes of cooking. The bake oven was much larger, stationary, of different construction, and generally used for different purposes. Sometimes the bake oven, as hereinbefore observed, was built into the huge chimney, beside the fireplace; more frequently, however, at least in later times, it had the distinction of an independent and separate existence, being erected at a convenient distance outside the kitchen. The main feature of the oven was a large flat smooth stone, or an iron plate of sufficient dimensions, forming the bottom, or baking surface. This was set horizontally in a bed of masonry at a convenient distance from the ground, usually about the height of a table; and over it was built, of brick or stone, a solid, hemispherical arch or dome, with an opening at one side, giving access to the baking surface. The oven was heated by covering the bottom, or baking surface, with thinly split wood, firing it, and keeping the bed of coals in place until a sufficient temperature was reached. When the coals and ashes had been removed with the "kitch," or scraper, and the dust carefully brushed out with an old broom, the bunches of dough or the unbaked pies were brought and skillfully thrust in, each to its proper place and each with the right side up, by means of a long wooden paddle-shaped implement called in English a peel; in Pennsylvania "Dutch," a "Schiesse." And those loaves and pies were good. Their crispy sweetness was remarkable. But the abundance with which they were made each bake-day, and ever needed to be made, was more remarkable still.

A feature of life in the autumn was the making of apple butter, a complicated and exacting but at the same time an enjoyable process. Some thirty, forty, or fifty bushels of apples were first gathered for cider, the best being laid aside for "peeling in." The cider-making was a task to delight the youthful heart. Upon the better equipped farms the apparatus was always ready. The apples were first poured into a hopper and thoroughly mashed between two huge fluted cylinders; the mill being turned by a horse walking in a circle and pulling a long sweep, or lever. The pomace was then set up in rings, or layers, upon the bed of the press, and held in place by ingeniously woven wisps of long rye straw. The straw not only held the pomace in place, one ring upon another, but also afforded abundant openings for the cider to escape when the pressure was applied. The pressure was usually obtained in one of two ways: by large wooden screws fixed in a strong frame above the pomace bed, and turned by long handspikes; or by a heavy lever, fastened to a deeply imbedded post or a tree, and carried over the pomace bed 18 or 20 feet to a point where another lever, by a simple mechanical arrangement, was applied to the first for pulling it down and holding it in place. The first of these levers was usually a huge log, a foot or two in diameter. It needed to be strong to withstand the tremendous strain put upon it. Next the cider was "boiled down" in a large copper kettle, holding from thirty to forty gallons; and in the meantime the whole family, frequently with the assistance of some of the neighbors, would be "peeling" and "schnitzing" the apples already selected for that purpose. After a kettle or two of cider had been boiled down, and a sufficient quantity of apples had been "schnitzed," the butter-making proper began. The great kettle was made about half full of cider, a lot of the "schnitzed" apples were poured in, and the fun began. After a little while the boiling mixture had to be stirred constantly. The stirer was constructed of two pieces of wood: one perforated piece, about four inches wide and long enough to touch the bottom of the kettle. Into the top end of this piece was mortised a handle, long enough to extend out horizontally some eight or ten feet from the fire. Two persons, particularly a young man and a young woman, could manipulate this contrivance very conveniently. As the kettle boiled more apples or more cider might be added from time to time; till finally, somewhere about daylight the next day, the mixture would be at the proper consistency, and would be dipped out, with a copper dipper from the copper kettle, and put into gallon crocks.

The German pioneer and his family had not many books. Together with the few volumes used by the boys and the still fewer used by the girls in their short terms at school, the Bible, the hymn book or prayer book, and the yearly almanac often made up the library. Of these, it would perhaps be an open question as to which was most used; but it was pretty certainly either the Bible or the almanac. The

German's moral and religious habits were usually deep-seated and unimpeachable; but at the same time he had important and constant use for his almanac. Indeed the latter was often almost a *sine qua non* to his correct performance of religious duties. It is sometimes no easy matter, even in modern life, to keep the names of the days of the week in their proper places without a calender; and numerous instances are on record in which most devout persons missed their reckoning in those early days, and not only kept the wrong day for Sunday, but also did the other thing that was almost inevitable: worked on Sunday. Mr. Waddell tells us[3] of one Jacob Coger,—he must have been a German,— who was presented at the Augusta court, not long after the organization of the county, "for a breach of the peace by driving hogs over the Blue Ridge on the Sabbath." Now, I suspect that it was not because Coger was a German, or an irreligious man, nor even because he lived in a Presbyterian community, that he was found in error, but simply because he did not have an almanac!

But the German farmer of several generations ago had many other than religious uses for his almanac. In some things he was too religious—he was almost superstitious. The twelve signs of the zodiac and the phases of the moon had many meanings for him. Oak timber was to be cut in one phase; pine in another. When a child was born the name was written down in the Bible, and frequently with it the record of the particular sign of the time—the fish, the scales, or the twins. There was another set of conditions, closely related to the foregoing, that was very studiously regarded in many things: what was commonly known as the "up-going" and the "down-going." Onions and potatoes had to be planted, and shingles be nailed on a roof, in the "down-going;" but corn and wheat and other things yielding above ground had to be planted, and the ground rail of a worm fence had to be laid, in the "up-going."

3. Scotch-Irish of the Valley of Virginia, p. 85.

As has already been remarked, the life of the early Germans was a busy and often a strenuous one. Work with the hands was taught as a virtue, and rigid economy was cultivated as a marked accomplishment. In times of haying and harvest the women frequently joined in the labor of the field. In such a life of early rising and late toiling, there may seem to have been a small place for pleasure or for the broader views of living. And yet that life had a lighter and brighter as well as a darker and sterner side. Wants were few and easily satisfied. With the stimulating breath of God's great out-doors giving untaught vigor to heart and eye and limb, there was a healthy joy in living—just living. And that joy was carried with a robust energy into every task, so that labor itself was more a pleasure than a burden. Upon special occasions these pleasures were heightened by companionship and the enthusiasm of numbers, when a log-rolling, a corn-husking, an apple bee, a quilting, or a marriage called the neighborhood together.

Then, at all times, there was the warm home hearth, where the boys and girls were generally found in their few hours of leisure; and, best of all, love was there also, and bound the circle firm and close, though perhaps the word itself was not often spoken. They had their seasons of relaxation and their times for serious and exalted thought. There were at least a few days in the calendar that were looked forward to, and when they came the innate poetry and higher sentiments of many hearts welled up and sought expression. The Christmas tree in America is said to be a gift of the Pennsylvania Germans;[4] and the oft-repeated story of the *Christ Kindlein* brought ever a renewal of peace and joy, deep and pure and holy.

4. Ladies' Home Journal, December, 1906.

CHAPTER XIII.

SOME EARLY INDUSTRIAL ENTERPRISES.

Besides their activities as farmers, millers, and tanners, the early Germans of the Shenandoah Valley took an active and often a leading part in the establishing and maintaining of larger industrial enterprises. As early as 1742 Vestal's Iron Works were organized in Frederick County;[1] and although information is not at hand concerning the several individual movers in the project, it is likely that the Germans were represented more or less directly, inasmuch as they were numerous among the inhabitants of the district. In Kercheval's day there was a place on Cedar Creek, probably on the line between Frederick and Shenandoah, known as "Zane's old iron works."[2] He tells us that the industry had been operated by "the late Gen. Isaac Zane." I am informed by Mr. T. K. Cartmell, of Winchester, that the enterprise was also known as Marlboro Iron Works; and that Isaac Zane, Jr., of Philadelphia, received a deed for the land, where the works were located, in 1765. About the middle of the 18th century, the Ephrata Brethren established at Staufferstadt, or Strasburg, a pottery industry, which has been continued by other hands, through successive generations, to the present time.[3]

On a day in the latter part of October, 1781, as the news of Cornwallis' surrender was being vociferously received in Woodstock, Shenandoah County, a wealthy German and his family came into the town. It was Dirck Pennybacker, son of Col. John Pennybacker of the American army. Dirck Pennybacker had moved from Pennsylvania, a few years before, to a place near Sharpsburg, Md., and there had built an iron-

1. Norris' History of the Lower Valley, p. 81.
2. Kercheval's History of the Valley, pp. 50, 100, 104.
3. Sachse's German Sectarians, Vol. II, p. 356.

working establishment; but a great freshet had swept away the labor of his hands, and now he was coming to try his fortunes in Virginia. Passing on through Woodstock, he went across the Massanutten Mountain into what is now Page County, and built Redwell Furnace on the Hawksbill Creek. After awhile, as the industry enlarged, the Pennybackers reached over the Massanutten and established a forge and associated iron works on Smith's Creek, a few miles below New Market. The place is still known as Pine Forge; and some of the massive limestone walls of the buildings yet remain. Mr. P. E. Frederick owned and operated Pine Forge for some years prior to the Civil War, and occasionally thereafter as late as about 1885.

In 1810 Benjamin Pennybacker, son of Dirck and father of U. S. Senator Isaac Samuels Pennybacker, built for his home the spacious "White House," still standing and doing good service at Pine Forge. George M. and Joel Pennybacker, sons of Benjamin and brothers to the Senator, bought early in the 19th century large quantities of mountain land in western Shenandoah and Rockingham. In the former county they built, a few miles west of Woodstock, the well-known Liberty Furnace, which for many years supplied the iron used at Pine Forge.[4] In Rockingham County, in Brock's Gap, they also built a furnace; but the ore there proved worthless. As a monument to their labor, however, the old stack remains and an oak tree has grown up through it.

The Pennybackers were the pioneers in the iron-working industry in Shenandoah and Page; but others, both Germans and English, soon followed them in the same business. John Arthur built in 1809 the famous Columbia Furnace, still in operation, ten miles west of Woodstock. The Blackfords and

4. These statements follow the account furnished the writer by Joel Pennybacker's daughter, Miss M. M. Pennybacker, of Linville Depot, Va.; but I am informed by Dr. S. J. Hoffman, of Woodstock, that Liberty Furnace was built in 1822 by Walter Newman, Esq. It is possible that Newman and the Pennybackers may have co-operated in the enterprise, or that one party succeeded the other.

Arthurs had a furnace in Powell's Fort, and probably one or two more near the western border of Shenandoah. Columbia Furnace came in time into the possession of George F. Hupp, of Strasburg, a paymaster in the War of 1812, and later an extensive iron master. Shortly prior to the Civil War the same property passed into the hands of another German, Samuel Myers, who owned at the same time the furnace near Shenandoah Alum Springs. After the Civil War, Columbia became the property of John Wissler, Esq., who operated it with great success till 1883. At that date it was purchased by Mr. H. C. Pearson.[5]

The establishment of these early furnaces gave an impetus to industry in various ways. Not only were men needed to build the structures and arrange the equipment; to dig ore and haul it to the furnaces; to haul away the pig iron and the products of forge and foundry; but many laborers were also needed to cut timber, burn charcoal, and transport it to the places of consumption. Practically all of these early furnaces, forges, and foundries were dependent upon the supplies of charcoal produced in the vicinity—that is, in adjacent sections of the Valley. The burning of charcoal, therefore, became an important industry in itself, and was evidently rather widely distributed, considering the fact that all the transportation had to be done with wagons. The writer has frequently seen in cultivated fields, at a distance of eight or ten miles from the nearest furnace, the places that had been occupied by coal-pits probably a half-century or more before. These spots are usually circular, forty feet or more in diameter, and are easily recognized by the black color of the soil. Frequently small pieces of charcoal may still be turned up by the plough. The wood generally used was pine, cut

5. For the information herewith presented the writer is under special obligation to Miss M. M. Pennybacker, of Linville Depot; Mr. Joel F. Kagey, of Hawkinstown; Miss Sarah M. Spengler, of Front Royal; and Dr. S. J. Hoffman, of Woodstock. The reader is also referred to Hardesty's Atlas for Rockingham County, p. 414.

in cord-wood lengths. Oak and other varieties were also used, but the best charcoal was made from pine. The four-foot sticks were first used in building up a square pen, or chimney, by laying a sufficient number of them one upon another, lapping at the corners. Around this chimney as a center the wood was stacked on end, with the tops of the sticks leaning in perceptibly, and the stack was enlarged by successive rings until it covered a circle of thirty feet or more in diameter. Upon the top of the ground stack was made a smaller one of similar formation, and the whole was finished out in a rather flat convex heap, resembling somewhat, when covered with leaves and earth, a huge ant-hill. The fire was started at the bottom of the chimney—the hole in the center; and the covering of damp leaves and earth was to prevent the wood from burning rapidly in a blaze, since the charcoal must be formed by a slow, smouldering fire. The burning of charcoal is carried on to a considerable extent in the western sections of Shenandoah County to-day. Some of the furnaces still use charcoal, combining it with coke. Moreover, rather large quantities are shipped to other sections; and one may frequently see the wagons of the colliers, with their huge black "bodies," lumbering in and out of Woodstock and adjacent towns.

One of the most important of the early iron-working establishments in the Valley was located in the northeastern part of Augusta County, near the Rockingham line, on Mossy Creek. It was known as Miller's Iron Works; and the site is marked to-day by the old stone walls and chimneys, and by the village of Mossy Creek. The iron works were founded by Hery Miller, a German,[6] sometime prior to the Revolutionary War. An account of Henry Miller's career has probably never been published before; and inasmuch as the fol-

6. This fact I have from a letter written Feb. 8, 1907, by a descendant, Mr. G. Moffett Miller, of Jameson, Mo.—Mr. Miller died early in May, 1907.

lowing one, given to the author by Mr. Samuel Forrer,[7] in a letter of January 31, 1907, contains so much of interest in a small compass, it is presented verbatim:

From all I can gather, Henry Miller and Daniel Boone of Kentucky fame were cousins, and hunted and trapped together and traded with the Indians. Miller, finding evidences of iron ore deposits, turned his attention to getting land grants and buying tracts from speculative owners in the Mossy Creek valley. He settled here sometime about 1748 or 1749;[8] and at one time owned over 30,000 acres of land. A great body of his land was divided among his children, and the remainder was sold for distribution of proceeds. He died in 1796, which date I have found on his tombstone on my farm, where he was buried. He built the house in which I reside in 1784. He died in North River Gap, at one of his sugar camps, where he was superintending the making of maple sugar, which was the only sugar obtainable in those days. The exact date at which he built the furnace and forge, known as Mossy Creek Iron Works, is not known, but is generally believed to be soon after he located here. The iron works were in the hands of his son, Samuel Miller, for many years after Henry Miller's death. My maternal grandfather, John Keneagy, came from Lancaster County, Pennsylvania, and bought the iron works, and settled his son Henry on the property in 1834. Henry Keneagy lived here about ten years, when my father, Daniel Forrer, and mother took possession in 1844. Mr. Waddell writes me that he always took the Millers to be of English or Scotch origin; but the name Miller is found among the Germans as well as among the English and Scotch.[9]

The Mossy Creek iron was manufactured into stoves and cooking implements (classed as hollow ware) and bar iron which was used for horseshoes, wagon tires, and general purposes. All of the bar iron was hammered under large hammers weighing 500 and 600 pounds each, and was sold all through this Valley, in Fredericksburg, Charlottesville, and also in the mountain country which is now West Virginia. It was transported altogether by wagons.

7. Mr. Forrer's family came to Pennsylvania from the town of Winterthur, Switzerland, about the middle of the 18th century. His father operated the Mossy Creek iron works prior to the Civil War, as will appear.

8. The date was probably several years later, if Miller and Boone were companions prior to Miller's settlement on Mossy Creek; for Boone was born only in 1735, and moved south from Pennsylvania in 1752, his family settling in North Carolina.

9. It has already been noted that Henry Miller was a German.

In an autumn issue of the *Republican Farmer* of 1811, published at Staunton, was found an advertisement of Miller's Iron Works, by Samuel Miller (son of Henry) and John M. Estill, administrators. The sale was set for September 6, 1811; and together with the furnace and forge were to be sold 8000 acres of land, the whole "supposed to be the most valuable property of the kind in Virginia."[10]

It is probable that this sale had been purposely delayed for a number of years after Henry Miller's death, in order that minor heirs might attain to their majority. It is also probable that Samuel Miller purchased the iron works at this time.

That this establishment was of more than usual importance is further shown by the fact that on March 30, 1837, a company of gentlemen in Staunton secured a charter from the Virginia legislature for building a turnpike to a point on the Harrisonburg and Warm Springs Turnpike at or near Miller's Iron Works. The company was allowed a capital of ten thousand dollars, and the road was to be known as the Staunton and Iron Works Turnpike.[11]

At some time early in last century the Millers built a paper mill near the site of the present Mossy Creek church. This mill was operated till a period near the middle of the century. About 1850 another paper mill was built a mile or two further up the creek, near the village of Mt. Solon. This mill finally came into the hands of Felix T. Sheets, who operated it till it was destroyed by fire about 1870. The material used for making paper at Sheets' mill—and doubtless at the earlier one also—consisted chiefly of rags gathered from every store and every accessible dwelling house throughout the Valley. The articles produced were printer's paper, wrapping paper, and paper boards, such as box boards and bonnet boards. Most of the newspapers of Augusta and Rockingham used the Mossy Creek paper. At one time the *Richmond Whig*

10. Waddell's Annals of Augusta, p. 386.

11. Acts of Assembly of Virginia, 1837.

used a great deal of it. The wrapping paper was made from straw, woolen rags, and some cotton rags, and was used by most of the local merchants.[12]

Near Churchville, about nine miles southwest of Mossy Creek and the same distance northwest of Staunton, was once a nail factory, supposed to be one of the oldest in the country. It was provided with a tilt-hammer, driven by water power, wherewith the iron was first forged into long flat plates. These plates were then cut by another machine into nail lengths, but the heads of the nails were forged by hand. This "plant" was owned and operated by a blacksmith named William Freal, a Pennsylvania German.[13]

If there was one class of enterprises more important than others in the development of the Shenandoah Valley three-quarters of a century ago, it was the building of turnpikes. From 1830 to 1840 a dozen or more such roads were constructed according to specifications required in charters granted by the State legislature. These specifications usually required that the road be of a certain width, within a certain maximum grading, and be covered with macadam of a certain thickness—often a foot. The construction of several of the most important of these roads may be noticed more particularly in this connection, as appropriate to our subject and as illustrating the part taken by the citizens of German descent in the leading industrial enterprises of their repective localities.

The turnpike from Harrisonburg, in Rockingham County, to Warm Springs, in Bath County, was provided for by an Act of Assembly passed January 29, 1830. The distance between the two terminal points is 75 or 80 miles, and the route passes around or over several large mountains. The persons

12. For information regarding these paper mills the writer is indebted chiefly to Mr. Samuel Forrer, of Mossy Creek, and to Mrs. S. F. Miller, of Bridgewater.—See also Howe's Antiquities, p. 177.

13. Staunton Semi-Weekly News, Jan. 9, 1902.

heading the enterprise and those who should join them later were incorporated as the Warm Springs and Harrisonburg Turnpike Company; a capital of $40,000, to be increased as necessary, was authorized; the shares of stock were to have a par value of fifty dollars each; and leading citizens interested in the project were appointed at different places, chiefly along the route of the proposed highway, to open books and receive subscriptions. The men appointed at Harrisonburg for this purpose were the following: Joseph Cravens, Isaac Hardesty, George W. Piper, William McMahon, and Joseph Cline. At Rifeville,[14] Daniel Smith, Daniel Rife, John Allebaugh, Joseph Coffman, and Jacob Dinkle were appointed. Samuel Miller, Jonathan Shipman, Harvey McDowell, Andrew Erwin, and John Brower were designated at Miller's Iron Works, which was one of the places along the route named in the charter. Appointments were also made at Jenning's Gap, Staunton, Warm Springs, and Lewisburg; but these stations were mainly outside of the German territory, and consequently not more than two or three German names are found in the whole number of appointees of these places. Among the fifteen names already mentioned, however, of men at Harrisonburg, Rifeville, and the Iron Works, at least nine were Germans.

The most famous and most constantly used road in the Valley, if not in the State, is the one already frequently mentioned, passing through Winchester, Woodstock, New Market, Harrisonburg, and Staunton, following in general the line of an ancient Indian trail and the later wagon road and stage road of the white men. On March 3, 1834, the Valley Turnpike Company was incorporated, and authorized to build a pike from Winchester to Harrisonburg, a distance of about 70 miles. Subscriptions were to be received, in shares of $25 each, to the sum of $250,000; and as soon as three-fifths of

14. Rifeville must have been in the vicinity of Dayton or Bridgewater. The name is now extinct.

the stock should be subscribed by individual citizens, the State board of public works was to subscribe the balance on the part of the Commonwealth. The company was empowered to use as much of the old wagon road—termed in the charter the old stage road—as was found desirable. Inasmuch as the committees appointed at the different stations to receive subscriptions were so largely made up of Germans, the several lists are given in full; and, for convenience, they are arranged in tabular form, as follows:

Winchester:—John Heiskell, John M. Broome, Nathan Parkins, Isaac Hollingsworth, Obed Waite, Edgar W. Robinson, David M. Barton, Charles H. Clark, Abraham Miller.

Newtown:—Joseph Long, John Allemong, John W. Grove, Joseph S. Ritenour, James G. Brooking.

Middletown:—David S. Danner, John Smith Davidson, Alexander Catlett, Anderson Brown, Abraham Brinker.

Strasburg:—David Stickley, William McCord, Anthony Spangler, William Morris, Samuel Fisher.

Woodstock:—Philip Williams, Jr., Absalom Rinker, Samuel Ott, William Moreland, Lorenzo Sibert, John Koontz, John Haas.

Mt. Jackson:—Reuben Bird, Christopher Hickle, Philip Pitman, Rees Allen, Joseph Samuels.

New Market:—Patrick McManus, Samuel Coffman, John Strayer, George Pennybacker.

Sparta:—Isaac Thomas, John Cowan, Peter Koontz, Derrick Pennybacker, Hiram Martz, George Rhodes.

Edom Mills:—John Chrisman, George H. Chrisman, Jacob Lincoln, Christian Kratzer, David Henton, Jesse Ralston.

Turlytown:—Samuel Cootes, Jacob Trumbo, John Rader, Sr., Shem Cochenour, John Shaver, John Oiler.

Dayton:—Samuel H. Coffman, John Brower, Martin Miller, John Herring, Martin Speck, George Airy, Sr.

Harrisonburg:—Robert Gray, John Kenny, James Hall, Isaac Long, Isaac Hardesty, James M. Huston.

At a meeting of the stockholders on June 11, 1838, over four years after the charter was granted, the work was still in process. Other—perhaps additional—appointments were made to the committees for soliciting subscriptions. It was reported at this meeting that J. R. Anderson of Richmond had been appointed chief engineer. Bushrod Taylor was president. Philip Pitman, Wright Gatewood, Philip Williams, and Joel Pennybacker[15] were directors, representing the stockholders; John B. Breckenridge, Isaac Hardesty, Samuel Harnsberger, Reuben Moore, and James C. Shipman were directors on the part of the State. Bushrod Taylor was twice reëlected president: on June 10, 1839, and on June 6, 1840. On June 4, 1841, Joel Pennybacker was elected to that office.[16]

On March 30, 1837, an Act was passed by the General Assembly incorporating the Harrisonburg and Staunton Turnpike Company. This road of twenty-five miles was evidently intended to be a continuation of the Valley Turnpike from Winchester to Harrisonburg; and the two companies appear to have been united at an early date. For this part of the road a capital of $100,000, in $25 shares, was authorized; and the following subscription committees were appointed:

Harrisonburg:—John Kenny, Samuel Shacklett, John F. Effinger, Algernon Gray, Jacob Rohr, Hugh Bruffy, and M. Harvey Effinger.

Mt. Crawford:—Edward Stevens, John Roller, Robert M. Grattan, Michael H. Harris, Peter Dinkle, James C. Shipman, William T. Newham, and George Kiser.

Mt. Sidney:—John Seawright, Adam Link, Jacob Baylor,

15. The iron master.

16. For much of the information herewith presented I am indebted to Hon. J. G. Neff of Mt. Jackson, and to Miss M. M. Pennybacker of Linville Depot.

Michael Mauzy, Samuel Hansberger, James Bourland, and William S. Hainger.

Staunton:—William Poage, Philip Fishburn, Robert Anderson, Samuel M. Woodward, Benjamin Crawford, John C. Sowers, and Jefferson Kinney.

Although one or two of these stations were getting beyond the German strongholds, at least eleven of these twenty-nine men were of that nationality.

The writer is informed by Hon. Jacob G. Neff, of Mt. Jackson, Va., who is now president of the Valley Turnpike Company, that the total cost of the whole road was $425,000. Three-fifths of this amount, as we have seen, was subscribed by the private citizens along the route. Hundreds of the energetic and progressive farmers took stock; and in Shenandoah and Rockingham the German names predominate; in Augusta and Frederick the balance is perhaps in favor of the English and Scotch-Irish.

Another early enterprise of considerable importance was the development of Orkney Springs, in western Shenandoah County, as a summer resort. On March 27, 1858, the Orkney Springs Company was incorporated by the Virginia legislature, and authorized to manage a capital stock of $100,000, and to acquire and hold as much as 5000 acres of land. David McKay, James M. Bradford, Samuel Cootes, Naason Bare, and J. Q. Wingfield were the promoters of the enterprise. Of the five, Cootes and Bare were Germans. For many years Orkney was one of the most popular resorts for health and pleasure in the country and it has not yet altogether lost its prestige.

For a number of years the Steenbergens, a family that appears to have belonged to the German nobility, occupied a prominent place in the commercial and industrial life of Shenandoah County and the Valley of Virginia. They were regarded as the wealthiest people in the county. William Steenbergen, the first of the name to locate in the Valley, married, about the year 1800, a daughter of Col. Taverner Beale, of Revolutionary note; and, after inheriting considerable property through his wife, built the limestone mansion still standing on the bluff just east of Smith's Creek, two miles above Mt. Jackson, and known as Mt. Airy. Mt. Airy was for a considerable period in the possession of Capt. John Meem; and the eminence which it occupies commands an excellent view of the famous Meem's Bottoms, lying between Smith's Creek and the North Branch of the Shenandoah River. When building Mt. Airy, William Steenbergen, or Baron Steenbergen, as he was sometimes called, imported for the structure two mantel-pieces from Italy, at a cost of more than a thousand dollars. He and his sons, William and Beale, were extensively engaged in the cattle business. In 1810 or 1811, William Steenbergen, likely the elder, was awarded several premiums on cattle at Georgetown, D. C., by the Columbian Agricultural Society. One steer, believed to be the largest ever raised in Virginia, attracted special attention. It was killed the following day at Krouse's slaughter-house, and the net beef weighed nearly 2000 pounds.[17] At one time Beale Steenbergen rounded up all the fat beeves in the country. After collecting all in the Valley, he put his agents on all the roads leading into Baltimore, and for awhile created an actual beef famine. He made a great deal of money by the scheme, but doubtless had cause to regret his shrewdness ever afterward. Because of this "corner in cattle" he was practically ostracized by his family and neighbors, and finally left the Valley.[18]

This incident may fairly suggest a general truth, as well as a fitting word for the conclusion of our present study. There

17. Schuricht's German Element, Vol. II, p. 24.

18. For information concerning the Steenbergens I am under obligation to Gen. G. S. Meem, Seattle, Wash.; Mrs. S. F. Miller, Bridgewater, Va.; Miss Mary C. Pittman, The Plains, Va.; Mr. Joel F. Kagey, Hawkinstown, Va.; and Eld. A. J. Kagey, dec'd, late of Mt. Jackson, Va.

doubtless always have been individuals among the Valley of Virginia Germans who have allowed their greed for material gain to override their sense of right; but they have always done so at their peril, and they have often met rebuke at their own doors. Although this people have a talent for acquisition, they have also a keen sense of justice, and are not often found willing to win gold or position at the sacrifice of principle.

Appendix.

A.

List of Unclaimed Letters in the Harrisonburg Postoffice, Sept. 30, 1809.

(From the Staunton *Deutsche Virginier Adler* of Nov. 18, 1809.)

Verzeichnisz der Briefe

Welche in der Postoffice zu Härrisonburg (Virg.) am 30-sten September 1809, liegen, und wenn solche nicht vor den 30sten nächsten December abgefordert werden, als todte Briefe an die General Postoffice zurückgesand werden.

A. Samuel Adams, Johann Albright, Johann Argabright, Johann Armetrout.

B. Andreas Bair, Samuel Blackburn, Rechtsgelehrter, Johanna Bruen, Abraham Brenneman, Katherine Baker, Benjamin Braun, James Breedlove.

C. Johann Clabough, Richard Custow.

D. Joseph Davis, Louis Driver, Johann Dunnavan.

F. Johann Firebough, Christian Funk 2, Herr Free.

G. Wilhelm Garrott, Samuel Gilmore.

H. Jacob Hesflinger, Oberst Benjamin Harrison 2, Wilhelm Herring, Joseph Harrison (?), Samuel Hemphill, Andreas Huling, Michael Harnasch.

K. Heinrich Kephart, Jacob K - - ling.

L. Karter Lightfoot, Ludwig Launceford.

M. Samuel Miller, Marie Mefford 2, Joseph Mouzy, Violetta Mouzy, Andreas M'Clelan, Johann Meadows.

N. Johann Niebls.

O. Marie Ocheltree, Edmon Ong.

P. Wilhelm Pence, Josua Parry, Thomas Porter.

R. Georg Rader, Johann Right, Wilhelm Rawley.

S. Robert Stringfelter, Jacob Scott, Robert Sanford, Jacob Schowalter, Peter Swope, Salomon Schetters.

T. Daniel Tharp, Ezekiel Thomas.

V. William Vickers.

W. Christoph Wervel, Peter William.

—Tutwlieler, P. M.

B.

List of Unclaimed Letters in the Woodstock Postoffice, January 1, 1821.

(From the *Woodstock Herald* of January 10, 1821.)

"A List of Letters remaining in the Postoffice at Woodstock, Va., which if not taken out before the 31st of March next, will be sent to the General Post Office according to law."

B. Col. Sam Bare 2, Henry Bowman, John Barb, Michael Bright, Jonas Burner, Wm. Byers, Adam Barb, Robert Batie, George Bowman, Jacob Burner, Jacob Beard, Wm. Bosserman, P. P. Balden.

C. Com'dt 13th Regt. Jacob Coverstone, John Coffman.

D. Richard Duncan, Elizabeth Donelson.

E. John Effinger.

F. Elizabeth Fry, Christiana Fawver, Sarah Fry, Joshua Foltz, Jacob Fravel, Thomas Frazier.

G. Henry Grant, Emanuel Graybill, Mary Grandstaff.

H. Margaret Helsley, George Hottle, John Hausafluck, Henry Hockman, Daniel Helsel, Philip Hoffman, Jacob Houser, Nath'l Humpston, Thomas Homston, Samuel Hickle.

K. Jacob Kniesley, Mary Knop.

L. John Lock, Henry Linn, Philip Long.

M. Daniel McIntorf, Hezekiah Moreland.

O. Michael Ott.

P. Richard Proctor, Aaron Proctor, Isaac Peer, Jos. Painter, John Poke, Jos. Parker, Christena Peer.

R. John Rols, Augustine Reedy, Jacob Roemer, John Ryman, John Rumbough, Adam Rodeffer, John Rodeffer.

S. Nichs. Schmucker, Samuel Steart, John Snyder, Abm. Smootz, Jesse Smith, Jacob Sigler, Jos. Sonenstine, Daniel Sheetz.

T. Samuel T. Turner.

W. John Wimer, Emanuel Windle, Benj. Williams, Lewis Williams, Daniel Windle, Margaret Windle, Daniel Webb, James Waugh, George Will.

Z. George Zircle.

—A. Fravel, P. M.

C.

Names of Persons whose Wills are Recorded in Augusta County Will Book No. 6,

Covering the Period from 1778 to 1786.

James Alexander
James Archer
Gabriel Alexander
Jas. Anderson
David Allen
John Archer
Robt. Alexander
John Anderson
Thomas Bradshaw
Wm. Blackwood
David Bell
James Buchanan
Robert Burns
Samuel Black
James Bell
Jemima Bradley
Adam Broaback
Robt. Bratton
Wm. Burke
David Cunningham
Chas. Campbell
Wm. Christian
Rebecca Caruthers
George Crawford
Elizabeth Clark
Robt. Campbell
Chris. Clemmons
Robt. Caldwell
John Christian
Isaac Carson
Valentine Cloninger
Chas. Donnelly
Casper Eakert
John Estill
John Flesher
John Francis
Lanly Graham
James Gamble

Archibald Gilkenson
Elizabeth Guy
James Gilmore
Edward Hinds
Archibald Henderson
James Hogshead
Saml. Henderson
James Henderson
John Henderson
Wm. Johnson
James Kirk
William Kerr
John Logan
Andrew Lewell
James Lessley
William Long
Jacob Lockhart
Matthew Lettimore
Barnerd Lance
John Mitchell
John McDonough
John McMahon
Richard Madison
Wm. McClintock
Robert Mills
Adam Murray
Morris Ofriel
Nathan Ragland
Eph. Richardson
John Ramsay
Daniel Ramsay
Robert Rusk
Matthew Robenson
——— Ramsay
Edward Rutledge
Jos. Skidmore
Margaret Sproul
Leonard Shounds
James Sawyers
Thomas Stevenson
William Tees
Moses Thompson
James Tate.
Wm. Thompson
John P. Vance
Jacob Vanlear
Edward Warner
Francis Were
James Wallace
William Woods
Thomas Waddle
Isaac ———
John Young
John Young

D.

Names of Persons whose Wills are Recorded in Frederick County Will Book No. 4,

Covering the Period from 1770 to 1783.

Gabriel Amiss
Peter Antle
Francis Allen
Wm. Abernatha
Lewis Bird
John Branson

Charles Burk
Abraham Brehon
Henry Bedinger
Henry Brinker
Jeremiah Beall
Christian Blank
John Berry
Saml. Blackburn
Thomas Barron
Richard Calvert
John Chinoweth
Wm. Chinoweth
Wm. Calmes
Martin Crydar
James Colvill
Jacob Christman
Thomas Craig
Peter Catlet
Henry Carrer
David Denny
William Death
Samuel Earle
Godfrey Eylor
William Ewing
Mary Fulton
George Fogelsong
William Frost
Christian Fogelsong
Andrew Frictley
Humphrey Fullerton
Thomas Lord Fairfax
Timothy Fuly
Richard Foley
David Glass
Charles Grim
Mathias Grove
Richard Hulse
Joseph Hawkins
Luke Hood
Sigismund Henly
John Haton
Job Hastings
George Harrison
John Hope
James Hamilton
Stephen Hotzenpeller
Robert Haning
Thomas Helm
George Hamton
Peter Helviston
John Hotsenfelar
Isaac Hukman
Michael Humble
Wm. Hankins
George Hendry
John Humphreys
Wm. Iolliffe
James Jones
Godfrey Ilor
James Iolliffe
John Iolliffe
Elizabeth Iolliffe
Jacob Koughnauer
Wm. Kerfoot
Geo. Lyndemooth
Saml. Litler
John Lerhen (?)
John Laurence
John Larrick, Sr.
Peter Lehne
Peter Lerew
Geo. Laubinger

Peter Mauk
Elizabeth Milburn
Angus McDonald
Frederick Mauk
Vallingtine Miller
William Neil
Nicholas Princler
Wm. Pritchard
John Painter
Oullerey Pitzer
Joseph Pollard
Thomas Provens
Isaac Parkins
Henry Peyton
Michael Pevice
Henry Rees
Edward Reed
William Russell
Robert Russell
George Ross
Ann Reed
Josiah Ridgway
Daniel Stout
John Stickley
Sarah Shepherd
Frederick Steep
Peter Sperry
Taliaferro Stribling
Laurence Stephens
George Smith
Benj. Sedwick
Ralph Thompson
Zebulon Tharp
David Watts
James Willson
Robert Willson
Peter Wolfe
Wm. Weathers
Moses Walton
John Bell
Samuel Bevin
Thomas Babb
Sarah Beckett
Joseph Bowman
John Byrns
Mary Barrett
James Barnett

E.

Names of Persons who Sold Land in Rockingham County from 1777 to 1793.

From the First Deed Book, No. 0.

Philip Armentrout
John Ashburner
Catherine Alstott
John Alstott
A. Armentrout
Saml. Bear
John Brunk
David Byers
Michael Bowyer
Benj. Berry
John Breeden
Henry Black

James Beard
Wm. Campbell
Ludwig Circle
Thomas Campbell
Wm. Chestnut
Chas. Calahan
Peter Conrad
Jos. Claypool
Valentine Cook
George Davis
James Denniston
Hugh Duglas
John Drake
James Dyer
Wm. Dever
Edward Ervin
Evan Evans
John Eddy
Jacob Elsworth
Gasper Faught
Geo. Freedly
John Fowler
James Finney
Mary Fitch
M. Fifer
Nicholas Fogle
George Fisher
Isaac Gum
Michael Gibbs
Jacob Gross
Conrad Good
John Gordon
Thomas Harrison
Robert Henderson
James Harris
Jacob Harnsberger

Wm. Hook
Peter Harman
B. Johnston
Joshua Jackson
John Jordan
George Koogler
Deter Kouts
John Kring
George Keisel
Elisha Knox
Jacob Kisling
Abram Lincoln
Thomas Laugton
Peter Lam
John Madison
Wm. Morris
Nicholas Mace
John Miller
Jacob Nicholas
Hy Null
William Oler
Wm. Pickerin
Saml. Philips
Aug. Price
John Petty
Adam Pipher
Jos. Rutherford
Peter Roller
Cornelius Ruddell
John Robinson
Brewer Reeves
Robt. Shankland
Daniel Smith
Nath. Scott
Adam Shearman
James Skidmore

Adam Sellers
Jacob Shirey
Jacob Spitler
John Spratt
John Tanner
Catherine Teeter
N. Troarbough
John Thomas
Peter Vanimer
John Voice
J. Vanferson
Ludwig Waggoner
Michael Wise
Martin Whitzel
John Wilson
John Warren
Conrad Young
Ludwig Zircle

F.

Names of Persons whose Wills are Recorded in Shenandoah County Will Book A,

Covering the Period from 1772 to 1784.

Joseph Abell
Frederick Andrick
Reuben Allen
Adam Broadback
Henry Bohman
Jacob Burner
Ann Crum
Elias Coffield
James Cornagie
Richard Campbell
Jacob Copenhaber
Joseph Clevinger
Abram Denton
Philip Darting
Adam Darting
Mary Dust
Isaac Durst
Christo Dosh
Wm. Downey
Christian Dellinger
Rachel Egan
Adam Funk
Joseph Frye
John M. Foltz
Jacob Guyger
Christopher Gistert
Ulry Gfeller
John Gilcock
George Huddell
Peter Hoop
Wm. Hoover
Harding Henry
John Hoy
William Hunt
John Hall
Abraham Hendrich
George Keller
George Maurer
Jacob Miller
Wm. Miller
Jno. Mackinturf, Sr.
Jacob Miller

Anthony Nisely
Jacob Offenbacker
Jeremiah Odell
Samuel Odle
Jacob Offenbocker
Ulrich Peters
Henry Pfiffer
Abraham Pickenberger
Jacob Roharer
David Rotheheffer
Susanna Rantz
Peter Ruffner
John Ruddell
Henry Rickaboker
Stephen Showman
Francis Slaughter
Martin Snyder
Henry Surber
Jacob Snyder
Joseph Smith
Michael Sommers
John Lievely
Lawrence Snapp
Wm. White
Philip Wisman
Adam Yeager

G.

Members of the House of Burgesses from the Valley Counties from 1742 to 1775, and of the Virginia Conventions of 1775 and 1776.

Frederick County.

Samuel Earle—1742; 1745-7.
Lawrence Washington—1744.
[A?] Campbell—1745-7.
George Fairfax—1748-9.
Gabriel Jones—1748-54.
George William Fairfax—1752-5.
———Perkins—1754-5.
Hugh West—1756-8.
Thomas Swearingen—1756-8.
George Washington—1758-65.
Thomas Bryan Martin—1758-61.
George Mercer—1761-5.
Robert Rutherford—1766-72.
James Wood—1766-76.
Isaac Zane—1773-6.
Charles Mynn Thruston—1775.

Augusta County.

John Madison—1748-54.
John Wilson—1748-72.
James Patton—1754-5.
Gabriel Jones—1756-8; 1769-71.
Israel Christian—1758-65.
William Preston—1765-8.
Samuel McDowell—1772-6.
Charles Lewis—1773-4.
George Matthews—1775.
Thomas Lewis—1775-6.
John Harvie—1775.
George Roots—1775.

Berkeley County.

Thomas Hite—1772-4.
Robert Rutherford—1772-6.
John Hite—1775.
Adam Stephen—1775.
William Drew—1775-6.

Dunmore County.

Francis Slaughter—1772-5.
Joseph Watson—1772-3.
Abraham Bird—1775-6.
Jonathan Clarke—1775.
Peter Muhlenberg—1775.
John Tipton—1776.

(*Compiled chiefly from Stanard's Colonial Virginia Register.*)

H.

Members of the Virginia Senate from the Valley Counties, 1883 to 1907.

(After 1893, Augusta should be understood as having with

it the City of Staunton, and Frederick as having with it the City of Winchester.)

Augusta County.

Absalom Koiner—1883-9.
Edward Echols—1890-97; '99-00; '06-07.
John N. Opie—1898-05.

Clarke, Frederick, and Warren.

John T. Lovell—1883.
J. M. McCormick—1884-5.
Marshall McCormick—1886-7.
T. W. Harrison—1888-92.

Clarke, Page, and Warren.

T. W. Harrison—1893-4.
Thomas D. Gold—1895; 1900-03.
E. H. Jackson—1896-9.
M. J. Fulton—1904-7.

Rockingham County.

John F. Lewis—1883-5.
J. B. Webb—1883-4.
George B. Keezell—1885-7; 1896-07.
John Acker—1888-91.
Thomas K. Harnsberger—1892-5.

Shenandoah and Page.

H. H. Riddleberger—1883.
Amos K. Grim—1884-7.
H. J. Smoot— 1888-91.
M. L. Walton— 1892.

Shenandoah and Frederick.

M. L. Walton—1893-5.
J. G. McCune—1896-9.
S. L. Lupton—1900-03.
F. S. Tavenner—1904-7.

I.

Members of the Virginia House of Delegates from the Valley Counties, 1883 to 1907.

Augusta County.

Marshall Hanger—1883.—
James H. Skinner—1883.
Edward Echols—1884-9.
John N. Opie—1884-5.
A. B. Lightner—1886-7; '90-91.
J. H. Crawford—1888-9.
George M. Cochran—1890-91.
George W. Koiner—1892-5.
H. J. Williams—1892-3.
Thomas R. N. Speck—1894-5.
Silas H. Walker—1896-9; 1902-7.
C. W. Simms—1896-7.
J. W. Churchman—1898-07.
John W. Todd—1900-1.

Clarke and Warren.

Alexander M. Earle—1883.
David Meade—1884-5.
H. H. Downing—1886-7; 1890-91; '94-5.
A. Moore, Jr.—1888-9.
William T. Kerfoot—1892-3.
S. S. Thomas—1896-9.
A. L. Warthen—1900-01.
Blackburn Smith—1902-5.
M. M. Johnson—1906-7.

Frederick County.

Holmes Conrad—1883.
R. T. Barton—1884-5.
John V. Tavenner—1886-7.
John M. Silver—1888-91.

Joseph A. Miller—1892-3.
Charles F. Nelson—1894-5.
James K. McCann—1896-7.
E. C. Jordan—1898-05.
Richard E. Byrd—1906-7.

Page County.

A. K. Grim—1883.
R. G. Mauck—1884-7.
Thomas J. Graves—1888-91.
C. E. Graves—1892-3.

Page and Rappahannock.

B. W. Petty—1894-5.
Richard S. Parks—1896-01.
G. C. Elkins—1902-3.
J. Hunton Wood—1904-5.
D. S. Louderback—1906-7.

Rockingham County.

Henry B. Harnsberger—1883.
Philander Herring—1883-4.
John F. Soule—1884-5.
George G. Grattan—1885.
J. B. Webb—1886-9.
John Acker—1886-7.
J. E. Sanger—1888-9.
T. K. Harnsberger—1890-1.
W. H. Blakemore—1890-5; '98-01.
Charles E. Fahrney—1892-5.
W. Harvey Zirkle—1896-7.
B. G. Patterson—1896-7; 1900.
D. M. Switzer—1898-9.
Frank Ralston—1901.
J. T. Robson—1902-5.
George E. Sipe—1902-3.
H. M. Rogers—1904-7.
P. B. F. Goode—1906-7.

Shenandoah County.

George J. Grandstaff—1883-5.
F. E. Rice—1886-7.
P. W. Magruder—1888-93.
Jacob G. Neff—1894-5.
W. A. Sager—1896-7.
Joseph M. Bauserman—1898-9.
Josiah Stickley—1900-01.
Samuel J. Hoffman—1902-5.
B. B. Bowman—1906-7.

(*The lists from 1883 to 1907 have been compiled chiefly from the Warrock-Richardson Almanac.*)

J.

Some German Members of the United States Congress from the Valley of Virginia.

Senate.

Isaac Samuels Pennybacker (1805-1847), of Shenandoah County: 1845-7.

Harrison Holt Riddleberger (1844-1890), of Shenandoah County: 1883-9.

House of Representatives.

Isaac Leffler: 1827-9. (Leffler may have belonged to a section west of the Valley.)

John Paul, of Rockingham County: 1882-3.—Judge Paul's mother was German; his father's family was French.

Isaac Samuels Pennybacker (1805-1847), of Shenandoah County: 1837-9.

Green B. Samuels, of Shenandoah County: 1839-41.

Daniel Sheffey (— 1830), of Augusta County: 1809-17. —Mr. Sheffey was elected from southwest Virginia, but located at Staunton later.

Thomas V. Swearingen, of Jefferson (?) County: 1819-22.

Jacob Swoope, of Augusta County: 1809-11.

K.

Some German Members of the Virginia Legislature from the Valley of Virginia.

Not already Mentioned in Appendixes G, H, and I.

Augusta County.

Charles M. Roller.
Daniel Sheffey: 1823.
H. W. Sheffey: 1852-3; Speaker of the House of Delegates during the Civil War.
Nicholas K. Trout: 1865 (?).—Member of Virginia Senate.

Berkeley County.

Adam Stephens.—Representative in the convention of 1788.

Frederick County.

Henry Bedinger: 1846.
Robert Y. Conrad: 1840.—Member of Virginia Senate.
M. R. Kaufman: 1860.
Daniel E. Wotring (1830—).

Jefferson County.

T. W(?). Swearingen: 1805-16.

Page County.

Andrew Keyser: 1852-3.
Henry W. Keyser.
M. Spitler: 1856.

Rockingham County.

Samuel A. Coffman.
J. Conrad: 1836.
John Koontz: 1795-8.
K. Martz: 1846.

John D. Pennybacker (—1904): 1859-63.—Member of Virginia Senate.

John E. Roller: 1869-73.—Member of Virginia Senate.

A. Waterman: 1831-4.

Shenandoah County.

Samuel Bare (—c. 1844): Member of Legislature about 1830-1.

Samuel Coffman: 1831-4.

Joel Pennybacker: 1840.—Member of Virginia Senate.

Philip Pittmann: 1864-5.—Member of Virginia Senate.

Absalom Rinker: c. 1836.

Jacob Rinker.—Was a member of the State Legislature for many years, following the Revolutionary War.

W. M. Seibert: 1860.

Joseph Stover Spengler (1790—1876).

Philip Spengler (1761—): c. 1815.

Joseph B. Strayer.

The foregoing lists (Appendixes J. and K.) have been compiled from various sources. They are not regarded as complete.

Revolutionary Pensioners Living in Valley Counties in 1835.

In the year 1835 the Secretary of War prepared and published a list of all Revolutionary Pensioners then living in the various States, from which list the following names have been secured. It is possible that a few of the men may have served only in the War of 1812, and not in the Revolution; but certainly the great majority of them were soldiers in the struggle for independence, and most of them had doubtless enlisted from the respective counties in which they were living in 1835. No pension was granted except for actual service for a period of at least six months.

The lists for Rockingham were published by Mr. Charles E. Kemper of Washington, D. C., in the *Rockingham Regis-*

ter of January 2, 1903. The other lists were furnished the author, by Mr. Kemper's kindness, within the last few months: and, so far as is known, they have not been published before.

L.

Frederick County.

Under Act of March 18, 1818.

William Albert, Penn. Line.
Cornelius Beazley, Penn. Line.
James Beckman, Va. Line.
Christopher Bedinger, Penn. Line.
John Begeant, Va. Line.
William Braithwait, Va. Line.
William Burke, Va. Line.
Dennis Bush, Va. Line.
John Campbell, Penn. Line.
Samuel Cox, Va. Line.
Thomas Crawford, Va. Line.
Thomas Foster, artificer, Va. Line.
John Grove, Penn. Line.
Daniel Haley, Va. Line.
James Hamilton, Va. Line.
John Haney, Md. Line.
Simon Harrell, Va. Line.
John Harris 4th, Va. Line.
John Hefferlin, Va. Line.
Nathaniel Henry, Lt., N. Y. Line.
Samuel Hickie, Va. Line.
Jacob Hunt, Md. Line.
Frederick Imhoff, Penn. Line.
Claude F. Jeannerel, Va. Line.
James Johnson, Penn. Line.
John Keger, Va. Line.
William Kingore, Va. Line.
Archibald McDonald, Va. Line.

Alexander McMullen, Va. Line.
James Martin, Penn. Line.
Daniel Miller, Va. Line.
Richard Murry, Va. Line.
Dennis Obriean, Md. Line.
James Oliver, Va. Line.
Christian Orendorf, Capt., Md. Line.
Moses Perry, Va. Line.
Lewis St. John, Va. Line.
George Seifert, Va. Line.
Jeremiah Sergeant, Va. Line.
Robert Sherman, Va. Line.
John Smith 4th, Penn. Line.
James Thompson, Va. Line.
G. Van Landengham, Va. Line.
John Williams 2d, Penn. Line.
George Wright, Va. Line.

Under Act of June 7, 1832.

James Barr, Va. Militia.
Henry Beatty, Va. Militia.
Jacob Berlin, Penn. Militia.
George Black, Va. Line.
Geo. Blakeman, Ensign, Va. Militia.
Humphrey Brook, Aiddecamp, Va. Line.
Philip P. Buckner, Ser., Va. Militia.
John Campbell, Va. Militia.
John Colbert, Va. State Troops.
Peter Edwards, Va. Cont. Line.
James Foster, Va. Militia.
John Grim, Va. Militia.
Samuel Hart, N. J. Militia.
George Hensell, Va. Militia.
Michael Humble, Va. State Troops.
Henry Knipe, Ser., Va. Militia.
Conrad Kramer, Q. Ser., Va. Line.

John Krim, N. J. Militia.
Peter Lauck, Va. Line.
George Lonas, Va. Line.
Basil Lucas, Ser., Va. Militia.
Jas. M. Marshall, Lt., Va. Line.
Thos. Mitchell, Seaman, Va. Navy.
William Monroe, Va. Line.
Hugh Parrell, Va. State Troops.
Wm. Phillips, Va. Line.
John Piper, Va. State Troops.
Andrew Pittman, Va. Militia.
James Rieley, Va. Militia.
John Schultz, Va. Line.
Jacob Shade, Md. Militia.
Thomas Smart, Penn. Militia.
Alex. Smith, Mass. Militia.
John Smith, Col., Va. State Troops.
George Snapp, Va. Line.
Jacob Sperry, Va. Militia.

Invalid Pensioners.

George Black, 12th Va. Reg.
William Bishop, 12th Va. Reg.
John Bryant, 7th Inf.
Samuel Griffith, 5th Reg. U. S. Inf.
Andrew McGuire, 1st Va. Reg.
Robert White, Lt., 12th Va. Reg.

M.

Page County.

Under Act of June 7, 1832.

Henry Aleshite, Penn. Line.
Owen Campbell, Va. Line.
Reuben Cave, Va. State Troops.
Richard Jenkins, Va. Militia.

Andrew Keyser, Va. Line.
Joseph Sampson, Va. Line.
Thomas Tharp, Va. Line.

N.

Rockingham County.

Under Act of March 18, 1818.

Jacob Conrad, Va. Line. Died June 3, 1824.
Jacob Smith, Va. Line. Age 75.

Under Act of June 7, 1832.

Chris. Ammon, Ser., Va. Mil. Age 75.
Geo. Argubright, Va. Mil. Age 75.
James Barleys, Va. Mil. Age 74.
Benj. Berry, Va. Mil. Age 76.
Peter Brown, N. Y. Mil. Age 86.
Wm. Bryan, Va. Mil. Age 72.
Andrew Byrd, Va. Line. Age 79.
Richard Custer, Va. Mil. Age 77.
Leonard Davis, Va. Mil. Age 72.
Ph. Haitsman, Penn. Mil. Age 75.
Law. Howderskell, Va. Mil. Age 82.
Andrew Huling, Va. Mil. Age 73.
Chris. Kapplinger, Va. Troops. Age 84.
Jacob Kisling, Va. Troops. Age 74.
Philip Koontz, Va. Line. Age 82.
Thomas Lewis, Lt., Va. Mil. Age 74.
Michael Lore, Va. Troops. Age 79.
Michael Mayer, Va. Mil. Age 89.
James Meadows, Va. Line. Age 74.
John Nicholas, N. C. Mil. Age 78.
James Palmer, Va. Mil. Age 70.
John Pence, Sr., Va. Mil. Age 79.
Conrad Radeer, Va. Troops. Age 78.
Henry Radeer, Va. Mil. Age 77.
Lawrence Raynes, Va. Mil. Age 74.

James Rogers, Del. Mil. Age 78.
Jose Rogers, Del. Mil. Age 75.
David Rolstone, Va. Mil. Age 73.
James Routon, Va. Mil. Age 72.
Melchior Segrist, Pa. Mil. Age 79.
George Stepler, Va. Mil. Age 75.
Matthew Tate, Va. Mil. Age 73.
John Taylor, Va. Mil. Age 77.
Henry Whetzell, Va. Mil. Age 76.

Revolutionary Pensioners still Living in 1840.

Elizabeth Brown, aged 83.
Andrew Huling, aged 75.
Philip Koontz, aged 95.
James Meadows, aged 81.
Henry Hammer, aged 84.
Leonard Davis, aged 79.
Francis Yancey, aged, 70.
William Bryan, aged 78.
Agnes Vanpelt, aged 77.
David Ralston, aged 79.
Magdaline Bible, aged 75.
Mary Gibbons, aged 80.
Philip Hartman, aged 83.
Matthew Tate, aged 87.
James Palmer, aged 77.

O.

Shenandoah County.

Under Act of March 18, 1818.

Daniel Anderson, Va. Line.
Philip Barr, Va. Line.
John Bly, Va. Line.
George Clower, Va. Line.
Leonard Cooper, Capt., Va. Line.
Thomas Dodson, Penn. Line.

Joachim Fetzer, Va. Line.
Archibald Finley, Va. Line.
Isaac Gibbons, Dragoon, Penn. Line.
Joseph Golloday, Va. Line.
William Grady, Va. Line.
Daniel Gray, Dragoon, Va. Line.
Peter Grim, Va. Line.
Drury Jackson, Va. Line.
Benj. McKnight, Va. Line.
Lewis Miller, Va. Line.
Collin Mitchum, Cor., S. C. Line.
Abner Newman, Va. Line.
Thomas Purdour, Va. Line.
John Rolls, Va. Line.
John Smith 5th, Va. Line.
Elias Turner, Va. Line.

Under Act of June 7, 1832.

Jeffrey Collins, Va. Mil.
George Fletcher, Va. Mil.
Joshua Foltz, Va. Line.
Jacob Helsey, Va. Mil.
Moses Henry, Va. Line.
Thomas Hudson, Va. Troops.
Jacob Kepps, Va. Mil.
John Lary, Va. Line.
Jacob Leneweaver, Va. Mil.
Christian Miller, Ser., Va. Mil.
David O'Rourke, Ser., Va. Mil.
Henry Roarer, Va. Troops.
Jacob Roland, Penn. Mil.
Robert Russell, Va. Troops.
Martin Zea, Va. Troops.

Invalid Pensioners.

John Berry, 9th Va. Reg.
Jesse Brown, 2d Reg. U. S. Inf.

Dennis O'Ferrell, 11th Va. Reg.
Willis Ramsey, 20th U. S. Inf.
John Stansbury, U. S. Inf.
William Tipton, Parker's Reg.

P.

Bibliography.

Archives.

Spottsylvania County Records: 1721 to the present. These records are fairly complete, and cover the period of the first settlements in the Valley of Virginia, but do not appear to contain any references to persons or places in that section. There are, however, records referring to the Germans of Germanna and adjacent sections. The records of Spottsylvania, from 1721 to 1800, were printed in abstract and published in a single volume in 1905, by Fox, Duffield & Co., New York.

Orange County Records: 1734 to the present. The records are in good condition and, with reference to wills and deeds, about complete. They contain frequent entries of Valley Germans beginning with the year 1735.

Frederick County Records: 1743 to the present. The records of deeds and wills are practically complete from the beginning. Many of the original documents were presented in German, and some suffered not a little in translation by clerks who were much more English than German.

Augusta County Records: 1745 to the present. The records of Augusta are in excellent condition; and, like those of Frederick, are of great interest and historical value.

Shenandoah County Records: 1772 to the present. A great many of the original papers must have been in German; and many of the signatures are recorded in German script.

Rockingham County Records: 1777 to the present. Many of the old records in Rockingham were destroyed by fire, some wholly, some partly, during the Civil War. A number of these have been restored as fully as possible; but some are perhaps in a condition that is irreparable, even though they are not altogether destroyed.

The Virginia State Library and the Virginia Historical Society both have at Richmond many documents of interest and value relating to the people and places in the Valley.

For the later periods, the records of Berkeley County (1772—) and Jefferson County (1801—), West Virginia; Page County (1831—), Warren County (1836—), and Clarke County (1836—), Virginia, will also doubtless be found valuable; though the present writer has not consulted them.

Books and Pamphlets.

Anbury, Major Thomas.—Travels through the Interior Parts of America; in a Series of Letters. Two vols., 906 pp., 8vo, illust. London, 1791: Printed for Wm. Lane, Leadenhall-Street.—The letters were written in 1776-1781. In the second volume are some from Charlottesville, Richmond, Winchester, Frederick, Md., and other places in adjacent sections. Much is told of the Hessians, the natives, the physical features of the country, etc.

Barringer, Dr. P. B., *et al.*—The University of Virginia: Its History, Etc., with Biographical Sketches and Portraits of Founders, Benefactors, Officers and Alumni. Two vols., 1064 pp., 4to, illust. New York, 1904: Lewis Publishing Co.—These volumes contain sketches of James Bumgardner, Jr., Holmes Conrad, H. H. Henkel, A. M. Henkel, D. B. Lucas, John Paul, C. B. Rouss, and other Valley of Virginia men of German descent.

Bernheim, G. D.—History of the German Settlements and of the Lutheran Church in North and South Carolina, From the Earliest Period of the Colonization of the Dutch, German and Swiss Settlers to the Close of the First Half of the Present Century. Pp. xvi—557, 12mo. Philadelphia, 1872: The Lutheran Book Store, 117 N. 6th Street.

Boogher, W. F.—Gleanings of Virginia History. An Historical and Genealogical Collection, Largely from Original Sources. Pp. viii—442, 8vo. Washington, 1903: Published by the Author.—Contains, among other things, several valuable rosters and schedules of the French and Indian War and the Revolution, from Hening's Statutes, records of the U. S. Pension Office, etc., that relate to the Valley counties of Virginia.

Bowman, Peter.—*Ein Zeugnisz von der Taufe.* Printed by Laurence Wartmann, Harrisonburg, Va., 1817.—Bowman was an elder in the Dunker Church, and lived in Rockingham County. The writer has never seen a copy of his book, and knows of only one, which is in the possession of Gen. J. E. Roller, Harrisonburg.

Braun, Johannes.—*Circular-Schreiben an die Deutschen Einwohner von Rockingham und Augusta, und den benachbarten Counties. Erster Band.* Pp., x—409, 16mo. Harrisonburg, Va., 1818: Laurentz Wartmann, Printer.—Brown was for many years a leading minister of the German Reformed Church, and published various works. The book here under review was well bound in sheep, and consists of five parts: Pp. 1-115, Reasons for supporting Bible Societies; pp. 119-234, Extracts from the Ninth Annual Report of the Committee for the British and Foreign Bible Society; pp. 235-276, Short Extracts from the Works of Dr. Claudius Buchanan: pp. 278-373, An Essay on Slavery and Serfdom; pp. 377-409, A Thanksgiving Sermon on the Conclusion of Peace, delivered at Salem Church, Augusta County, April 13, 1815; with extracts from other sermons.

(2) *Eine kurze Unterweisung Christlichen Religion, nach dem Heidelbergischen Catechismus, in den Deutschen und Englischen-Sprachen. bey Johannes Braun, Diener des Evangelii.* Pp. 72, 16mo. Harrisonburg, Va., 1830: Lawrence Wartmann, Printer.—On each left-hand page is the German text; on each right-hand page is the corresponding English.

Brock, Dr. R. A.—Virginia and Virginians: 1606-1888. Eminent Virginians, By R. A. Brock; History of Virginia, From Settlement of Jamestown to Close of the Civil War, By Virgil A. Lewis. Two vols., 8vo, illust. Vol. I—pp. 1-408—Early Virginians and History of Virginia; Vol. II—pp. 409-870—more Virginia history and more Virginians, chiefly men of more recent times. Richmond and Toledo, 1888: H. H. Hardesty, Publisher.—Two big, handsome volumes, with much of interest and value in them; but unserviceable to a great extent for lack of indices.

Bruce, Thomas.—Southwest Virginia and Shenandoah Valley. Pp. x—259, 8vo. Richmond, 1891: J. L. Hill Publishing Co.—Appears to have been written chiefly for advertising purposes, but contains much of interest: among other things, sketches of the Valley towns of Luray, Shenandoah, Grottoes, Berryville, Front Royal, Waynesboro, Basic City.

Brumbaugh, M. G.—A History of the German Baptist Brethren in Europe and America. Pp. 559, 8vo, illust. Mt. Morris (now Elgin), Ill., 1899: Brethren Publishing House.—Gives much of interest concerning one of the religious bodies now largely represented in the Valley of Virginia.

Burkholter, Peter.—*Eine Verhandlung, Von der äusserlichen Wasser-Taufe, und Erklärung einiger Irrthümer.* Pp. 60, 16mo. Harrisonburg, Va., 1816: Laurentz Wartmann, Printer.—Burkholder was a noted leader of the Rockingham Mennonites. Only two copies of this pamphlet are known: one of these is in the possession of the writer.

Cartmell, T. K.—Historical, Biographical, and Genealogical Studies of the First Settlers and Their Descendants of the Lower Shenandoah Valley. In preparation.—Mr. Cartmell was for 25 years clerk of the county court of Frederick

County, and has many advantages in the preparation of such a work.

Casey, Joseph J.—Personal Names in Hening's Statutes at Large of Virginia, and Shepherd's Continuation. Pp. 141, 4to. New York, 1896: Published by the Author, 26, E. 129th St.—This is an index of Hening and Shepherd by proper names: a very helpful work.

Chandler, J. A. C.—Makers of Virginia History. Pp. 356, 12mo, illust. New York, 1904: Silver, Burdett and Company.—Dr. W. H. Ruffner, a Valley German and an eminent Virginian, is presented among the other worthies; but the sketch of him is rather indifferent.

Cooke, John Esten.—Virginia: Chapter XXIII, pp. 322-330: "The Virginians of the Valley."—This part is mainly from Kercheval, on the Germans. Mr. Cooke is in a common error as to the dates of first settlements, priority of the different classes, etc.; but he gives a true idea of the character of the people.

Crozier, W. A.—Virginia Colonial Militia: 1651-1776. Pp. 144, 8vo. New York, 1905: Published by the Genealogical Association.—A very valuable work, containing hundreds of names, chiefly from original sources. Some of the lists are taken from Hening.

(2) Virginia County Records: Spottslyvania County, 1721-1800. Being Transcriptions, from the Original Files at the County Court House, of Wills, Deeds, Administrators' and Guardians' Bonds, Marriage Licenses, and Lists of Revolutionary Pensioners. Pp. 576, 8vo. New York, 1905: Published for the Genealogical Association by Fox, Duffield & Co.—A valuable source book, containing records (in abstract) of some German families east of the Blue Ridge, but of none in the Valley.

Diffenderffer, F. R.—The German Immigration into Pennsylvania through the Port of Philadelphia, and "The Redemptioners." Pp. 1-328, Publications of the Pennsylvania-German Society, Vol. X, 1900.

Engle, J. M.—A History of the Engle Family in the Shenandoah Valley and Family Connections. Gen. Wm. Darke, Moores, Dukes and Molers, and Incidents of the Civil War. Pp. 36, 16mo, illust. Washington, 1906: Published by the Author, Sixth Auditor's Office, Treasury Department.—Contains many genealogical and other facts of interest, and is generally reliable; but lacks literary form.

English, W. H.—Conquest of the Country Northwest of the River Ohio, 1778-1783, and Life of Gen. George Rogers Clark. With numerous sketches of men who served under Clark and full lists of those allotted lands in Clark's grant for service in the campaigns against the British Posts, showing exact land allotted to each. Two vols., pp. 1186, 8vo, illust. Indianapolis and Kansas City, 1897: The Bowen-Merrill Co.—A voluminous and valuable work, containing much from original matter. It pays high tributes to Maj. Joseph Bowman and other Valley Germans.

Falkenstein, G. N.—History of the German Baptist Brethren Church. Pp. 154, 8vo, illust. Lancaster, Pa., 1901: The New Era Printing Co.—Reprinted from the Pennsylvania-German Society Annual of 1900.

Fast, R. E., and Hu Maxwell.—The History and Government of West Virginia. Pp. x—514, 12mo, illust. Morgantown, 1901: The Acme Publishing Co.—Contains some interesting facts concerning the German element in the Valley and adjacent sections, and has a valuable bibliography.

Flory, J. S.—The First Period of Literary Activity among the Dunkers. In preparation.—Professor Flory has had excellent opportunities for obtaining valuable information on his subject. His address is Bridgewater, Va.

Foote, W. H.—Sketches of Virginia, Historical and Biographical. Second Series, 2d ed., revised. Pp. xiv—596, 8vo. Philadelphia, 1856: J. B. Lippincott & Co.—Mr. Foote was pastor of the Presbyterian Church at Romney, Va. His book contains much of interest and value concerning the early history of the Valley, with special reference to the Scotch-Irish, but also with incidental reference to the Germans and others.

Fretz, A. J.—A Brief History of Bishop Henry Funck and other Funk Pioneers, and a complete Genealogical Family Register with biographies of their descendants from the earliest available Records to the Present Time. With Portraits and other Illustrations. With an Introduction by John F. Funk, of Elkhart, Ind. Pp. 874, 12mo. Elkhart, Ind., 1889: Mennonite Publishing Co.—A mine of information, not only concerning the well known and innumerable Funk family, but also concerning related families: the Stovers, Monks, Rosenbergers, Showalters, Hecklers, Meyers, Austins, Fretzs, Krouts, Shenks, Ashenfelters, Ruebushs, Hunsickers, Wismers, *et al.*

Funk, Benj.—Life and Labors of Elder John Kline, the Martyr Missionary. Collated from his Diary. Pp. 480, 8vo, illust. Elgin, Ill., 1900: Brethren Publishing House.—John Kline was a Dunker preacher of Rockingham, whose labors covered the period from 1835 till his martyrdom in 1864. His travels and ministrations extended over the Shenandoah Valley, and westward across the Ohio River. The book contains innumerable entries of German names in the Valley and elsewhere.

Funkhouser, Jacob.—A Historical Sketch of the Funkhouser Family. Pp. 100, 8vo, illust. Harrisonburg, Va., 1902: The Rockingham Register Press.

Garr, J. W. and J. C.—Genealogy of the Descendants of John Gar, or more particularly of his son, Andreas Gaar, who emigrated from Bavaria to America in 1732. With Portraits, Coat-of-arms, Biographies, Wills, History, Etc. Pp.

xv—608, 8vo. Cincinnati, 1894: Published by the Author, John C. Garr (now of Jacksonville, Fla.).—This book is excellently arranged, for the tracing of genealogy; and contains much about the Germans of Madison County, Va.

Gilbert, D. M.—The Lutheran Church in Virginia, 1776-1876. A Historical Discourse Delivered before the Lutheran Synod of Virginia, at its Forty-Seventh Convention Held in Strasburg, Shenandoah County, Virginia, August 3-8, 1876. Pp. 58, 8vo. New Market, Va., 1876: Henkel & Co., Printers.—Contains much historical and biographical matter.

(2) The Praises of the Lord in the Story of Our Fathers. A Historical Discourse, delivered in Grace Evangelical Lutheran Church, Winchester, Virginia, on Sunday Morning, May 13, 1877. Pp. 33, 8vo. New Market, Va., 1877: Henkel & Co., Printers.—Chiefly a history of the Lutheran congregation at Winchester, but contains also numerous more general facts.

(3) A Chapter of Colonial, Luthero-Episcopal Church History. An address delivered at the laying of the Corner-Stone of the Emanuel Evangelical Lutheran Church, Woodstock, Virginia, Friday, August 8, 1884. Pp. c. 30, 8vo., reprinted from the *Lutheran Quarterly* of October, 1884.—An interesting account of the early Lutherans in the Valley of Virginia, and of Gen. Muhlenberg's career: an exhaustive discussion of his double church relation, with the Lutherans on the one hand, with the Episcopalians on the other.

(4) Early History of the Lutheran Church in Georgia. Pp. 20, 8vo., reprinted from the *Lutheran Quarterly* of April, 1897.—The facts herein presented are connected with the Virginia Lutherans only in a general way.

Grumbine, L. L.—The Pennsylvania-German Dialect. Pp. 37-99, Publications of the Pennsylvania-German Society,

Vol. XII, 1903.—Of great interest in studying the language used several generations ago by the Valley of Virginia Germans, and still used in familiar conversation by a few families and in a few localities.

Hale, John P.—Trans-Allegheny Pioneers: Historical Sketches of the First White Settlements West of the Alleghenies, 1748 and After. Pp. 330, 12mo, illust. Charleston, W. Va., 1886: Published by the Author; later, Cincinnati: S. C. Cox & Co., 72 W. 4th St.—This book needs an index. It does not give much about the Valley Germans, but contains some interesting facts about the Ruffners, from Page County, who settled in Kanawha, and others originally from the Valley.

Hardesty, H. H.—Historical and Geographical Encyclopedia, Special Virginia and County Editions. Giving a History of the Virginias, Biographical Sketches of Eminent Virginians, written by R. A. Brock; Military History by Counties, Giving the first Roster ever compiled of the Soldiers of the Lost Cause, for each County Edition, with record of the Military Organizations of the County, and History of its Honorable Part in the Great Drama of the late War; Also, a Department devoted to Family and Personal Sketches. New York, Richmond, Chicago, and Toledo, 1884: H. H. Hardesty & Co.—Only the Rockingham County edition has been examined. In this, pages 305-430, folio, are of special interest: the bulk of the book is of a general character. The muster rolls of military companies are of particular value.

Hark, J. Max.—*Chronicon Ephratense.* A history of the Community of Seventh-Day Baptists at Ephrata, Lancaster County, Pa. Translation by Hark. Lancaster, Pa., 1889.—The Ephrata Brethren were an early offshoot of the Dunkers, and are often confused with them. The former had several communities in Virginia during the third quarter of the 18th century.

Hartzler, J. S., and Daniel Kauffman.—Mennonite Church History. Pp. 422, 8vo, illust. Scottdale, Pa., 1905: Mennonite Book and Tract Society.—Considerable space is devoted to the Mennonites in Europe, as well as to each of the branches of the church in America. The congregations in the Valley of Virginia and adjacent districts receive extended notice in an excellent chapter by Bishop L. J. Heatwole.

Hays, Daniel.—A history of the Non-Resistant Religious Bodies of the Shenandoah Valley. In preparation. In this work Elder Hays will tell of the Quakers, Mennonites, and Dunkers, and of their experience during the Civil War.

Heatwole, D. A.—A history of the Heatwole Family, from the Landing of the Ancestor of the Race, up to the Present Time. Pp. 24, 16mo. Dale Enterprise, Va., 1882: Office of the *Watchful Pilgrim.*

Hütwohl, Jacob, Jr.—*Chronik der Familie Hütwohl.* Pp. 71, 8vo, illust. Boppard on the Rhine, 1901: Otto Maisel, Printer.—A more extended account of the Heatwoles, written by a German member of the family. Especially interesting on the causes and circumstances of German emigration.

Heckman, G. C.—German Colonization in America. Pp. 13-29, Pennsylvania-German Society Publications, Vol. V, 1895.

Hening, W. W.—The Statutes at Large; Being a Collection of all the Laws of Virginia, from the First Session of the Legislature, in the year 1619. In thirteen 8vo. volumes of over 600 pages each, covering the legislation up to October, 1792. The books were printed for the editor at Richmond (Vol. XIII at Philadelphia), and were issued during the period from 1819 to 1823. In 1836, Samuel Shepherd published at Richmond three volumes more, covering the legislation from 1792 to 1806.—This series of volumes by

Hening, with Shepherd's Continuation, are a real treasure house to the history student, and probably form the most valuable source-book extant on the history of the State to the end of the 18th century. The first volume in which any references to the Valley Germans appear is No. 4, covering the period from 1711 to 1736. These references are indirect for the most part. Vol. V, 1738-1748, contains several Acts of special interest relative to the dividing of the counties of Frederick and Augusta, the killing of wolves and paying therefor, the fixing of court days, etc. Vol. VI, 1748-1755, records various Acts relating to Frederick and Augusta counties, and to the oncoming war with the French and Indians. Vol. VII, 1756-1763, is the most interesting and valuable of all for Valley German history. The Military Schedule of 1758 and the Acts for establishing towns are of special interest.

Henkel, A. L.—Biographical Sketch of Rev. Paul Henkel. Born December 15, 1754; Died November 27, 1825. Pp. 4, 8vo. New Market, Va., 1890: Henkel & Co., Publishers.

Henkel, Socrates.—History of the Evangelical Lutheran Tennessee Synod, Embracing An Account of the Causes which gave rise to its Organization; Its Organization and Name; Its Position and Confessional Basis; Object of its Organization; Work, Development, and various Sessions; Its Policy; And its Future. Pp. 275, 8vo. New Market, Va., 1890: Henkel & Co., Publishers.

Henkel, Socrates, *et al.*—The Christian Book of Concord, or Symbolical Books, of the Evangelical Lutheran Church; Comprising the Three Chief Symbols, the Unaltered Augsburg Confession, the Apology, the Smalcald Articles, Luther's Smaller and Larger Catechisms, the Formula of Concord, and an Appendix. To which is Prefixed An Historical Introduction. Second Edition, Revised. Translated from the German. Pp. viii—780, 8vo. New Market, 1854: Solomon D. Henkel and Brs.—On this moumental work the Henkels and their helpers labored seven years. The successful accomplishment of the task was a notable achievement in the religious and literary progress of the Valley of Virginia Lutherans.

Hoffman, W. J.—Popular Superstitions. Pp. 70-81, Publications of the Pennsylvania-German Society, Vol. V, 1895.

Holsinger, H. R.—History of the Tunkers and The Brethren Church: Embracing the Church of the Brethren, the Tunkers, the Seventh-Day German Baptist Church, the Old German Baptists, and the Brethren Church; Including their Origin, Doctrine, Biography and Literature. Pp. 826, 8vo. Lathrop, California, 1901: Printed for the Author by the Pacific Press Publishing Co., Oakland.—This book contains an account of certain men and movements among the Valley of Virginia Dunkers.

Hotchkiss, Jed, and J. A. Waddell.—Historical Atlas of Augusta County, Virginia. Maps from Original Surveys, by Jed Hotchkiss; Its Annals, by J. A. Waddell. Pp. 94, large folio. Chicago, 1885: Waterman, Watkins & Co.—An excellent work, specially valuable for its maps. The historical and biographical notes are also of interest pertinent to our subject.

Howe, Henry.—Historical Collections of Virginia; Relating to its History and Antiquities, together with Geographical and Statistical Descriptions. Pp. 544, 8vo, illust. Charleston, S. C., 1846: Babcock & Co., Publishers.—One of the most helpful histories of Virginia ever published. It contains a separate sketch of each county, and other valuable features. There are, however, a few grave errors; one, for instance, in the account of the Tunkers of Botetourt County; pp. 203, 204, wherein the common mistake is made of describing the Tunkers (Dunkers) in terms of the mystical and ascetic Ephrata Brethren. The book is becoming rare.

Hurst, J. F.—Short History of the Church in the United

States, A. D. 1492-1890. Pp. 132, 16mo. New York, 1890: Chautauqua Press, 150 Fifth Avenue.—Contains valuable information concerning the characteristics and movements of some of the religious bodies largely represented in the Valley of Virginia.

Jefferson, Thomas.—Notes on the State of Virginia. Pp. 344, 16mo. Philadelphia, 1825: H. C. Carey & I. Lea, Publishers.—Written in 1781 and 1782. A number of facts are presented relating to the geography, population, customs, religion, distribution of militia in the several counties, etc., but not much relating particularly to the Valley or its inhabitants. The book is listed here chiefly because of the trustworthiness of the author and the remoteness of the period it represents. Many of the various histories of Virginia contain, each a little, in reference to the Valley and its people; but it has not been deemed necessary to include more than two or three in this bibliography.

Jensen, J. C.—American Lutheran Biographies. Milwaukee, 1890.—Contains sketches of some prominent Valley of Virginia Germans.

Keagy, Franklin.—A History of the Kägy Relationship in America from 1715 to 1900. Pp. 675, 8vo, illust. Harrisburg, Pa., 1899: Harrisburg Publishing Co.—A book finely printed, bound, and illustrated. The author, a citizen of Chambersburg, Pa., spent over twenty years in preparing the work.

Kemper, W. M., and H. L. Wright.—Genealogy of the Kemper Family in the United States. Descendants of John Kemper of Virginia. With a Short Historical Sketch of His Family and of the German Reformed Colony at Germanna and Germantown, Va. Pp. 248—xix, 8vo. Chicago, 1899: Geo. K. Hazlitt & Co., Printers, 373 Dearborn St.

Kennedy, J. P.—Journals of the House of Burgesses of Virginia. Two vols., folio. Vol. I, 1770-1772, pp. xxxv—333;

Vol. II, 1773-1776, pp. xxiii—301. Richmond, 1905.—Contain frequent references to, and occasional petitions from, the Valley counties and citizens. A number of German names appear.

Kercheval, Samuel.—A History of the Valley of Virginia. Revised and Extended by the Author. Third Edition, pp. 403, 8vo. Woodstock, Va., 1902: W. N. Grabill, Printer. —A work published first in 1833, and still holding rank as the best and fullest authority on the early conditions in the Valley.

Körner, Gustav.—*Das Deutsche Element in den Vereinigten Staaten von Nordamerika, 1818-1848.* Pp. 461, 8vo. Cincinnati, 1880: A. E. Wilde & Co.—This work treats of the Germans in the several sections and States of the Union; pp. 393-410 being devoted to Maryland and Virginia. Professors M. Schele de Vere and George Blättermann and Dr. Carl Minnigerode are put forth as distinguished Germans in the Old Dominion. The book has appended a list of 55 "Sources."

Kuhns, Oscar.—The German and Swiss Settlements of Colonial Pennsylvania. Pp. 268, 12 mo. New York, 1901: Henry Holt & Co.—A good outline of the historical back ground is given; Pennsylvania-German family names, manners and customs, religious life, etc., are discussed; and an extended bibliography is appended.

Lathrop, J. M., A. W. Dayton, *et al.*—An Atlas of Frederick County, Virginia. From actual Surveys. Pp. 42—, folio. Philadelphia, 1885: D. J. Lake & Co.

Lathrop, J. M., B. N. Griffing, *et al.*—An Atlas of Rockingham County, Virginia. From actual Surveys. Pp. 58, folio. Philadelphia, 1885: D. J. Lake & Co.

(2) An Atlas of Shenandoah and Page Counties, Virginia. From actual Surveys. Pp. 60, folio. Philadelphia, 1885: D. J. Lake & Co.—These county atlases are finely

executed and of great value. The maps not only show the several counties as wholes, but each district separately. Every road and residence is located, and the name of each resident is given.

Learned, M. D.—The Pennsylvania-German Dialect, Part I. Baltimore, 1889.

Lederer, John.—The Discoveries of John Lederer, In three several marches from Virginia, to the West of Carolina, and other parts of the Continent: Begun in March 1669, and ended in September 1670. Together with a General Map of the Whole Territory which he traversed. Collected and translated out of the Latine from his Discourse and Writings, By Sir William Talbot, Baronet. Pp. 30, 8vo. Rochester, N. Y., 1902: 300 copies reprinted for G. P. Humphrey.—The book was first printed in 1672, in London. Lederer was a German, and evidently a scholarly man. His map is remarkably accurate, considering the time and circumstances of its execution; and his accompanying essay is, except in one or two minor particulars, exact and reliable. Lederer was, so far as is known, the first white man to cross the Blue Ridge and enter the Valley.

Lewis, Virgil A.—West Virginia. Its History, Natural Resources, Industrial Enterprises, and Institutons. Pp. 390, 8vo, illust. Charleston, 1903: The Tribune Printing Co. —Contains a few statements of interest concerning the Shenandoah Valley and its people.

(2) History and Government of West Virginia. Pp. 408, 12mo, illust. New York, Cincinnati, Chicago, 1904: American Book Co.—Gives a number of interesting facts about the early Germans in the Valley and adjacent sections.

Loy, M., *et al.*—The Distinctive Doctrines and Usages of the General Bodies of the Evangelical Lutheran Church in the United States. Pp. 193, 12mo. Philadelphia, 1893: Lutheran Publication Society.—A work that is helpful in determining the religious relationship of the Valley of Virginia Lutherans.

McIlhany, H. M., Jr.—Some Virginia Families. Being Genealogies of the Kinney, Stribling, Trout, McIlhany, Milton, Rogers, Tate, Snickers, Taylor, McCormick and other Families of Virginia. Pp. 274, 8vo, illust. Staunton, Va., 1903: Stoneburner & Prufer, Printers.

Mann, W. J.—Life and Times of Henry Melchior Muhlenberg. Pp. xvi—547, 8vo. Philadelphia, 1887: G. W. Frederick, 117 N. Sixth St.

Meade, William.—Old Churches, Ministers, and Families of Virginia. In two vols., pp. 986, 8vo. Philadelphia, 1872: J. B. Lippincott & Co.—Volume II contains much of interest and value concerning the people of the Valley counties—the Germans and Scotch-Irish, as well as the few English.

Moore, Thomas.—The German Element in the Shenandoah Valley. In preparation as a Bachelor's thesis at Roanoke College, Va.

Morris, J. G.—Fifty Years in the Lutheran Ministry. Pp. viii—630, 8vo. Baltimore, 1878: Printed for the Author by James Young, 112 W. Balt. St.—Gives much of interest concerning movements and men connected with the Valley of Virginia.

Norris, J. E.—History of the Lower Shenandoah Valley Counties of Frederick, Berkeley, Jefferson, and Clarke: Their Early Settlement and Progress to the Present Time; Geological Features; A Description of their Historic and Interesting Localities; Cities, Towns, and Villages; Portraits of some of the Prominent Men, and Biographies of Many of the Representative Citizens. Pp. 812, 8vo, illust. Chicago, 1890: A. Warner & Co.—A huge volume containing much of interest and value, but rather poorly arranged.

Palmer, Dr. W. P., Sherwin McRae, H. W. Flournoy, *et al.*—

Calendar of Virginia State Papers and Other Manuscripts, Preserved in the Capitol at Richmond. Eleven 4to vols., of 600 or more pages each, containing reprints of papers dated from 1652 to 1869. The books were printed at Richmond, and were issued from 1875 to 1893.—In interest and value to the student of Virginia history, these volumes deserve to be ranked with Hening's *Statutes*. Vol. I, 1652-1781, is of special interest in reference to the first German settlers of the Valley.

Paul, John.—Address delivered at the Laying of the Corner Stone of the Rockingham County Court House, October 15, 1896. Pp. 19, 8vo. Harrisonburg, 1896: *Spirit of the Valley* Press.—A masterly presentation of the history of Rockingham County from the standpoint of the legal profession.

Peyton, J. L.—History of Augusta County, Virginia. Pp. vii—395, 8vo. Staunton, 1882: Samuel M. Yost & Son; Frank Prufer & Son, Binders.—A very readable volume, containing much valuable information, chiefly concerning the Scotch-Irish; but there is much also, incidentally, concerning the Germans and others. From it one gets a rather strong impression of the extent to which the Germans have entered into the important enterprises of Staunton in the more recent times—say, since 1850.

Pott, August Friedrich.—*Die Personennamen, insbesondere die Familiennamen und ihre Entstehungsarten; auch unter Berücksichtigung der Ortsnamen.* Pp. 721, 8vo. Leipzig, 1853: F. A. Brockhaus.—A voluminous and apparently serviceable work on the origin of family names. The author (1802-1887) was a distinguished philologist, and the founder of modern scientific etymology.

Richards, H. M. M.—Descendants of Henry Melchior Muhlenberg. Pp. 1-89, Publications of the Pennsylvania-German Society, Vol. X, 1900.

Richards, R. R.—The German Migration into the Valley of Virginia. Prepared as a Bachelor's thesis at Roanoke College, Va., in 1904.

Richardson, W. H.—The Picturesque Quality of the Pennsylvania German. Pp. 1-27, Publications of the Pennsylvania-German Society, Vol. XIII, 1904.

Roller, J. E.—Address at Lebanon, Pa. Pp. 14-23, Publications of the Pa.-Ger. Society, Vol. XIV, 1905.—Of interest in Valley of Virginia German history.

Rosengarten, J. G.—The German Soldier in the Wars of the United States. Second Edition, Revised and Enlarged. Pp. 298, 16mo. Philadelphia, 1890: J. B. Lippincott Co.—An interesting work; but the author appears to have known but little of the German soldiers of Virginia, particularly of the Valley.

(2) The German Allied Troops in the North American War of Independence, 1776-1783. Translated and Abridged from the German of Max von Eelking. Pp. 360, 8vo, illust. Albany, N. Y., 1893: Joel Munsell's Sons.—Gives a good deal concerning the Hessians and others at Charlottesville, Va., Winchester, and elsewhere.

(3) German Influence in America. Pp. 4, 8vo. Reprinted from Lippincott's Magazine of April, 1902.

(4) Popp's Journal, 1777-1783. Pp. 29, 8vo. Philadelphia, 1902.—A translation of the journal, with finely executed maps, of a Hessian soldier. It contains interesting comments on Winchester, Va., the surrounding country, and other Valley of Virginia subjects.

(5) American History from German Archives, with Reference to the German Soldiers in the Revolution and Franklin's Visit to Germany. Pp. 1-93, Publications of the Pa.-Ger. Society, Vol XIII, 1904.

Ruffner, Henry.—Address to the People of West Virginia; Shewing that Slavery is Injurious to the Public Welfare, and that it may be gradually abolished, without Detriment to the Rights and Interests of Slaveholders. Pp. 40, 8vo. Lexington, Va., 1847: Printed by R. C. Noel.—A masterly treatise, showing not only what the title indicates, but also giving much of interest regarding the conditions then prevailing in the Valley of Virginia and elsewhere. The pamphlet is at present very rare, only one copy being known to be extant.

Rupp, I. D.—History of Lancaster County, Pennsylvania, Lancaster, 1844.

(2) A Collection of Upwards of Thirty Thousand Names of German, Swiss, Dutch, French and other Immigrants in Pennsylvania from 1727 to 1776. With a Statement of the names of Ships, whence they sailed, and the date of their arrival at Philadelphia, Chronologically Arranged, together with the Necessary Historical and Other Notes. Second Revised and Enlarged Edition, with German Translation. Pp. x—495, 12mo. Philadelphia, 1898: Leary, Stuart & Co.—A compilation from the records of the port of Philadelphia, of great value to the historian and genealogist. The names of the ancestors of practically all the German families found in the Valley of Virginia to-day, may be found in this book. An alphabetical index would add very much to its serviceableness.

Sachse, J. F.—The German Pietists of Provincial Pennsylvania, 1694-1708. Pp. xviii—504, 8vo, illust. Philadelphia, 1895: Printed for the Author.—Gives graphic portrayals of many forces and figures moving in Pennsylvania about the time of the beginning of the migration to the Valley of Virginia.

(2) The German Sectarians of Pennsylvania, 1708-1800. A Critical and Legendary History of the Ephrata Cloister and the Dunkers. Two vols., 8vo, pp. xxxvi—1041, illust. Philadelphia, 1899, 1900: Printed for the Author.—Two elegant and interesting volumes. The second one contains

an account of the Ephrata community at Strasburg, Va., and others in the State.

(3) *Curieuse Nachricht,* from Pennsylvania, By Daniel Falckner. Translated from Falckner's original writing. Pp. 39-256, Publications of the Pa.-Ger. Society, Vol. XIV, 1905.—Falckner's work, published in Germany in 1702, did much to stimulate German immigration to Pennsylvania in the early years of the 18th century.

Saffell, W. T. R.—Records of the Revolutionary War: Containing the Military and Financial Correspondence of Distinguished Officers; Names of the Officers and Privates of Regiments, Companies, and Corps, with the Dates of their Commissions and Enlistments; Etc. Third Edition. Pp. 555, 8vo. Baltimore, 1894: Charles C. Saffell, 224 W. Fayette St.—Gives roster of Morgan's regiments from Virginia; but the list of Muhlenberg's German Regiment does not appear.

Schantz, F. J. F.—The Domestic Life and Characteristics of the Pennsylvania-German Pioneer. Pp. 1-97, Publications of the Pa.-Ger. Society, Vol. X, 1900.

Schuricht, Herrmann.—History of the German Element in Virginia. Vol. I, pp. 168, 8vo, 1898; Vol. II, pp. 224, 8vo, 1900. Baltimore: Theo. Kroh & Sons, Printers.—Schuricht goes too far in his enthusiasm for his race; he frequently strains the point on names that he supposes to be German; but in spite of all his faults he presents much that is indisputable and valuable. His is perhaps the most extensive work thus far published on the Germans of Virginia. It is the only one, devoted exclusively to the subject, that the present writer has seen.

Seidensticker, Oswald.—*Die Erste Deutsche Einwanderung in Amerika und die Gründung von Germantown im Jahre 1683.* Pp. 94, 8vo. Philadelphia, 1883.—An interesting collection of sketches of German-American people and life.

(2) *Geschichtsblätter: Bilder und Mittheilungen aus dem Leben der Deutschen in Amerika.* Edited by Carl Schurz. Second Volume. Pp. viii—276, 12mo. New York, 1885: E. Steiger & Co.—The parts of this book that bear more directly upon Virginia Germans relate to Gen. Peter Muhlenberg and his contemporaries; to Pennsylvania-German industrial habits; etc. A valuable bibliography is appended.

(3) The First Century of German Printing in America, 1728-1830. Preceded by a Notice of the Literary Work of F. D. Pastorius. Pp. x—254, 8vo. Philadelphia, 1893: Schaefer & Koradi.—A veritable gold mine to the antiquarian, although, as the author himself realized, the list of publications is far from complete. The most important of the early printing houses in the Shenandoah Valley are noticed.

Spaeth, Adolph.—Charles Porterfield Krauth. In two volumes. New York, 1898: The Christian Literature Co.

Spangler, E. W.—The Annals of the Families of Casper, Henry, Baltzer and George Spengler, who settled in York County [Pa.] respectively in 1729, 1732, 1732 and 1751: With Biographical and Historical Sketches, and Memorabilia of Contemporaneous Local Events. Pp. 605, 8vo, illust. York, Pa., 1896.—Many of the Spenglers came to Virginia, where they have won distinction in both civil and military life.

Stahr, J. S.—The Pennsylvania-Germans at Home. Pp. 53-70, Publications of the Pa.-Ger. Society, Vol. V, 1895.

Stanard, W. G. and Mary N.—The Colonial Virginia Register. A List of Governors, Councillors and Other Higher Officials, and also of Members of the House of Burgesses, and the Revolutionary Conventions of the Colony of Virginia. Pp. 249, 8vo. Albany, N. Y., 1902: Joel Munsell's

Sons.—Contains names of a half dozen or more Valley Germans.

Stapleton, A.—Memorials of the Huguenots in America, with special Reference to their Emigration to Pennsylvania. Pp. ix—164, 8vo, illust. Carlisle, Pa. 1901: Huguenot Publishing Co.—Many German families of Pennsylvania and Virginia are mentioned.

Thwaites, R. G., and Louise P. Kellogg.—Documentary History of Dunmore's War, 1774. Compiled from the Draper Manuscripts in the Library of the Wisconsin Historical Society, and published at the charge of the Wisconsin Society of the Sons of the American Revolution. Pp. xxviii —472, 12mo, illust. Madison, Wis., 1905: Wisconsin Historical Society.—Contains muster rolls, etc., from Augusta and other Valley counties.

Toner, Dr. J. M.—Index to Names of Persons and Churches in Bishop Meade's Old Churches, Ministers and Families of Virginia. Revised by Hugh A. Morrison, of the Library of Congress. Pp. 63, 8vo. Washington, 1898: The Southern History Association.—A valuable aid to a famous work.

Viereck, L.—German Instruction in American Schools. Pp. 531-708, Vol. I, Report of U. S. Commissioner of Education, 1900-1901.—A most valuable and interesting work. It presents the status of the study of German in American schools, colleges, and universities; many of the leaders in promoting the subject; together with the historical background of German-American relations, and an extensive bibliography.

Waddell, J. A.—Scotch-Irish of the Valley of Virginia. Pp. 79-99, Proceedings and Addresses of the Seventh Congress of the Scotch-Irish Society of America.—This address deals mainly, of course, with the Scotch-Irish; but the author admits that the Germans were in Augusta six years earlier. He also makes other references to the Germans.

(2) Annals of Augusta County, Virginia, From 1726 to 1871. Second Edition, Revised and Enlarged. Pp. 545, 4to. Staunton, Va., 1902: C. Russell Caldwell, Publisher.—Contains much of interest and value, though a few inaccuracies have been overlooked. The index needs revision and correction.

Walker, C. D.—Memorial, Virginia Military Institute. Biographical Sketches of the Graduates and Elèves of the Virginia Military Institute Who fell during the War between the States. Pp. 585, 8vo. Philadelphia, 1875: J. B. Lippincott & Co.—Contains sketches of a number of Valley men, four or five of whom bore German names; also a muster roll of the V. M. I. Cadet Battalion that took part in the battle of New Market, May 15, 1864.

Wayland, J. W., J. S. Flory, J. A. Garber, J. H. Cline, W. T. Myers, *et al.*—Bridgewater College: Its Past and Present. Pp. 298, 8vo, illust. Elgin, Ill., 1905: Printed by the Brethren Publishing House.—Tells of the struggle by the German Baptist Brethren (Dunkers) of the Valley of Virginia for higher education; gives sketches and portraits of some of the leaders; and contains a complete catalogue of the students of the college from 1880 to 1904.

Wenger, Jonas, *et al.*—History of the Descendants of Christian Wenger, Who Emigrated from Europe to Lancaster County, Pa., in 1727, and a complete Genealogical Family Register; with Biographies of his Descendants from the Earliest Available Records to the Present Time. Pp. 259, 12mo, illust. Elkhart, Ind., 1903: Mennonite Publishing Co.—The Wenger family is largely represented in the Shenandoah Valley.

Wenger, J. H.—History of the Descendants of Abraham Beery: Born in 1718; Emigrated from Switzerland to Pennsylvania in 1736: and a Complete Genealogical Family Register. Pp. 328, 12mo. South English, Iowa, 1905: Published by the Author.—The Beery family is also widely distributed in Rockingham and other Valley counties.

Withers, A. S.—Chronicles of Border Warfare, or a History of the Settlement by the Whites of North-Western Virginia, and of the Indian Wars and Massacres in that Section of the State, with Reflections, Anecdotes, etc. A New Edition, Edited and Annotated by Reuben Gold Thwaites. With a Memoir of the Author, and Several Illustrative Notes by the late Lyman Copeland Draper. Pp. xx—447, 8vo. Cincinnati, 1895: The Robert Clarke Co.—Does not contain much concerning the Shenandoah Valley proper, *i. e.*, the lower valley of Virginia. This is one of the most famous of the books on border warfare.

Wood, J. W.—History of the Wood Family. Pp. 24, 12mo. Luray, Va.—Contains many references to German families of Page County, Va., that intermarried with the Woods.

Woods, Edgar.—Albemarle County in Virginia. Giving some account of what it was by nature, of what it was made by man, and of some of the men who made it. Pp. 412, 8vo. Charlottesville, Va., 1901: The Michie Co., Printers.—Gives an account of the quartering of the German Convention troops near Charlottesville during the Revolution, with references to numerous German families of various periods. Over half of the book is devoted to notes on Albemarle families. The Appendix contains rolls of militia and military companies in the early Indian wars and the Revolution; lists of emigrants to other States; a necrology from 1744 to 1890; etc.

Zigler, D. H.—A History of the Dunkers in the Valley of Virginia. In preparation.—The author's address is Broadway, Va.

Clark.—Colonel George Rogers Clarke's Campaign in the Illinois in 1778-9 and Major Bowman's Journal. Pp. 119, 8vo. Cincinnati, 1869: Robert Clarke & Co.—Major Bowman and his company were from the lower Shenandoah Valley.

Henkel.—In Memoriam. Rev. Socrates Henkel, D. D. Pp. 29, 8vo. New Market, Va., 1901: Henkel & Co.—Contains biographical sketch, press notices, and personal tributes. Dr. Henkel was one of the foremost leaders of the Virginia Lutherans.

Kagy.—The Kagys: A Biography of the Kagy Relationship. Pp. 8, 8vo. Salem, Ill., 1884: Herald-Advocate Job Office Print.—Gives brief accounts of the Kageys of Pennsylvania and Virginia, as well as of those of Ohio and Illinois.

Koiner.—A Historical Sketch of Michael Keinadt and Margaret Diller, His Wife. The History and Genealogy of their numerous posterity in the American States, up to the year 1893. Pp. 171, 8vo, illust. Staunton, Va., 1893: Stoneburner & Prufer, Publishers.—An interesting history of a prominent family.

Lutheran Church.—Minutes of the Tenth Convention of the United Synod of the Evangelical Lutheran Church in the South, held in the Church of the Holy Communion, Dallas, N. C., July 10-15, 1906. Pp. 124, 8vo.

(2) Minutes of the Eighty-Sixth Annual Convention of the Evangelical Lutheran Tennessee Synod, Held in St. Thomas Church, S. C., August 8-12, 1906. Pp. 56, 8vo.

(3) Minutes of Seventy-Seventh Convention of the Evangelical Lutheran Synod of Virginia, Held in Mt. Tabor Church, Va., August 22-26, 1906. Pp. 45, 8vo. New Market, Va., Henkel & Co., Publishers.—These publications contain much information concerning several of the important religious bodies largely represented in the Valley of Virginia.

Officers and Soldiers.—A List of Non-Commissioned Officers and Soldiers of the Virginia State Line, and Non-Commissioned Officers and Seamen and Marines of the State Navy, whose Names are on the Army Register, and who have not received Bounty Land for Revolutionary Services. Documents No. 43 and No. 44. Pp. 19 and 51. Richmond, 1835: Printed by Samuel Shepherd, Printer to Commonwealth.—A few names of Valley men may be upon the lists; but, owing to the meager information given, it is very difficult to identify the individuals named.

Reformed Church.—Acts and Proceedings of the Classis of Virginia of the Potomac Synod of the Reformed Church in the United States. Sixty-Eighth Annual Session, May 23-28, 1906. Pp. 41, 8vo. Annville, Pa.: Hiester Printing and Publishing Co.—The classis herein referred to was held at Mt. Crawford, Rockingham County, Va. The report contains information on the religious, missionary, and educational activities of the church.

Seidensticker.—*Dr. Oswald Seidensticker. Professor an der Universität von Pennsylvanien. Ein Lebensbild.* Pp. 72, 8vo. Philadelphia, 1894: H. R. Grassman, 50 N. Fifth St. —Contains biography, memorial addresses, and a list of Seidensticker's works.

Articles in Magazines and Newspapers.

Baltimore Sun.—Virginia Heraldry. Sunday editions, July 31, 1904, to or near the present (March, 1907). The sketches of the Hites, July 16 and 23, 1905, and of the Bartons, October 8, 1905, are of special interest in Valley German history.

Gospel Messenger, Elgin, Ill.—Autobiographical Sketches, by Eld. B. F. Moomaw, of Virginia. October 6, 13, 20, 27, November 3, 10, 17, and December 8, 1891.—A good deal is told of the war experiences of Virginia Dunkers, by one who was in the midst of things.

Harrisonburg Daily News, Harrisonburg, Va.—September 22, 1903: Candidates Named by Democrats for November

Elections: Who and What they Are.—Sketches and portraits are given of Sen. George B. Keezell, Dr. H. M. Rogers, Mr. C. L. Hedrick, Mr. E. W. Carpenter, Hon. George N. Conrad, Col. D. H. Lee Martz, Mr. J. S. Messerley, Sheriff John A. Switzer: all prominent men of Rockingham County, and all of German lineage except one.

(2) April 6, 11, 22, 24, 1907: Some Ancient Muster Rolls. By J. W. Wayland.—Classified lists of the soldiers of Augusta and Frederick in the French and Indian War, together with names of persons furnishing horses, provisions, etc., for the campaigns. A number of Germans appear.

Harrisonburg Free Press, Harrisonburg, Va.—February 14, 1900: The Germans: Their Early Settlement in Rockingham County and the Valley of Virginia. By Charles E. Kemper.—Gives much also regarding the causes of the German immigration to America.

(2) History of Rockingham County. By J. H. Floyd. A series of ten articles, beginning May 23, 1900, and ending July 27, following. The period embraced begins with the first settlements near Winchester and continues to the present time. A good deal of attention is given to the rosters and muster rolls of Rockingham soldiers in the several wars.

Journal of the Presbyterian Historical Society, Philadelphia; Witherspoon Building.—The First German Reformed Colony in Virginia: 1714-1750. By William J. Hinke. In three instalments: Vol. II, No. 1 (June, 1903), pp. 1-17; No. 2 (Sept., '03), pp. 98-110; No. 3 (Dec., '03), pp. 140-150.—An account of the Germanna settlements.

McClure's Magazine, New York and London.—December, 1906; pp. 124-136: Reminiscences of a Long Life. By Carl Schurz.—One paper of a series. This one contains graphic sketches of the new, crude West of fifty years ago;

a study of the great German immigration of that period; an account of a visit to London; anecdotes of Kossuth, Jenny Lind, and Wagner.

Moorefield Examiner, Moorefield, W. Va.—South Branch Valley Genealogies. By H. E. Wallace, Jr. The series continues from January to August 24, 1905; the first two articles being two weeks apart, the rest appearing at weekly intervals. The families presented are the following: Van Meter, du Bois, Hopewell, Inskeep, Cunningham, and Heydt (Hite).

Old Dominion Home, Dayton, Va.—Vol. I, No. 2 (November, 1906); pp. 2-4: The Legend of Cook's Creek. By L. J. Heatwole.—Contains a good many facts of historical interest regarding the Cook's Creek section ot Rockingham County.

Our Church Paper, New Market, Va.—August 27, 1902: A Fortnight in the South. By H. E. J., in *The Lutheran.*—A sketch containing numerous facts relating to the Lutherans in Virginia and North Carolina. In the same issue are also the following: St. John's Church, Wytheville, by L. A. Fox; and an account of the 82d annual convention of the Lutheran Tennessee Synod, at Rader's Church, Rockingham Co., Va., Aug. 21-25, 1902.

(2) September 24, 1902: Pioneer Home Mission Work: Some Leaves from the Journal of the Rev. Paul Henkel. By H. E. J., in *The Lutheran.*—An account of tours in 1806 to Ohio and North Carolina.

Page Courier, Luray, Va.—In the spring or summer of 1885, as nearly as has been ascertained, James W. Wood, of Compton (now of Luray), Va., published a series of articles on Page County Families: The Woods, Stricklers, Keysers, and others.

Pennsylvania-German, Lebanon, Pa.—Vol. III, No. 1 (January, 1902), pp. 3-18: Gen. John Peter G. Muhlenberg.—An extended illustrated sketch, by the Editor, P. C. Croll.

(2) Vol. IV, No. 2 (April, 1903), pp. 243-253: Rev. Gerhart Henkel and His Descendants. By A. Stapleton.—Contains an account of the Henkel Press, New Market, Va.

(3) Vol. V, No. 2 (April, 1904), pp. 61-72: From Winchester to Harrisburg. By Dr. I. H. Betz.

(4) Ditto, pp. 81-89: Researches in the First Century of German Printing in America, 1728-1830. By A. Stapleton.—In the line of a supplement to Seidensticker's work.

(5) Vol. V, No. 4 (October, 1904), p. 183: Early German Printing in America: A Resume. By A. Stapleton.

(6) Vol. VI, No. 1 (January, 1905), pp. 230-235: The Germans and Our Independence. By F. G. Gotwald.

(7) Vol. VI, No. 2 (April, 1905), pp. 262, 263: Early German Printing in America: Supplement No. 2. By. A. Stapleton.

(8) Ditto, pp. 271-285: Pennsylvania-German Influence. By T. C. Zimmerman.

Pennsylvania Magazine of History and Biography, Philadelphia.—Vol. VI (1882), pp. 58-68: The German Almanac of Christopher Sauer. By A. H. Cassel.—This paper is of interest to Valley Germans, because many of the Sower almanacs were used in Virginia, and some were sent as far south as South Carolina and Georgia.

(2) Vol. VIII (1884), pp. 328-340: A Partial List of the Families Who Arrived at Philadelphia between 1682 and 1687.—Among the number were some Germans whose descendants may have reached the Valley of Virginia within the next century.

(3) Ditto, pp. 414-426: A History of the Upper Germantown Burying-Ground. By Dr. P. D. Keyser.—Con-

tains names of many German families found later in Virginia.

(4) Vol. IX (1885), pp. 82-88: Inscriptions in the Upper Germantown Burying-Ground. By Dr. P. D. Keyser.

(5) Vol. X (1886), pp. 241-250; 375-391: German Emigration to the American Colonies, and Distribution of Emigrants. By A. D. Mellick, Jr.—A most readable and thought-stimulating paper.

(6) Vol. XII (1888), pp. 76-96: The Quarrel between Christopher Sower, the Germantown Printer, and Conrad Beissel, Founder and Vorsteher of the Cloister at Ephrata. By S. W. Pennypacker.

(7) Vol. XIII (1889), pp. 184-206: Frederick Augustus Conrad Muhlenberg, Speaker of the House of Representatives, in the First Congress, 1789. By Oswald Seidensticker.—Makes some interesting references to Gen. Muhlenberg and other members of the family.

(8) Ditto, pp. 265-270: An Exhortation and Caution to Friends concerning Buying or Keeping of Negroes. By George Keith. Edited by G. H. Moore.—"Given forth by our Monthly Meeting in Philadelphia, the 13th day of the 8th Moneth, 1693, and recommended to all our Friends and Brethren, who are one with us in our Testimony for the Lord Jesus Christ, and to all others professing Christianity."—A Quaker protest, said to be the first printed document of the kind in America. The reasons for protesting against slavery are summed up under five heads—religious, ethical, and legal.

(9) Vol. XIV (1890), pp. 297-312; 387-402: The Register of the Ephrata Community. By J. F. Sachse.—Valuable sources for German names and facts historical and biographical: period covered, c. 1728 to c. 1813.

(10) Ditto, pp. 403-413: Memoir of Israel Daniel Rupp, the Historian. By Oswald Seidensticker.—Rupp was the

compiler and editor of the "Thirty Thousand Names," and other valuable works.

(11) Vol. XXI (1897), pp. 488-492: A Letter of Gen. Daniel Morgan and Two from Gen. Peter Muhlenberg to Col. Taverner Beale of Virginia. Contributed by G. W. Schmucker.—Chiefly in regard to military conditions and proceedings, with personal and family touches.

(12) Vol. XXII (1898), pp. 452-457: The Pennsylvania-Dutchman, and Wherein He Has Excelled. By S. W. Pennypacker.

(13) Vol. XXIII (1899), pp. 157-183: A Defence of the Hessians. By. J. G. Rosengarten.—A reliable article that throws much new light on an old question.

Rockingham Register, Harrisonburg, Va.—History of Rockingham County. By G. F. Compton.—Of the early periods, chiefly. The series of articles was begun on February 5, 1885; the 27th installment appeared on August 27, following; and was "to be continued"; but the publication does not seem to have been resumed. The sudden ending of the series is a matter for regret, since these papers probably make the nearest approach, thus far, to a complete history of Rockingham.

(2) June 14 and July 26, 1895: Historical Sketches of the Valley Mennonites. By L. J. Heatwole.—Authoritative papers of interest.

(3) January 2, 1903: Heroes of the Revolution from Rockingham. By Chas. E. Kemper.—A list of the Revolutionary pensioners living in Rockingham County in 1835.

Shenandoah Valley, New Market, Va.—July 28, 1904; pp. 2, 3: Report of the Meeting of the United Lutheran Synod at New Market, July 27—, 1904.—Contains much valuable historical matter concerning the Lutheran Church in Virginia and elsewhere.

(2) Ditto, Supplement, giving a historical account of St. Matthew Lutheran Church, by Rev. Dr. J. A. Snyder, and of Emmanuel Lutheran Church, by Rev. E. L. Wessinger. Both these churches are at New Market.

(3) August 4, 1904: Report of the Meeting of the United [Lutheran] Synod at New Market, Concluded.—More historical facts.

(4) November 17, 1904: A Sad Fortieth Anniversary. Extracts from the diary of George M. Neese, of entries made in October, 1864, giving historical and personal facts, in connection with Sheridan's burning, relating to Gen. Muhlenberg, Capt. Ramsay Koontz, and other Valley Germans.

(5) December 1, 1904: Outline of the Genealogy of the First Four Generations of the Branner Family in Virginia. By J. C. Branner.

(6) September 27, 1906: Roster of Confederate Veterans, who attended the Reunion, near New Market, Va., Sept. 7, 1906, of the Neff-Rice Camp, U. C. V.

(7) January 10, 1907: Revised Roster of Capt M. M Sibert's Military Company, 1859.

(8) January 24, 1907; pp. 1, 2: Address before Neff-Rice Camp, U. C. V., New Market, Va., January 19, 1907, by Gen. John E. Roller.—Makes frequent allusions to the Valley of Virginia Germans.

Shepherdstown Register, Shepherdstown, W. Va.—November 15, 1906: Sketch of the Lutheran Church at Mecklenburg (Shepherdstown), by John Byers; reprinted from the *Baltimore American.*

Strasburg News, Strasburg, Va.—August 21, 1903: Report of the Centennial Celebration, August 13, 14, 1903, at St. Paul's Lutheran Church.—Contains long historical addresses by D. M. Gilbert, H. E. Jacobs, and C. J. Smith.

Virginia Magazine of History and Biography, Richmond.—Vol. II (1893), No. 4, pp. 399-404: A Register of the Persons who have been either Killed, Wounded or taken Prisoners by the Enemy, in Augusta County, as also such as have Made their Escape, 1754-1758.—A number of German names are found in the list.

(2) Vol. IX (1902), No. 4, pp. 337-352; Vol. X (1903), No. 1, pp. 33-48; No. 2, pp. 113-130: The Germans of the Valley [of Virginia]. By J. W. Wayland.—A rather comprehensive account of the German people of Northern Virginia, prepared chiefly from secondary sources.

(3) Vol. X (1902-3), No. 1, pp. 84-86: Adam Mueller (Miller), First White Settler in the Valley of Virginia. By C. E. Kemper.

(4) Vol. XI (1903-4), No. 2, pp. 113-131; No. 3, pp. 225-242; No. 4, pp. 370-393; Vol. XII (1904-5), No. 1, pp. 55-82; No. 2, pp. 134-153; No. 3, pp. 271-284: Moravian Diaries of Travel Through Virginia. Edited by W. J. Hinke and C. E. Kemper.—Diaries, translated from the German, of Moravian missionaries who, from 1743 to 1753, went up and down the South Branch and Shenandoah Valleys, and into Eastern Virginia. We have herein prolific and valuable sources of history.

(5) Vol. XII (1904), No. 2, pp. 202, 203: Moravian Missionaries and the Scotch-Irish. By J. A. Waddell.—A defence of the Scotch-Irish.

(6) Vol. XII (1904-5), No. 3, pp. 313-317: The Dunkers and the Sieben-Taeger. By J. W. Wayland.—An exposition of certain errors and confusions, with references to authorities.

(7) Vol. XII (1904-5), No. 4, pp. 337-352; Vol. XIII (1905-6), No. 1, pp. 1-16; No. 2, pp. 113-138; No. 3, pp. 281-297; No. 4, pp. 351-374: The Early Westward Movement of Virginia, 1722-1734. As Shown by the Proceed-

ings of the Colonial Council. Edited and Annotated by C. E. Kemper.—These documents, with the Moravian Diaries, form the most valuable sources yet published for early Valley of Virginia history.

(8) Vol. XIV (1906), No. 2, pp. 136-170: The Germans in Madison County, Virginia. Documents Translated and Annotated by W. J. Hinke.—Should be included in this bibliography, because there was more or less communication between the Madison Germans and those of the Valley, and some of the former moved into the Valley.

Virginische Volksberichter, Und Neumarketer Wochenschrift, New Market, Va.—The German newspaper published by Ambrose Henkel from 1807 to 1809. An almost complete file is preserved by the Henkel Publishing House.

Der Westen, Chicago.—June 12, 1892: Lord Fairfax in Virginia. By Andreas Simon.—The same journal published a sketch of Daniel Sheffey, son of a German shoemaker of Maryland, who came to the Valley of Virginia and won great distinction as a lawyer and politician.

West Virginia Historical Magazine, Charleston.—Vol. I, No. 2 (April, 1901), pp. 31-38: The Ruffners—I—Peter. By W. H. Ruffner.—Peter was the first of the name in Virginia. He settled in Page County in 1739.

(2) Vol. I, No. 3 (July, 1901), pp. 33-41: The Ruffners—II—Joseph. By W. H. Ruffner.—Joseph, the eldest son of Peter, was born in 1740, on the Hawkshill. At the age of 24 he married Ann Heistand, of the vicinity. All of his eight children, except one who died young, ultimately went to Kanawha County.

(3) Vol. I, No. 4 (October, 1901), pp. 46-54: The Ruffners—III—David: First Article. By. W. H. Ruffner.—David was the eldest son of Joseph. He was born in 1767; in 1789 he married Ann Brumbach, a Mennonite, of near Harrisonburg. In 1796 he followed his father to Kanawha—the site of the present city of Charleston.

(4) Vol. II, No. 1 (January, 1902), pp. 45-53: The Ruffners—III—David: Second Article. By W. H. Ruffner.

(5) Vol. II, No. 2 (April, 1902), pp. 60-74: The Ruffners—IV—Henry: First Article. By W. H. Ruffner.—Henry, the oldest son of David, was born in Page County (then Shenandoah) in 1790, and was taken to Kanawha in 1796. He was the first Presbyterian of the family. For nearly thirty years between 1820 and 1850 he was a professor and, later, president, at Washington College, Lexington, Va. In 1847 he wrote his celebrated pamphlet against slavery.

(6) Vol. II, No. 3 (July, 1902), pp. 36-44: The Ruffners—IV—Henry: Second Article. By W. H. Ruffner.

(7) Vol. I, No. 3 (July, 1901), pp. 28-33: The Oldest Town in West Virginia. By W. S. Laidley.—Between Shepherdstown and Romney, the author decides for Romney—upon rather flimsy grounds.

(8) Vol. II, No. 2 (April, 1902), pp. 5-18: The Van Meter Family in America. By Miss A. H. Van Meter; Addenda by W. S. Laidley.—In the same issue, pp. 19-30, is an article on Gabriel Jones, "The Lawyer," by R. T. Barton, which contains much of interest in Valley history.

(9) Ditto, pp. 31-35: Col. David Shepherd, First Lieutenant Commandant of Ohio County, Virginia. By G. L. Cranmer.—David was the son of Capt. Thomas Shepherd, for whom Shepherdstown, W. Va., was named.

(10) Ditto, pp. 38-53: The Millers and their Kin. By Dr. J. L. Miller.—Gives an account of Jacob Miller, founder of Woodstock, Va., and others of his race.

(11) Vol. II, No. 3 (July, 1902), pp. 16-36: Braddock's March Through West Virginia. By W. P. Craighill.—Gives much of interest concerning the lower Valley.

(12) Vol. III, No. 2 (April, 1903), pp. 99-119: Jost Hite, Pioneer of the Shenandoah Valley, 1732. By W. S.

Laidley.—An interesting and valuable article, but in error in regarding Hite as the first settler in the Valley.

(13) Ditto, pp. 119-127: Notes Relating to the Elting and Shepherd Families of Maryland and Virginia. By S. G. Smyth.

(14) Ditto, pp. 127-144: Augusta Men in French and Indian War. By Dr. J. L. Miller.— An interesting list, containing some German names among a much larger number of Scotch-Irish and English names.

William and Mary College Quarterly, Williamsburg, Va.—Vol. IV (1895-6), pp. 62, 63: The Rev. John Casper Stoever, Sr. By Dr. A. G. Grinnan.—Mr. Stover was pastor of the Lutheran church in Madison County, Va., prior to 1738.

(2) Vol. IX (1900-1), pp. 132, 133: First Settler in the Valley. By Lizzie B. Miller.—Contains a copy of the naturalization paper of Adam Miller of Germany, who settled on the Shenandoah River in 1726-7.

(3) Vol. X (1901-2), pp. 120-123: Memoranda copied from the Note Book of Maj. Isaac Hite, of Belle Grove, Frederick Co., Va.—The notes are made up of a protracted record of births, deaths, and marriages of members of the Hite family.

(4) Vol. XIII (1904-5), pp. 247-256; Vol. XIV (1905-6), pp. 9-19; 186-193: Record of the Peaked Mountain Church, Rockingham County, Virginia. Edited by W. J. Hinke and C. E. Kemper.—Translated from the German originals. Contains, among other things, an agreement between the Reformed and Lutherans; list of church officers; record of baptisms; etc. A valuable document.

Woodstock (now *Shenandoah*) *Herald,* Woodstock, Va.—This paper was founded in 1817, by B. L. Bogan. It is edited at present by Capt. J. H. Grabill, who has files of the paper of 1821 and several years following, containing facts of great interest.

INDEX

TO

The German Element of the Shenandoah Valley of Virginia.

This Index is arranged according to the following plan: Under each letter personal names come first; then geographical names; thirdly, names and terms of a more general character.

At a few places notes correcting or amplifying the text have been inserted.

—2

www.ingramcontent.com/pod-product-compliance
Lightning Source LLC
Chambersburg PA
CBHW071639270326
41928CB00010B/1979

* 9 7 8 0 7 8 8 4 1 6 4 5 3 *